D1644160

From High Priests to Desecrators

WRITING ON WRITING

Other titles in this series

Hardy: The Margin of the Unexpressed
by Roger Ebbatson

Literature and Addiction
edited by Sue Vice, Matthew Campbell and Timothy Armstrong

Shakespeare and the New Europe
edited by Michael Hattaway, Boika Sokolova and Derek Roper

The Lover, the Dreamer and the World:
The Poetry of Peter Redgrove
by Neil Roberts

Childhood in Fiction and Autobiography since 1940
by John Hodgson

Cover design by Catherine Cozier

From High Priests to Desecrators

Contemporary Austrian Writers

**Edited by Ricarda Schmidt
and Moray McGowan**

Sheffield Academic Press

Copyright © 1993 Sheffield Academic Press

Published by Sheffield Academic Press Ltd
343 Fulwood Road
Sheffield S10 3BP
England

Typeset by Sheffield Academic Press
and
Printed on acid-free paper in Great Britain
by Biddles Limited
Guildford

British Library Cataloguing in Publication Data

From High Priests to Desecrators:
Contemporary Austrian Writers.—(Writing
on Writing Series, ISSN 0966-7423; No. 5)
I. Schmidt, Ricarda II. McGowan, Moray
III. Series
830.9

ISBN 1-85075-429-2

1000173209

CONTENTS

Preface

The range of papers published here will, we hope, be a reminder of the thematic and formal variety of contemporary Austrian literature, a variety which one modest volume cannot hope to encapsulate in its entirety. The often sought 'Austrianness' of this literature is a chimera, even though some authors, and perhaps even more so their reception—as several of the contributions here show—would be hard to imagine on the literary scene of any other German-speaking country. Our title would seem to posit either a bipolarity of possible positions for the contemporary Austrian writer—enthronement within the established culture or angry rejection of it and by it—or a linear range of possibilities between these two extremes. It seems to us entirely appropriate that a number of our contributors felt unable or unwilling to relate their analysis of a given writer or writers to this intentionally schematic model, itself meant as a provocation, an invitation to dissent and differentiation.

The papers published here were first given at a conference held at the University of Sheffield on 25–27 March 1991. We are most grateful to the Austrian Institute and its director, Dr Peter Marginter, for the generous support of that conference and this publication. We would also like to thank Waltraud Anna Mitgutsch, whose reading from her work was a memorable highlight of the conference.

Ricarda Schmidt
Moray McGowan
June 1992

LIST OF CONTRIBUTORS

Thomas E. Bourke is Senior Lecturer in German at University College Galway.

Allyson Fiddler is Lecturer in German at University College Swansea.

Axel Goodbody is Lecturer in German at the University of Bath.

Herbert Herzmann is Lecturer in German at University College Dublin.

Brian Keith-Smith is Senior Lecturer in German at the University of Bristol.

Moray McGowan is Professor of German at the University of Sheffield.

Michael Mitchell is Senior Lecturer in German at Stirling University.

Andrea Reiter has taught at the Universities of Salzburg and Southampton and the National University of Ireland.

Mike Rogers is Lecturer in German at the University of Southampton.

Sigrid Schmid-Bortenschlager is Professor of German and Comparative Literature at the University of Salzburg.

Ricarda Schmidt is Lecturer in German at the University of Sheffield.

Fritz Wefelmeyer is Senior Lecturer in German at the University of Sunderland

John J. White is Professor of German and Comparative Literature at King's College, University of London.

Juliet Wigmore is Lecturer in German at the University of Salford.

From Provocation to Appropriation*

Sigrid Schmid-Bortenschlager

For reasons which will become apparent, my title reverses the temporal or causative sequence suggested by the overall conference title. If one relates the latter to the Austrian literary scene, certain names spring to mind almost irrespective of one's view of the potentially extremely ambivalent terms used: the association of the term High Priest with Peter Handke is almost inevitable; in the case of Desecrator the names of Thomas Bernhard and Elfriede Jelinek immediately suggest themselves.

Let us, for the moment, remain with these examples. In choosing to translate 'desecrator' as 'Nestbeschmutzer' I have focused on a narrower meaning than that of the English term, which does not specify what is being desecrated. The German expression's reference to the fouling of one's own nest is much more specific, though this nest does not absolutely have to be Austria, as in the two examples cited; it could just as well be literature which is being befouled, an aspect which, for Jelinek at least, is also important.

However, let us turn to the particular literary scandals which have swept Austria in the last few years: the production of Thomas Bernhard's play *Heldenplatz* in celebration of the one-hundredth anniversary of the Burgtheater in 1988, Elfriede Jelinek's play *Burgtheater*, produced in Bonn in 1985 as an unofficial anticipation of this anniversary, and the controversies surrounding the publication of Jelinek's novel *Lust* in 1990.

It is significant that two of these cases are connected, directly or indirectly, with the Burgtheater, and moreover that the accusations, insults and smear campaigns which they provoked

---

*   Translated by Moray McGowan.

were to be found primarily in those media whose consumers certainly do not form this theatre's audience. Here, as elsewhere, it can be seen that the strategy of defining and establishing Austrian identity after 1945, as a cultural identity symbolized by the reconstructed State Opera House, St Stephen's Cathedral and Burgtheater, has been successful (see Schmid 1984). In Austria, whoever calls the Opera or the Burgtheater into question, calls Austria itself into question.

I shall give a brief word on the individual cases. In the case of Thomas Bernhard the provocation of the Austrian popular psyche began when Claus Peymann, a German, a 'Piefke' indeed, became director of the Burgtheater in 1986. This appointment, a matter of considerable significance in Austrian cultural politics, was hotly debated in the media. One can only speculate about whether the fact that Peymann was well-known as a director of Bernhard's work was a factor in the decision. The second step was Peymann's commissioning of Bernhard to write a play on the occasion of the hundredth anniversary of the Burgtheater, which led in turn to public dissatisfaction just before the premiere. At this point the text of the play was largely unknown: but one knew what to expect from Bernhard, and this alone sufficed for emotions to overheat, for quotations to be invented, and so on. Not only the press, but also the parliament was drawn into the affair, which led, if one can believe the statements of some of those involved, to Bernhard being insulted on the street in Vienna. However, it hindered neither the premiere nor its artistic and commercial success. Shortly afterwards the documentation of the scandal was published by the Burgtheater in book form, a book which forms an ideal object for an analysis of the relationship of art and commerce (*Heldenplatz: Eine Dokumentation*).

Two years earlier, a more modest scandal was provoked by Elfriede Jelinek's play *Burgtheater*, in which, in her now familiar style and in barely disguised form, she constructed a collage of quotations from films from the National Socialist period through which famous members of the Burgtheater acting dynasty of the Hörbigers and the Wesselys had acquired artistic and commercial success. Jelinek seeks to show how actors in the apparently harmless field of entertainment were also underpinning the Nazi regime and the propagation of its ideology, and how after the fall of the regime fellow-travelling was rapidly reinterpreted as resistance.

In the case of Jelinek's novel *Lust* too the media campaign, as is typical for best-sellers, preceded the appearance of the book. Magazines like *Lui, Brigitte, Playboy* and *Stern* discovered an interest in literature and published interviews with Jelinek which, like those she gave on television, had a structure comparable to that of Jelinek's other texts: skilful montages of ready-made fragments on the themes of women, sexuality and emancipation (see Vogel 1990). In the *Lust* scandal, the text itself was absent; it was completely replaced by the person of the author—a variation on the first two cases, in which the text was also noticeably absent, being in one case replaced by the image of the author Bernhard, in the other by the images of the persons cited by the text as examples, namely the acting dynasty of the Wesselys and the Hörbigers (Jelinek's precise identification of these historical figures led to her in turn being accused of being guilty of the death of Paul Hörbiger: see Lingens 1985).

Significant here is on the one hand the very noticeable personalization of literature and the redundancy of the text that goes with it, but also the evidently almost unlimited ability of the cultural market to make successful publications out of provocations, which, on closer view, means robbing would-be provocations of their effect precisely through the process of apparently publicizing them in the media.

This would seem to imply that texts, if allowed a legitimacy as such, can indeed have an effect, and that it is therefore necessary to convert them into other forms of discourse, to transform and to disguise them in order to make them consumable. If for example one engages in a close reading of Elfriede Jelinek's *Lust*, then the text awakens uncertainties, defensive postures, feelings of displeasure. The text mixes primitiveness and refinement, and makes us aware that here, as always with Jelinek, we are being offered a satirical collage of quotations. This awareness has the power to create distance and destabilization of familiar patterns of reception and of thought. By transferring the 'scandal' onto the author as producer of this violent pornography, who would appear to embody the role of the 'domina', the uncertainties created by the text can be diverted onto the harmless level of an individual moral condemnation of the author (see Lingens 1985: 13-16).

A similar personalizing effect could be seen in the *Burgtheater* scandal: neither the role of performing artists under a dictatorship nor the essential corruptibility of artists were discussed. Instead, Paula Wessely confesses that in her youthful folly she may have played roles which she should not have played: 'Ja, es tut mir leid, daß ich damals nicht den Mut gefunden habe... ', so ran the caption for a picture of Wessely in *Profil*. The text completed the quotation:

> ...die Dreharbeiten zu *Heimkehr* einfach abzubrechen. Vielleicht habe ich aber doch einiges von dem wiedergut-gemacht, indem ich konkreten Menschen, jüdischen Kollegen und Freunden, in dieser Zeit konkret geholfen habe (Lingens 1985: 13, 16).

Automatically, one feels sympathy for this motherly old lady who, at her advanced age and so long after the event, is being subjected to this controversy. Admiration for her stature seems to underline the pettiness of her attacker Jelinek.

Similarly in the case of Thomas Bernhard, his portrayal of the latent and sometimes far from latent anti-Semitism in Austria is glossed over as his typical and familiar tendency to exaggeration: a registered trademark, tried, tested and harmless.

Literature has its established place in the market: there are best-sellers, which actually get read; there is the so-called serious or highbrow literature, which one talks about, which gets bought, but is not read; and then there are the many literary texts which are produced but rarely sold (since they appear under small imprints almost unknown in the marketplace) and thus also rarely read.

Literature has its role in a state like Austria which has an image of itself as a cultured state: we need artists, and in exchange they are assigned certain roles and positions. One of the most important roles is, undoubtedly, that which 'Her Majesty's Loyal Opposition' is said to have in Great Britain. Of Thomas Bernhard it is said that he was delighted at the news of Heimito von Doderer's death, since that left free the throne of *the* Austrian author. The increasingly sophisticated strategies of social control subsequently divided this throne into two, which came to be occupied by Handke and Bernhard, who between them had the task of fulfilling the double role of High Priest and Desecrator. It now looks as though Elfriede Jelinek may fill the Desecrator role vacated by Bernhard's death, an almost ideal solution, since then women would be represented too.

It is undoubtedly true that the literary market has always thrived on scandal and personalization. However, the structures were previously rather different. Let us recall two phases in postwar Austrian literature which were accompanied by scandal: firstly the appearances by the Wiener Gruppe in the 1950s, secondly the appearance of Handke and Wolfgang Bauer on the German-language stage at the end of the 1960s and the beginning of the 1970s.

The history of the Wiener Gruppe has been chronicled by Gerhard Rühm (see Walter-Buchebner Gesellschaft 1987). In this case too the popular press reacted with editorials and readers' letters in favour of censorship and the banning of decadent art, as in the following characteristic reactions to Achleitner, Artmann and Rühm's *hosn rosn baa*:

> 'Nix steht drin', müßte man aber über die Wortmalereien und Reimereien des Oberösterreichers Achleitner und des dekadent wirkenden Großstädters Rühm sagen... Wenn aber die beiden von der Art ihres Landsmannes abweichen, dann führt sie ihre eigene Art (also ihre Ab-Art) zu mundartlichem Gestammel oder zu Unart und Unrat. Ihre Vorliebe für das Trübe und Schmutzige ist dann gerade hervorstechend: sie tut einem körperlich weh (*Wiener Zeitung*, 11 December 1959).

The decisive difference from the most recent 'scandals', however, lies in the fact that in the above case the reaction at least took place *after* the performance or publication of the texts, or during the performance itself, so that the text, as a catalyst of reactions, still had a function *as a text*; the above example shows this neatly, in so far as the reviewers have been influenced to attempt a language game themselves (*Unart–Unrat*). They react more to the form than to the content of the texts. Moreover, the reactions take place within the literary market itself, not only in the popular press: Gerhard Fritsch lost his job as an editor of the establishment literary magazine *Wort in der Zeit* after he had printed Wiener Gruppe texts, which, one might note, led to the demise of this magazine and enabled Fritsch to found what was more or less his own magazine, *Literatur und Kritik*. Heimito von Doderer, who worked in the 'more sensitive' sphere of highbrow journalism as editor of the literary page of the popular paper *Kurier*, had to bow to the pressure of a censorship which identified itself with the 'gesundes Volksempfinden': he was unable to print the texts in question and resigned his post in protest.

Scandals of comparable publicity value accompanied the breakthrough of a new generation of playwrights some ten to fifteen years later, represented particularly by Peter Handke and Wolfgang Bauer. But here too it was the actual performance which served as catalyst for the public reactions; the marketing of the scandal followed the premiere and did not precede it, even though interesting parallels to later events are beginning to emerge in the respective publicity strategies. Here too a close interest is shown by newspapers whose readers are certainly not the typical consumers of modern theatre, not the potential audience. For example, on 28 January 1968 the Austrian local press, evidently inspired by an Austria Press Agency report about the production of Handke's play *Publikumsbeschimpfung* in the Blaubeuren theatre near Ulm, carried headlines like 'Publikum trank Sekt weg' or 'Gegenseitige Beschimpfung'.[1] The connection between actor and champagne evidently sets in train a series of associations stretching from comments on the dissolute lifestyle of actors to outbursts of pure envy, which seem to ignore the fact that alcohol on the stage is almost always fake. The play and its turbulent performance history remained newsworthy, confirming its ability to provoke its intended public: on 13 February 1968 the *Salzburger Volksblatt* reported on a performance in Maastricht during which students carried a grand piano onto the stage to give a musical response to the

---

1. *Express*, 28 January 1968 and *Salzburger Volksblatt*, 28 January 1968 respectively. The *Vorarlberger Nachrichten, Kärntner Tageszeitung, Linzer Volksblatt* and *Kleine Zeitung* used identical or near-identical headlines. Information from the Viktor Matejka press cutting collection in the Dokumentationsstelle für Neuere Österreichische Literatur, Vienna.

play. Public reaction abroad, too, remained consistent to the play's intentions. On 26 July 1968, for example, the *Neue Zürcher Zeitung* reported on the 'Hilflosigkeit' of the actors in the face of the public reaction to the play in the Theater am Turm in Frankfurt, and even the supposedly so reserved London audience, according to the *Frankfurter Allgemeine Zeitung* of 6 April 1972, allowed itself to be provoked 'zurückzuschimpfen'. In Greece the military dictatorship was more cautious and banned the play as 'anarchistisch und regimefeindlich' (see *Süddeutsche Zeitung*, 22 January 1972).

If one is to believe the press reports, the reactions to Handke's play consisted largely of the audience being stirred into action, playing along with the action, insulting the actors back: the audience takes possession of the stage, participates in the action, destroys the boundary which the footlights conventionally represent. These were, after all, the years around 1968, and it is noticeable in the reviews and reports that small experimental theatres obviously coped better with the audience activity this play provoked than did the larger, established, more famous theatres, where—for example in Claus Peymann's otherwise highly praised production—the actors were nonplussed by such interruptions. Of course one must beware of nostalgic distortion; in most cases one is not talking about a spontaneous reaction to the text or the performance. After the first few performances a pattern developed: the audience went to *Publikumsbeschimpfung* in order to disrupt, to insult the cast back, to react. Here too the media prepared the way for a pseudospontaneity. But nonetheless the reactions were provoked by the actual cultural event rather than its mediation, and were expressed directly.

A little while later, at performances of Wolfgang Bauer's *Magic Afternoon*, the audience had returned to normality: it no longer stormed the stage, but reverted to traditional methods of expressing approval or dissent: applause and boos, and 'murrendes Verlassen des Saals'.[2]

2. E.g. *Neue Zeit* (Graz), 10 November 1969, observed a 'Massenflucht älterer Zuschauer' at the Freie Volksbühne, Berlin, production. See also *BZ* (Berlin), 10 December 1969: 'Murrend verärgert, beleidigt verließen ganze Reihen reiferer Jahrgänge das Theater und auch jüngere buhten,

To stress the parallels and the differences once again, in every case the popular press tailors its negative reaction to the prejudices of its readership, and at the same time significantly amplifies, even if it does not actually produce, the readership's antipathy towards modern art. This is a familiar phenomenon: those who do not concern themselves at all with modern art believe that they know best about it and are the most virulent in condemning it.

In each case the press colludes in creating an image of an author which makes knowledge of her or his texts superfluous. Interest is directed towards the scandal or the author who has provoked it, not towards the content and form of the texts themselves. The aggressions unleashed by literature are directed not at the literary texts themselves, but at their authors.

In all three periods considered here theatre, in which I include the cabaret texts of the Wiener Gruppe, is the form which provokes the largest public reaction and the largest subsequent reaction in the press. The group experience in the theatre evidently liberates aggressions more readily, or at any rate more visibly, than does the individual reading of a text (an exception is Jelinek's *Lust*, although one might ask whether interviews are not in themselves a kind of theatrical performance).

There are also differences: in the case of the Wiener Gruppe and the Graz playwrights (as, for our present purposes, I will call the early Handke and the early Bauer) the specific performances provide the primary catalyst for the negative reactions which are subsequently amplified, simplified and disseminated through the media. In the case of Bernhard and Jelinek the negative reactions actually precede the appearance of the text and take place in demonstrable ignorance of it.

In my earlier examples the chosen form of the literary text in question is the subject of the attack. In the case of Bernhard and Jelinek it focuses on the content; the form is if anything invoked as an excuse, insofar as these writers are noted as using exaggeration as a literary technique.

If we generalize this comparison, we can see that the reception

störten...denn ihnen fehlte...was sie selbst in so reichem Maße zu haben glauben, eine Ideologie'.

of literature moves further and further away from the actual literary product. Literature has not lost its potential to provoke, which manifests itself in the form of 'scandal'. It has, however, changed from being a form of protest with sometimes massive personal consequences (as in the cases of Fritsch and Doderer) to being a marketing strategy, a part of product management: the way in which the publishers and the Burgtheater management reacted to the attacks on *Lust* and *Heldenplatz* respectively scarcely allows any other interpretation.

We can assume that both Bernhard's accusation of the continuity of anti-Semitism and anti-intellectuality in Austria and Jelinek's critical engagement with the relationship between power and sexual pleasure are serious and important themes for the potential public as well as for the authors. However, with the transfer of the text's challenge, and the transformation of the displacement of familiar patterns of perception in the text into the familiar patterns of advertising strategies, the text is robbed of its potential effect. Coming to the text after multiple exposure to publicity about it in the media, it is scarcely possible for the reader not to relate the text immediately to its mediated reception, so that a prefabricated discourse pattern overlays one's own reception of the text itself, and steers it, repeatedly and irresistibly, in certain directions.

The shock which literary texts can unleash in the individual, the reason why they are still read, is thus dampened. Even if we distance ourselves from it, we are bound, negatively, to the image of the text as scandal. Moreover, this will be true not just for the specific text in question, but also for all past or future texts by this author. Our reception is predetermined and the question is no longer what this text confirms or changes in our own views and beliefs. Such questions are coloured by the suspicion that the whole thing is not that serious, that it is, rather, an advertising stunt to boost sales. In the terms of classical commodity aesthetics attention is diverted from the product to the aesthetics of its appearance in the marketplace as a sales-boosting scandal.

In this context one should note that the potential 'scandalousness' of the texts of Bernhard or Jelinek is itself partly a reaction to and product of simpler and more primitive

manipulative strategies of the—particularly the Austrian—
cultural industry. In the Kreisky era of the 1970s intellectuals and
artists temporarily gained a certain importance in the state.
Their declarations of support were in demand, the state (which
in Austria is frequently confused with the government) recalled
its function as a patron of the arts, out of an anxiety that the
extra-parliamentary opposition might, via students and artists,
interrupt the state's smooth functioning. Thus prizes, grants and
a social fund were established. In 1970 the first annual official
report on Austrian culture appeared. In the meantime it has
grown from 48 pages to 228. This work is not comprehensive: it
only lists support from the Federal Ministry for Education and
the Arts and omits support from other public, municipal or
regional sources. However it makes rewarding reading. It
shows—in its organization alone, let alone in the figures—the
real status of literature in the cultural market: it takes third last
place ahead only of cultural policy and photography; even film is
apparently more important, even though Austria does not have
a film industry worth speaking of.

The report shows clearly the interconnectedness, not to say
the nepotism, of the Austrian cultural scene. It is always the
same names which appear as members of juries, as prize-
winners, as authors whose books have received a publication
subsidy and which have been bought by public institutions in
large numbers (a frequent means of indirect subsidy). Bernhard
and Jelinek do not belong to these much-mentioned names,
whereas in the case of Handke one might think that new prizes,
like the Kafka prize or the Grillparzer prize, have only been
created so as to be able to award yet another prize to him.

The report shows too that in Austria one can live modestly, if
not actually well, from literature. Even authors who are not
particularly productive can survive: not, admittedly, by book
sales, but by readings, prizes, scholarships, commissions from
the state radio and television channels, by receiving various
types of payment in kind (such as exchanging your literary
estate for a flat or a pension). But this security is only ever
distributed in small portions, grants for one or two years, after
which the application process, the begging, has to begin again.
And while there is certainly no open censorship, and indeed

much attempt at objectivity, nonetheless something much more dangerous is encouraged: self-censorship, the adaptation to assumed expectations, which because it is usually unconscious or only half-conscious, is much harder to measure or counteract than direct intervention.

Few authors can afford to absent themselves from this process, in which constructive criticism is certainly desired, indeed encouraged, but only so that its impact can be absorbed and fed back gently into the system. The system's acceptance of relatively extreme criticism then becomes a challenge to all those who do not want to play along with the system, who want instead to develop new, more extreme forms of criticism which are no longer absorbable by the system: the radicality of a Jelinek, the exaggeration of a Bernhard are, among other things, reactions to this Austrian cultural system. But this radicality in turn makes their work exploitable material for scandal-mongering journalism, for the commodity-aesthetic marketing described above.

Austrian cultural politics has of late been discussed as 'sozialpartnerschaftliche Warenästhetik' (Menasse 1990) and, wrongly, been labelled as a typically Austrian phenomenon. I only partly agree with Menasse in this, for he neglects both the general effectiveness of the strategy of the 'Personalisierung von Literatur' and a particular reason for and further development of the Austrian model which cannot be explained by social partnership alone. The patronage function of the state is not only influenced by the desire for internal political order, a function which was politically significant only in the 1970s and has in the meantime become completely obsolete.

It is true that today the financial support of the state facilitates direct or indirect preventive control over the critical potential of the creative writer. But it provides above all for the timely channelling of criticism, which in a democratic society is of course desirable and necessary. It ensures that it can take into its service any dissatisfaction that has the potential to become public, by allocating to it the role of a safety valve. Market mechanisms such as those that strong, independent publishers would provide, would be harder to control; but while Switzerland, comparable in size and language situation, has both serious publishers and newspapers interested in literature, they do not exist in Austria (see Schmid-Bortenschlager 1982). In Austria, the safety valve function is achieved through the support given directly to individuals, and the resulting dependency and self-censorship.

At the same time, through indirect channels, the state gets its money back. Austrian culture, including, though marginally, literature (cheaper than music, with its expensive orchestras and soloists), is becoming integrated into Austria's largest industry, namely the tourist industry. The tourism value of the Vienna Opera or the Salzburg Festival is well known and accepted; in recent years it is noticeable how certain disadvantaged and underdeveloped regions or seasons are trying via culture to enter the international tourist market, for example the Rosegger-Tage in Alpl, the Rauriser Literaturtage, the Reichenau Festival and so on. There is hardly a castle, a lake, a monastery or even a farm without a festival. The establishment of cultural activities in areas of economic crisis such as Steyr connect the channelling of social dissatisfaction with the attempt at economic rejuvenation through tourism.

This development is important in our context because the tourist industry approaches literature with quite specific expectations as to its usefulness. It has, on the one hand, to be 'typisch österreichisch', that is, to confirm the tourist trademark 'Österreich', and on the other hand it must have a certain entertainment value. Comedies are most in demand, since one likes to laugh when on holiday; problems are something one would rather leave at home. Literature is therefore required to be either harmless or spectacular, like Felix Mitterer's production of *Munde* high up in the mountains.

Contemporary Austrian literature as it is widely perceived would thus seem to be in a dead-end street: either it conforms to the cultural market and supplies, if not intrinsically harmless work, then work which can be rendered harmless, or it takes up a radical stance and runs into the waiting trap of total media exploitation via scandal. There is a third possibility, that of publishing more or less independent of the attention of the media and the public, through small alternative publishers. This experience, very different from that of the works and authors discussed above, is in fact the reality of the majority of the literature written in Austria today.

WORKS CITED

Achleitner, F., H.C. Artmann and G. Rühm
    1959   *hosn rosn baa*. Vienna: Frick.
Bernhard, T.
    1990   *Heldenplatz*. Frankfurt: Suhrkamp.
Burgtheater Wien (ed.)
    1989   *Heldenplatz: Eine Dokumentation*. Vienna: Burgtheater Wien.
Jelinek, E.
    1984   *Theaterstücke: Clara S. Was geschah, nachdem Nora ihren Mann verlassen hatte. Burgtheater*. Cologne: Prometh Verlag.
    1990   *Lust*. Reinbek: Rowohlt.
Lingens, P.M.
    1985   'Wieweit verdient Paula Wessley Elfriede Jelinek?'. *Profil* 48, pp. 12-16.
Menasse, R.
    1990   *Die sozialpartnerschaftliche Ästhetik: Essays zum österreichischen Geist*. Vienna: Sonderzahl.
Schmid, G.
    1984   'Die falschen Fuffziger. Kulturpolitische Tendenzen der fünfziger Jahre', in F. Aspertsberger *et al.* (eds.), *Literatur der Nachkriegszeit und der fünfziger Jahre in Österreich*. Vienna: Österreichischer Bundesverlag, pp. 7-23.
Schmid-Bortenschlager, S.
    1982   'A-CH: Literatur(en) in Österreich und in der Schweiz. (K)ein Vergleich', in K. Bartsch, D. Goldschnigg and G. Melzer (eds.), *Für und wider eine österreichische Literatur*. Königstein: Athenäum, pp. 116-29.
Vogel, J.
    1990   'Oh Bildnis, oh Schutz vor ihm', in C. Gürtler (ed.), *Gegen den schönen Schein: Texte zu Elfriede Jelinek*. Frankfurt: Neue Kritik, pp. 140-56.
Walter-Buchebner Gesellschaft (ed.)
    1987   *Walter-Buchebner-Literaturprojekt: Die Wiener Gruppe*. Vienna: Böhlau.

Demythologizing the Austrian 'Heimat': Elfriede Jelinek as 'Nestbeschmutzer'

Allyson Fiddler

The marketing of Elfriede Jelinek's novel *Lust* (1989) on a 'pornography for women' platform has earned its author widespread acclaim as a controversial feminist writer *in aller Munde*.[1] Indeed her growing stature in academic circles, too, has been largely underpinned by her reputation as a feminist writer and evinced by critical readings of *Die Liebhaberinnen* (1975) and *Die Klavierspielerin* (1983) in particular. At home in Austria, however, the foundations of Jelinek's reputation were laid on a very different reception. There it was not her concern with unpalatable issues such as feminist pornography and female masochism but rather her bold deprecation of her own mother country which first aroused the public's disdain and won Jelinek her notoriety. This important aspect of Jelinek's reception was established with the première of her play *Burgtheater* (November 1985) but has been all but eclipsed by the predominant treatment of her by critics as a feminist. It is Jelinek's reputation as 'Nestbeschmutzer' which I wish to discuss in the following essay.

Of course 'Nestbeschmutzer' are certainly not uncommon in Austria and many of Jelinek's colleagues such as Wolfgang Bauer, Thomas Bernhard and Peter Turrini have also earned themselves this label. Nor is Austria short of stage scandals (see Landa 1988). It is not my intention then to claim that Jelinek is alone in her criticism of Austria but rather I wish to characterize the particular nature of Jelinek's criticism and to raise a few questions regarding the reception of this as 'Nestbeschmutzung'.

1. *Lust* is in fact better understood as a parody of pornography, as I have argued elsewhere. See Fiddler 1991.

Burgtheater has been chosen as a focus for this study principally because of the massive adverse reaction to the play. The fact that it is set in what is, for the Austrian national conscience, a particularly sensitive period—the Third Reich—is not, however, coincidental. Why is it that Jelinek's play has not been produced in Austria, where other 'Nestbeschmutzer', Thomas Bernhard for instance, now enjoy a certain standing and are even played in that highest of cultural establishments, featured in Jelinek's play of the same name, the Burgtheater? What is it, in other words, that makes Jelinek so unattractive to Austria's theatres?[2]

The 'Heimat' myth has been a constant preoccupation of Jelinek's from the beginning of her career. Before focusing on its treatment in the play *Burgtheater*, I should like first to define this myth and support my claim that it is a concern which is never very far from her mind. The national stereotype evokes an image of the Austrian people as peace-loving, simple, sociable and carefree folk, who spend their time enjoying the good things in life. This is, of course, an exaggerated cliché, but one in which many foreigners nevertheless believe. Austria's geographical character as an 'Alpenrepublik' allows a landscape of serene, beautiful, majestic, often snow-capped mountains and rolling green pastures to be the dominant image included in brochures sent to tourists who flock to Austria both in the summer and the winter holiday seasons. Helmut Sagmeister argues that it is not just foreigners who see Austria in this light and observes that all Austrians and most foreigners believe in the image of Austria as the 'Image einer harmonischen, heilen Welt' (Sagmeister 1982: 97).

The advent of the Waldheim era signalled a period of renewed self-examination in Austria such that this supposed harmony can surely no longer be taken for granted by its inhabitants. It is

2. Only recently has Vienna shown any interest in Jelinek. In its winter season 1991–1992 the Volkstheater staged productions of both *Was geschah, nachdem Nora ihren Mann verlassen hatte* and *Krankheit oder Moderne Frauen*. Plays by other 'Beschmutzer', such as Peter Turrini and Wolfgang Bauer, have been produced in Vienna, for example in the Akademietheater, a small but nevertheless prestigious 'zweite Bühne' to the Burgtheater. The Akademietheater premièred Jelinek's *Totenauberg* in September 1992.

questionable in fact whether the description recorded by Sagmeister has ever been a valid one, and authors such as Jelinek have in any case been trying to dismantle this myth for decades. In her earliest text *wir sind lockvögel baby!* (1970), a pop-trivia montage which carried a provocative, tongue-in-cheek dedication to the Austrian army, powerful notions of fatherland are destroyed when the Beatles—some of the many characters Jelinek borrows for her novel—return home after their long travels:

> die dicke edeltraud diese geschwulst und kein geringerer auf deren griffbrett george seine unverwechselbaren spässe meist derberer natur trieb war es welche den vieren wieder ihr vaterhaus ihre eltern die sie geboren und erzogen die pritschen die sie gefickt die pissoirwände die sie beschmiert kurz all das was für den durchschnittsmenschen von heute untrennbar mit dem begriffe heimat & scholle verbunden ist in erinnerung brachte (p. 83).

Here, then, it is the concept and connotations of a generalized and universally applicable 'Heimat' which are the target of Jelinek's criticism. By the time of *Die Liebhaberinnen* (1975), however, the criticism had already taken on an expressly anti-Austrian dimension. This text can be read as an anti-'Heimatroman' which unveils the stifling and oppressive nature of sexual relationships in the Austrian provinces and shows the interaction of the villagers to be based on power struggles and employment hierarchies rather than on the convivial, tranquil simplicity and friendship typical of many a traditional 'Heimatroman'.[3] The narrator's question in her 'vorwort', 'Kennen Sie dieses SCHÖNE land mit seinen tälern und hügeln?' (p. 7) is a rhetorical one which is the driving force for the plot and commentaries throughout. Jelinek's sub-text, as expressed through her narrator, is really 'I'll tell you a few things about this supposedly lovely country', and her refusal to provide us with descriptions of the forest and countryside are justified by her narrator's taunting but superfluous assurance that 'wir sind doch hier nicht in einem heimatroman!' (p. 82).

---

3. 'Heimatliteratur' does not have to show a blind adulation for nature and nation, however. See Pabisch's account (1977) of modern 'Dialektdichtung'.

In her prose text *Wolken. Heim* (1990), Jelinek's preoccupation
with possible corollaries of 'Heimat'—that is nationalism and
patriotism—takes on a compelling and contemporary focus.
Here, the author sets out to explore the question of German
national identity and, in a very dense montage of quotations
from Hölderlin, Fichte, Kleist, Heidegger and excerpts from
letters written by members of the Rote Armee Fraktion, she
brings to our attention the dangers inherent in a renewed sense
of German self-importance. In her forced praise of
'Germanentum', Jelinek has her narrator voice sentiments
which echo the cultural and imperial claims of National
Socialism.[4] In *Totenauberg* (1991) too, Jelinek has turned her
attention once again to satirizing her fatherland. More essay
than drama, it plays with the character of Martin Heidegger
and focuses on rural Austria with its stereotypical landscape of
mountains and snow.

The rural element in Austria's image is not one with which
Jelinek deals specifically in *Burgtheater*. It is voiced in the play
but does not feature in terms of the setting or plot as it does in
her novel *Oh Wildnis, oh Schutz vor ihr* (1985), a novel which is
committed to correcting the prevailing literary image of nature
as apolitical. Jelinek is concerned to show a correlation between,
on the one hand, the way in which nature is revered and
idealized as something idyllic, pure and worthy of the nation's
defence, and on the other, the appropriation of this image in
patriotic representations of the fatherland. A review of *Oh
Wildnis, oh Schutz vor ihr* by Gunhild Kübler pinpoints the
author's intention very clearly:

> Dem umfangreichen Buch lässt sich ein Klartext entnehmen,
> der auf die Gefahr einer braun-grünen Umweltschutzallianz in
> Österreich hinweist und Front macht gegen die verbreitete
> Auffassung, der Kampf für den Umweltschutz habe
> inzwischen den Klassenkampf abgelöst (Kübler 1985).

It is this expressly political dimension which is so characteristic
of Elfriede Jelinek's understanding of nature. As Kübler points

---

4. *Wolken. Heim* was written before the Berlin wall came down but
its publication is a timely and sinister warning of the dangers of a new
'Großdeutschland'.

out, Jelinek's concern is not with nature per se but with the capitalist economics and class struggle which it veils or from which it often detracts.

In turning now to look in more detail at *Burgtheater* and at the question of its reception, I shall argue that its plot and semi-montage structure (*Burgtheater* abounds in cultural references and quotation) inevitably detract from the author's intention of making a contribution to 'Vergangenheitsbewältigung': by modelling her characters on real-life Austrian personalities, Jelinek renders it difficult for her audience to understand the play as anything other than a vitriolic 'Schlüsselstück'. However, it is also a piece of linguistically experimental theatre, and as such it is important to examine the complex function of dialect in the play. The slapstick nature of much of the action and the fact that the play was written by a communist woman are without doubt additional factors to be considered but ultimately it is with the implications of the title of this play that the answer to Austria's disaffectedness with Jelinek lies.

In *Burgtheater* fascism rears its ugly head, not as a latent ideology in contemporary society, but as a reality, since the two parts of the play are set respectively in 1941 and in 1945, just before the liberation of Vienna. The characters in the play are a family of Burgtheater actors, consisting of husband and wife, Istvan and Käthe, the husband's brother Schorsch, a sister called Resi who serves the family as their maid, the couple's three children and two stereotypical 'Volksstück' and Burgtheater fixed part characters, the 'Alpenkönig' and the 'Burgtheaterzwerg'. The first part sees the actors having to come to terms with the new spirit of patriotism and nationalism which is being propagated by the Nazis and shows in particular Käthe's inability to speak the high German which is now required. Her brother-in-law Schorsch explains to her:

> SCHORSCH *gutmütig, brav*: Was i dir neilich scho sagen wollt, Kathi, mir missen unsane Rollen jetzn, vasteht, itzo a weng... ändern. Anpassn den veränderten Zeitläuften. Dem Verlangen vom Hoamatl... staatspolitisch besonders wertvoll! (Jelinek 1984: 104)

Käthe remains oblivious to Schorsch's message that she ought not to be constantly singing the praises of Austria and things

Austrian and is reprimanded by him in a tone which is charged with irony since it is clear that he too has not mastered the 'Schriftdeutsch' which they are required to speak:

> SCHORSCH: Ich hob dir vorhin scho ernsthoft gesokt, Katherl, daß des net ollweil so weitergeht mitn Semmering und die Alpen und die Liadln. Man konn jo nicht immer lochen, net wohr. Der Ernst der Stunde verlangt gebieterisch noch einem in Großdaitschlond ollgemein verständlichen Schriftdaitsch, Alpen- und Donaugaue fiegen sich. Ein neuer Erdenbürger! Willkommen! (p. 105)

The only significant piece of 'action' occurs in the 'Allegorisches Zwischenspiel' at the end of the first part, when the 'Alpenkönig', a member of the Austrian resistance movement, comes down in his 'Märchenkahn' to ask for a contribution from the family. The actors are incensed and tear the 'Alpenkönig' apart on stage, leaving behind a pile of limbs and pools of blood.

By the end of the war, in Part 2, Käthe has progressed from her earlier praise of 'Österreichertum' (p. 105) to a stage of national if not linguistic assimilation. She now speaks of 'Uns Daitschen' (p. 131). With the impending liberation of Vienna, there is a general atmosphere of fear as to what will become of the family under the Russians. The 'Burgtheaterzwerg', who has been hidden away by the maid, Resi, and moved about from place to place in order to avoid discovery and inevitable exter-mination by the Nazis, is finally uncovered by the family. The dwarf realises his power over the actors and demands Käthe's daughter Mitzi's hand in marriage as a bribe for his silence:

> Schlußendlich kurz und gut: Wenn Sie nicht wollen, daß ich sag, was Sie olle gemocht haben im 38er Jahr und danach, dann missen Sie mir dieses junge Madl scho geben. Sunsten sag i's, sunsten sagi's glei der empeerten Effentlichkeit! (p. 141)

This blackmail is foiled when Schorsch arrives back from a short stay in prison, declaring that he has managed to get himself photographed writing out a cheque for the patriotic Austrian resistance movement. Käthe is not to be consoled, however, as her beloved Burgtheater will now be occupied by the Russians! After a number of unsuccessful attempts, she manages to stab herself and lies bleeding to death throughout the closing actions of the play, muttering her regrets as follows:

KÄTHE *richtet sich plötzlich auf, verletzt, stöhnt undeutlich*:
Es ist mir schon wieder nicht gelungen. Derweil hat der Russe
mein Burgteatta bezwungen. Er richtet sich dorten häuslich
ein. Nein! ... Haltets eahm auf! Ringsum schlagen nämlich
Millionen deutsche Herzen. *gurgelnd* (pp. 148-49)

The nature of the plot, together with the texture and
construction of Jelinek's play, has focused reaction to *Burgtheater* towards one particular interpretation. Before I present
this interpretation let me explain what I mean about its texture.
The text of *Burgtheater* is assembled from a number of different
sources: it incorporates a great many clichéd Austrian songs and
sayings, such as 'Grieß enk Gott alle miteinander' (p. 103),
'Brüderlein fein, Brüderlein fein, einmal muß geschieden sein!'
(p. 115)[5] and 'Mir sein mir! I bin i!' (p. 116);[6] snippets from Nazi
propaganda films and parodies of quotes from well-known
classics such as Grillparzer's *König Ottokars Glück und Ende*;
and, finally, Jelinek's own 'original' contributions to the
dialogue. The author's statement that 'Das Stück ist an realen
Personen orientiert, die in der Zeit des Faschismus berühmte
Schauspieler waren' (Jelinek quoted in Löffler 1985: 88) confirmed the public's suspicions that *Burgtheater* was about Paula
Wessely, her husband Attila Hörbiger and his brother Paul, all of
whom were able to carry on with their careers as actors during
the war. Paula Wessely acted in a number of propaganda films,
one of which was *Heimkehr*, from which there are quotations
and to which there are allusions in Jelinek's play. Schorsch tells
Käthe, for example, that 'A daitsches Madel in Polen wirst jetzt
spün... Konnst scho onfongen, den Akzent lernen, gö!' (p. 110),
a clear reference to Wessely's role in *Heimkehr* as a persecuted
German in Poland. There are echoes too of the stirring 'Wir
werden heimkehren' message of the film such as Istvan's

5. The former is an exaggerated form of the song sung by the 'Chor der
Tiroler' in the first act of Carl Zeller's operetta *Der Vogelhändler* and the
latter is a famous song from Ferdinand Raimund's *Das Mädchen aus der
Feenwelt oder der Bauer als Millionär*.
6. The Duden dictionary *Wie sagt man in Österreich?* gives
the following definition of this particularly Austrian saying: '"wir sind
wir": Ausdruck einer in Österr. häufigen Gesinnung der ignoranten
Abkapselung, die, getragen vom eigenen Selbstbewußtsein, sich über
alles Fremde erhaben dünkt'.

promise that 'In unsarem Bette wird unser Herz pletzlich wissen: Ringsumschlagen Millionen deutsche Herzen! Daheim bist du, endlich daheim!' (p. 130), words which paraphrase the original text of the film (see Löffler 1985: 91).

There are further details in the play which can be interpreted as caricatured parallels and distortions of facts from the Wessely and Hörbiger biographies. The exact family constellation, for example, of husband, brother, wife and three daughters is replicated in *Burgtheater*. Paul Hörbiger did donate money to a resistance group and was briefly arrested by the Gestapo when this was disclosed. His sudden arrest, however, and the limited extent of his resistance have not been satisfactorily explained. Sigrid Löffler maintains that even Paul Hörbiger's memoirs do not clarify this episode:

> Wieso Hörbiger, der öffentliche Ja-Sager und heimliche Nein-Schreiber, plötzlich in die Fänge der Gestapo geriet, ist nicht zur Gänze aufgeklärt. Seinen eigenen Memoiren zufolge habe 'meine, wenn auch bescheidene Tätigkeit in der Widerstands-bewegung' vor allem in der Ausstellung eines Schecks auf 3000 Reichsmark für eine vage definierte Widerstandsgruppe bestanden (Löffler 1985: 91).

Paula Wessely's contemplated suicide after the war has been documented, although the attempt by the fictional mother to murder her daughter (pretending to remove a coffee stain from Mitzi's dress, Käthe pours petrol over her and sets her alight, Jelinek 1984: 138) met with cries of outrage. Peter Michael Lingens, the then editor of *Profil*, wonders how Jelinek can justify presenting this 'lie' in the midst of so many true correlations. Wouldn't the public assume that this attempted infanticide had also occurred? (Lingens 1985: 14)

The letters sent by members of the public to newspapers and to the magazine *Profil* bear testimony to an overwhelming defence of Paula Wessely and Attila Hörbiger and a false accusation that Jelinek is guilty of a 'holier than thou' attitude: 'Frau Jelinek hat die NS–Zeit nicht persönlich erlebt, aber vielleicht hätte sie nach einigen Recherchen im Verwandten- oder Bekanntenkreis auch eine Reihe von "Mitläufern" gefunden?' (Tamussino 1985: xi). Another reader asks:

Was berechtigt diese Frau Jelinek zu der unglaublichen Anmaßung, sich als Anklägerin der Familie Hörbiger–Wessely aufzuspielen, nur weil diese großen Schauspieler sich vor fast 50 Jahren nicht entschließen konnten, eine große Karriere, ein gesichertes Bühnenengagement, ihr Heim, ihre Heimat, ja ihre ganze Existenz aufzugeben und freiwillig in die Emigration zu gehen?

She ends her letter with a rallying cry to other like-minded Austrians: 'Deshalb steige ich für sie auf die Barrikaden und hoffe, daß das auch viele andere Österreicher tun' (Würzburger 1985: 8).

Only rarely have critics or lay commentators used Jelinek's politics as a way of explaining what they condemn as her biased views of the past. Having first admitted that 'ich habe das Stück *Burgtheater* weder gesehen noch gelesen', one member of the public, Fritz Potyka, professes that Jelinek's communism is enough to render her play void of literary value:

Wenn man zusätzlich erfährt, daß die Autorin Elfriede Jelinek eingeschriebenes Mitglied der Kommunistischen Partei ist, dann weiß man zur Gänze, woher der Wind weht und wo die Hintermänner zu suchen sind. Also ist die ganze Sache literarisch wertlos (Potyka 1985: xi).

A reviewer writing under his or her initials (A.M.) for *Deutsche Wochenzeitung* bemoans what he/she sees as a fashionable tendency amongst the 'Kulturschickeria...sich kritisch und empört über die "Gefahr des Faschismus" zu äußern'. This, for the journalist, is a shocking anomaly when 'halb Europa hier und heute unter roter Tyrannei schmachtet' (A.M. 1986). One critic even turns the tables and calls Jelinek a fascist: 'Ich behaupte, hier formuliert sich unter dem Schutzschild der Vergangenheitsbewältigung ein wahrhaft faschistischer Geist' (Schmidt–Mühlisch 1985). Since it is not often explicitly cited as a contributory factor, it is difficult to assess just how far Jelinek's communism was held against her. She was certainly pilloried by the right-wing press and in particular by the *Kronen-Zeitung's* Michael Jeanée (formerly with Germany's *Bild am Sonntag*), and the communist paper *Volksstimme* for its part went to some considerable length to defend Jelinek and to point out that she was being made to stand for all progressive contemporary

artists in Austria. In an open letter to Vienna's mayor, Helmut
Zilk, Gerald Graßl quotes Jeanée's opinions and explains how
the *Krone* journalist had twisted Zilk's words of praise for
Wessely and Hörbiger and encouraged his readers to unite
against Jelinek and her like:

> Des Bürgermeisters Rede ist kurz...'Und alle Hetzer und
> Jelineks und Schmierer sind gänzlich ohne Bedeutung und
> Wichtigkeit und Kraft. Und das ist gut so.'...Unterschwellig
> wird nun hier der Eindruck den 'KZ'-Lesern vermittelt, als
> hätten Sie mit der Gratulation Wessely–Hörbiger gleichzeitig
> einen demonstrativen Akt gegen die Schriftstellerin Elfriede
> Jelinek setzen wollen (Graßl 1985: 9).[7]

Jelinek learned a sobering lesson from the furore and personal
attacks which the interpretation of the play as a drama *à clef*
provoked. In *Oh Wildnis, oh Schutz vor ihr*, we hear her
sarcastic warning against basing any work of literature on real
people:

> Auch über die derartig schöne Heimat bitte keine Kunst
> ausschütten! Auf so einem Stückel Papier, was geht da schon
> drauf? Also nicht übertreiben, die Natur geht nämlich drauf!...
> Keine Lügen über Personen verbreiten, gelt, sonst setzts was.
> Das ist eine Haltung gegenüber der wahrheitsgemäßen Kunst:
> daß sie lieber wahrheitsgemäßigt stattfinden sollte. Wenn
> Menschen darin verschlüsselt, aber erkennbar, enthalten sind,
> dann her mit dem Gericht, dem Gerücht und den Anwälten,
> die vor Gericht dann zudringlich werden und Geld verdienen
> wollen. Nicht Vorbilder in der Kunst beschämen! (p. 33)

Despite its overwhelming reception as a 'Schlüsselstück'
Jelinek insisted that *Burgtheater* was essentially about
opportunism and about the susceptibility of artists to ideology (it
is thus doubly reminiscent of Klaus Mann's *Mephisto*). Her main
focus had been, she claimed, to show how language and culture
could be appropriated and used to propagate particular
ideological messages. Nevertheless, it is easy to see how the
restrictive parameters of the play—dealing with one particular

---

7. For a fuller picture see Gerhard Moser's overview (1986) of the
adverse criticism Jelinek has received. Moser argues that grant and subsidy cuts as well as censorship have been some of the problems which
progressive (he does not say communist) writers have had to endure.

family of actors and making concrete references to true events from their past—should have led to a refusal on the part of the public to see any wider relevance and general applicability of its desired 'Vergangenheitsbewältigung' and to an almost exclusive fixation by critics with Jelinek's cruel denunciation of some of the country's most popular personalities.

The treatment of language in Jelinek's play is of paramount importance and this fact is made clear for all who read stage directions such as 'es muß so gesprochen werden, daß es ausgesprochen sinnvoll klingt, mit Betonungen und allem' (p. 149), or in particular the explicit instruction which precedes the action:

> Sehr wichtig ist die Behandlung der Sprache, sie ist als eine Art Kunstsprache zu verstehen. Nur Anklänge an den echten Wiener Dialekt! Alles wird genauso gesprochen, wie es geschrieben ist. Es ist sogar wünschenswert, wenn ein deutscher Schauspieler den Text wie einen fremdsprachigen Text lernt und spricht (p. 102).

This calls to mind another Austrian playwright's instructions for directing his plays. Ödon von Horváth was so disappointed with the productions of his plays, and in particular with the production and misinterpretation of *Geschichten aus dem Wienerwald*, that he wrote a retrospective 'Gebrauchsanweisung' for it, in which he stated:

> Es darf kein Wort Dialekt gesprochen werden! Jedes Wort muß hochdeutsch gesprochen werden, allerdings so, wie jemand, der sonst nur Dialekt spricht und sich nun zwingt, hochdeutsch zu reden. Sehr wichtig! Denn es gibt schon jedem Wort dadurch die Synthese zwischen Realismus und Ironie. Komik des Unterbewußten (Horváth 1971: 663).

Although the required effect is slightly different—Horváth's actors should give the impression of dialect speakers trying to speak 'Hochdeutsch' whereas Jelinek's actors should preferably be Germans imitating an artificial, exaggerated dialect—the reasons for these linguistic frictions are similar. Horváth's claim that his entire *œuvre* was concerned with 'der ewige Kampf zwischen Bewußtsein und Unterbewußtsein' (p. 659) is a fitting description of Jelinek's concerns in *Burgtheater*. Horváth insisted that his work was conceived as a kind of continuation of the 'Volksstück', and, uncharacteristic though it may seem, his avowed aim was, 'ein wahrhaftiges Volkstheater aufzubauen, *das an die Instinkte und nicht an den Intellekt des Volkes appelliert'* (p. 662, my emphasis); Jelinek's intention is precisely the reverse. In writing *Burgtheater*, Jelinek aimed to provoke the reader or audience to *think* about the past and not to rehearse emotional or instinctive reactions and memories.

Like *Geschichten aus dem Wienerwald*, Jelinek's play is also more accurately a parody of a 'Volksstück' than a 'Volksstück' proper; her subtitle, 'Posse mit Gesang', indicates the tradition which she is parodying. Jelinek is not concerned to expose the 'Kleinbürger' as Horváth does or indeed as do Carl Merz and Helmut Qualtinger in *Der Herr Karl*, to name another satirical work of relevance to our analysis of the role of language. The eponymous Herr Karl slips into 'Hochdeutsch' when he expounds aspects of the contemporary propaganda or ideology and thus practises the Austrian variation of 'Vergangenheitsbewältigung': 'Distanzierung statt Bewältigung' (Weber quoted by Landa 1988: 37). In *Burgtheater* the slippage from dialect to 'Hochdeutsch' is momentary and is not the main focus of Jelinek's demystification. The author turns her attention instead to the whole stock of socio-cultural characteristics which lie dormant and wait to be charged with different meanings as and when this becomes necessary. Her criticism thus lies firmly with the Viennese dialect if not as deeply implicated in fascism then certainly as a discourse which contains the vocabulary of Austrian culture and is ripe for exploitation.

Examples of this can be seen in the conclusions to both parts of Jelinek's play, which disclose by use of Freudian parapraxes, the possible 'true' meaning of certain well-established symbols of Austrian national identity. The hymn of praise for Austria from Grillparzer's character Ottokar von Hornek, according to Sagmeister, 'ein Muß in jedem traditionellen Lesebuch, ein Musterbeispiel für die Erfüllung des obersten Lehrziels, die Schüler mit den Wertbegriffen des Wahren, Guten und Schönen vertraut zu machen' (Sagmesiter: 1982: 95), appears in distorted, dialect form at the close to Part 1 of *Burgtheater*. Jelinek's version runs:

SCHORSCH: Allein was nottut und was Klotz gefällt.
ISTVAN: Der klare Blick, der offne richt'ge Zugewinn.
SCHORSCH: Da seicht der Österreicher hin vor Samojeden.
ISTVAN: Denkt sich sein Teil und läßt den Großsulz reden!
SCHORSCH: O gutes Gland, o Vaterland!
ISTVAN: Verrottend zwischenem Kind Italien und dem Spengler NACKTBRAND
SCHORSCH: liegst du, der wangenrote KLÜNGLING da:
ISTVAN: Erhalte Gott dir deinen LUDERSINN.
SCHORSCH: Und eingriffe gut, was andre versargen! (pp. 125-26).[8]

Chosen as the epitome of classical culture which evokes everything fine, noble and beautiful about Austria and the Austrians, Ottokar's speech was rewritten by Jelinek and charged with images of stupidity and opportunism. The close of the play functions in a similar fashion. Here, the noise and confusion of the action and dialogue gradually become focused into a litany of Austrian names, short phrases and symbols chanted by all the characters in unison. The characters mouth both distorted evocations of traditional culture and history: 'Der Grillkarzer', 'Die Hofwürg', 'Das Salzkammerblut', 'Die Saubertöte', 'Das Haus Habswürg', and events of recent political history which, by implication, are meant to be as 'urösterreichisch' as the previous list. These are, for example, 'Das Judensterndl', 'Das Musikkazett', 'Die Vergaserin', 'Ringstraßenmorderie' and so on. The subconscious, we are invited to think, slips through and spoils the naive, apolitical myth of Austrianness.

Christopher Wickham warns in 'Heimatdichter as "Nestbeschmutzer"' that for a 'Dialektdichter' to write critically of his or her 'Heimat' is 'tantamount to a stab in the back'

8. A comparison with Grillparzer's original (written in 1825) makes the extent of Jelinek's cruel parody quite clear:

> Allein, was Not tut und was Gott gefällt,
> Der klare Blick, der offne, richtge Sinn,
> Da tritt der Österreicher hin vor Jeden,
> Denkt sich sein Teil, und läßt die andern reden!
> O gutes Land! o Vaterland! Inmitten
> Dem Kind Italien und dem Manne Deutschland,
> Liegst du, der wangenrote Jüngling, da:
> Erhalte Gott dir deinen Jugendsinn,
> Und mache gut, was Andere verdarben! (Grillparzer 1960: 1037).

(Wickham 1987: 194). Clearly, Jelinek is not a 'Dialektdichter'; exceptionally, she uses dialect in *Burgtheater*, where it is not an authentic medium but rather an artificial ploy. However, it is no mere coincidence that Jelinek should have chosen to write her play in dialect, albeit in this caricatured 'Meta-Wienerisch' (Kaufmann 1985). She is well aware of the central position which language plays in the formation of social and cultural identity and aware, therefore, also that any 'Heimat' critique which is exercised through dialect is inherently severe. Wickham explains:

> Because dialect implies a whole gamut of cultural associations, the explicit rejection of these via the medium of dialect is not only disorienting but a threat to an entire, harmonized world view. The epithet 'Nestbeschmutzer' seems generously mild when seen in this light (p. 194).

If dialect symbolizes a pre-rational stage of development which is dominated by vulnerability and irrationality as Wickham suggests, then it is tempting to interpret Käthe's inability to learn to speak 'Hochdeutsch' in psychoanalytical terms, that is as symptomatic of a society which refuses to give up the freedom and spontaneity of the Imaginary (Viennese dialect) for the strictures and laws of the Symbolic ('Hochdeutsch'). For Martin Walser, who defines 'Heimat' as 'der schönste Name für Zurückgebliebenheit' (1968a: 40), dialect occupies a positive position in its function as mechanism of control watching over the imitation process inherent in people's use of 'Hochdeutsch' (1968b: 56).

To a certain extent dialect functions in Jelinek in a Walserian fashion. Nazi terminology disintegrates and becomes laughable when it is expressed in dialect: 'Der Ernst der Stunde verlangt gebieterisch noch einem in Großdaitschlond ollgemein verständlichen Schriftdaitsch, Alpen- und Donaugaue fiegen sich. Ein neuer Erdenbürger!' (Jelinek 1984: 105). The important difference, however, is that Jelinek's point is not to show that these are alien ideas to the Austrian actors but rather that they are adopted unthinkingly and regurgitated in sentiment even if not quite linguistically intact. Thus, the 'Burgschauspieler' do not act out of an ideological conviction as Nazis, but have 'sich selbst zu kasperlmäßigen Puppen gemacht...deren

Gefährlichkeit in ihrem automatenhaften, spielerischen, ziellosen Aktionismus liegt' (Nyssen 1984: 162). Moreover, uttered in the same breath, the Austrian terms appear equally ideologically suspect: 'Ich hob dir vorhin scho ernsthoft gesokt, Katherl, daß des net ollweil so weitergeht mitn Semmering und die Alpen und die Liadln' (Jelinek 1984: 105).

Jelinek's treatment of Viennese dialect is, however, only a minor contributory factor in the condemnation she received in response to the play's eventual performance (three years after it was first published). Most critics express praise for the author's clever manipulation of language. Even Lingens, who is highly critical of the play, finds it 'sprachlich überaus gekonnt' (1985: 13). A far more likely complaint against the play and possible justification for its absence from the stage in Austria is that it contains offensive and shocking actions which may be deemed too disgusting for the average Austrian audience. Food is thrown all over the stage and played with by the children, the Alpenkönig's blood is splattered about as he is torn limb from limb, Resi, the maid, is alternately kicked and kissed by Käthe and there is even a smattering of bad language. German critics certainly protested their disgust quite vociferously:

> (*Burgtheater*) ist schlicht ein Machwerk, angereichert mit Widerlichkeiten und Perversitäten, deren dramaturgische Notwendigkeiten mit der Kneifzange des Möchte-Gern-Dramatikers im Stück festgemacht sind (Gerber 1985).

Perhaps this rather slapstick style of humour is considered too distasteful for an Austrian audience, or perhaps it is just too difficult for both the theatre establishment and the general public to accept this shocking and vulgar material from a woman's pen. Few commentators admit that this prejudices their opinion, though in one mostly positive letter to *Profil*, a reader admits that 'daß sie dabei eine Frau ist, macht sie noch böser' (Schuch 1985: 4). Such factors are difficult to investigate, though it is undoubtedly true that women playwrights are under-represented compared to other genres of literature and find it difficult to get their work produced. But this is a universal problem and not one which is specific to Austria. Topsy Küppers, director of the 'Freie Bühne' theatre in Vienna, is quoted as saying she would love to stage Jelinek but that it would be too costly to do so: 'Jelineks Stück ist eines der besten und schärfsten gesellschaftskritischen Kabaretts. Ich würde es sofort aufführen, aber leider fehlen mir die Mittel dazu' (quoted in Närr 1985).

To claim that Austrian directors have shied away from staging Jelinek because her work is too linguistically experimental or because it contains too many monologues and no strong plots would also be misguided. Many of Bernhard's plays bear similar characteristics, but have been staged despite his predilection for these techniques. The *FAZ* commentator Ulrich Weinzierl ponders on the unthinkable consequences that might have ensued had the play *Minetti* been written by Jelinek and not Bernhard. Unfortunately, he does not say whether his fears are due to Jelinek's sex or to her communism (Weinzierl 1985).

A more plausible theory than these is advanced by Peter Roessler who explores the lack of reaction to the publication of the play in 1982 (Roessler 1982: 85-91). Roessler describes the general tone of histories of the 'Burg' as one of sickly nostalgia and explains that the management's decision to retain the classics in its repertoire throughout the Nazi period was interpreted in retrospect in such a way as to make the classics connote resistance. If the Burgtheater was to play its role in the restoration then it had to be seen to possess and to have always possessed an 'übergesellschaftlicher Wert'. Even today, Roessler claims, the Burgtheater has to defend itself against any embarrassing questions regarding its history:

> Gemeinsamkeits-Symbol also als Innenfunktion—nach außen auratisches Symbol des Hochkulturlandes Österreich und damit Lockvogel für gebildete Touristen, deren gepflegtes Genießen durch Fragen nach der Vergangenheit peinliche Störung erfahren könnte (Roessler 1982: 90).

Roessler alleges in the light of this that the original, calculated reaction to *Burgtheater* was to hush it up. The publisher Jugend & Volk vetoed its planned publication of the play and when it did appear in *manuskripte* the press did not stir at all. This was, Roessler argues, a deliberately adopted strategy. His article ends with an appeal: 'Eine Aufführung des Stückes ist dringend zu fordern. Dann nämlich *muß* berichtet werden' (p. 91). The avalanche of publicity which the Bonn première launched—in the form of reviews and investigative articles on Wessely and

Hörbiger—lend Roessler's prediction a prophetic tone.

Jelinek's concern with demystifying the notion of 'Heimat' has, as I showed earlier, not been limited to this work only. Moreover, her critique has not always been presented in an Austrian context. That *Burgtheater* should be singled out and come to earn Jelinek the reputation of being anti-Austrian, then, reveals the logic of the critics' complaints since it is without doubt the play's interpretation as a 'Schlüsselstück' which accounts for most of the outspoken public condemnation which its author has received. Wessely and Hörbiger, it would seem, are so much an integral part of Austrian self-identity (ranking alongside Grillparzer as symbols of all that is great and good about Austrian culture) that any attack on them is tantamount to high treason. A *Profil* reader compounds this crass equation by casting Austria in National Socialist terms, as part of a 'Großdeutschland':

> Noch einmal: Heimkehr! Kaum ein schöneres Bekenntnis zum 'Deutschsein' als das von Paula Wessely im Film 'Heimkehr' gesprochene ist mir bekannt, es sei das von 'König Ottokars Glück und Ende' über Österreich. Nicht ins Nest scheißen, sonst müssen wir eine neue Definition für Verleugner finden (Huber-Straßhammer 1985: 8).

The fact that *Burgtheater* has not been produced in Austria suggests that theatres have not wished to seem to be endorsing Jelinek's version of the lives of two of the country's most cherished actors by allowing a performance run in Austria and have consequently boycotted it. It is likely that the possibility of a legal scandal, with a lawsuit against the author, put paid to any possibility of an Austrian production. While some critics called for a production at the Burgtheater itself (Henrichs and Löffler), others consulted lawyers and warned of the consequences: 'Wer immer sein (oder eines hingeschiedenen Anverwandten) "Lebensbild vor Entstellung schützen" will, hat hüben wie drüben gute Chancen' (Sichrovsky 1985: 101). Wessely's daughter, Elisabeth Orth, bemoaned the fact that her family had decided not to take legal action and was of the opinion that Jelinek's play ought to have 'ein gerichtliches Nachspiel' (Orth 1985: 94).

Roessler is right to point out that with its attack on the temple itself—that greatest of Austrian myths, the Burgtheater—the implications of Jelinek's 'Nestbeschmutzung' are potentially far-reaching. However, the effect of the play's staging has been a resultant narrowing down of its reception to an obsessive concern with the integrity of the 'disciples' of the eponymous institution. It is likely that this almost exclusive focus on the Wessely–Hörbiger element belies the full extent of Austria's disenchantment with Jelinek which is more realistically a reaction against her sex, politics and 'bad taste'. Both the critics and the lay public have deflected attention away from any consideration of the literary and dramatic merits of the play and have refused to enter into constructive discussion about the role of artists in the Third Reich. Instead they have merely questioned the right of anyone who was not alive in the National Socialist era to cast aspersions on the activities of those who were.

WORKS CITED

A. M.
    1986   'Selbstgerechte Kulturbanausen'. *Deutsche Wochenzeitung*, 10 January.
Bernhard, T.
    1977   *Minetti: ein Portrait des Künstlers als alter Mann*. Frankfurt: Suhrkamp.
Ebner, J., (ed.)
    1980   *Wie sagt man in Österreich? Wörterbuch der österreichischen Besonderheiten*. Mannheim: Duden.
Fiddler, A.
    1991   'Problems with Porn: Situating Elfriede Jelinek's *Lust*'. *German Life and Letters* 44, pp. 404-15.
Gerber, D.
    1985   ' "*Burgtheater*" oder "Wo habt ihr dessengleichen schon gesehen?" ' *General-Anzeiger für Bonn*, 12 November.
Graßl, G.
    1985   'Gegen "Hetzer" und "Schmierer" '. *Volksstimme*, 17 December.
Grillparzer, F.
    1960–1965 *König Ottokars Glück und Ende. Sämtliche Werke*. Ed. P. Frank and K. Pörnbacher. 4 vols. Munich: Hanser, I, pp. 973-1083.
Henrichs, B.
    1985   'A Hetz'. *Die Zeit*, 15 November.
Horváth, Ö. von
    1971   'Gebrauchsanweisung', in T. Krischke and D. Hildebrandt (eds.), *Gesammelte Werke*. Frankfurt: Suhrkamp, IV, pp. 659-65.

Huber-Straßhammer, W.
  1985   Letter. *Profil* 50.
Jelinek, E.
  1970   *wir sind lockvögel baby!* Reinbek: Rowohlt.
  1984   *Burgtheater* in *Theaterstücke: Clara S. Was geschah, nachdem Nora ihren Mann verlassen hatte. Burgtheater.* Cologne: Prometh Verlag (First published in *manuskripte 76*, 1982).
  1985a   *Die Liebhaberinnen.* Reinbek: Rowohlt (First published 1975).
  1985b   *Oh Wildnis, oh Schutz vor ihr.* Reinbek: Rowohlt.
  1989   *Lust.* Reinbek: Rowohlt.
  1990   *Wolken. Heim.* Göttingen: Steidl.
  1991   *Totenauberg.* Reinbek: Rowohlt.
Kaufmann, E.
  1985   'Nudeln und Blut'. *Die Wochenpresse,* 19 November.
Kübler, G.
  1985   'Spitze Schreie. Elfriede Jelineks "Oh Wildnis, oh Schutz vor ihr" '. *Neue Zürcher Zeitung,* 20 December.
Landa, J.
  1988   *Bürgerliches Schocktheater.* Frankfurt: Athenäum.
Lingens, P.
  1985   'Wieweit verdient Paula Wessely Elfriede Jelinek?'. *Profil* 48.
Löffler, S.
  1985   'Was habe ich gewußt—nichts'. *Profil* 48.
Mann, K.
  1981   *Mephisto: Roman einer Karriere.* Reinbek: Rowohlt (First published Amsterdam: Querido Verlag, 1936).
Moser, G.
  1986   'Kulturlose Wende?'. *Volksstimme,* 17 October.
Närr, M.
  1985   'NS-Zeit und Künstler—Schwamm drüber?'. *Die Wochenpresse,* 25 November 1985.
Nyssen, U.
  1984   'Nachwort' in E. Jelinek, *Theaterstücke. Clara S. Was geschah, nachdem Nora ihren Mann verlassen hatte. Burgtheater.* Cologne: Prometh Verlag.
Orth, E.
  1985   'Was hätte das für ein Theaterstück werden können'. *Profil* 48.
Pabisch, P.
  1977   *Anti-Heimatdichtung im Dialekt.* Vienna: Schendl.
Potyka, F.
  1985   Letter. *Die Presse,* 7/8 December.
Qualtinger, H.
  1973   *Der Herr Karl: Qualtingers beste Satiren. Vom Travnicek zum Herrn Karl.* Munich: Langen Müller.
Raimund, F.
  1924–1934 *Das Mädchen aus der Feenwelt oder der Bauer als Millionär: Historisch-kritische Säkularausgabe der Sämtlichen Werke.* 6 vols. Vienna: Anton Schroll.

Roessler, P.
1982   'Vom Bau der Schweigemauer', *TheaterZeitSchrift* 2, pp. 85-91.

Sagmeister, H.
1982   'Die Problematisierung der Heimat in der modernen Österreichischen Literatur', in G.J. Carr and E. Sagarra (eds.), *Irish Studies in Modern Austrian Literature*. Proceedings of the first Irish Symposium in Austrian Studies. 19–20 February 1982. Dublin: Trinity College, pp. 94-121.

Schmidt-Mühlisch, L.
1985   'Der arme Alpenkönig stirbt um des Führers willen'. *Die Welt*, 13 November.

Schuch, R.
1985   Letter. *Profil* 33.

Sichrovsky, H.
1985   'Paula Wessely: Der letzte Skandal?'. *Basta* 11, pp. 99-101.

Tamussino, U.
1985   Letter. *Die Presse*, 7-8 December.

Walser, M.
1968a   'Heimatkunde', in *Heimatkunde: Aufsätze und Reden*. Frankfurt: Suhrkamp, pp. 40-50.
1968b   'Bemerkungen über unseren Dialekt', in *Heimatkunde*, pp. 51–57.

Weber, N.
1980   *Das gesellschaftlich Vermittelte der Romane österreichischer Schriftsteller seit 1970*. Frankfurt: Peter Lang.

Weinzierl, U.
1985   'Sauberes Theater'. *Frankfurter Allgemeine Zeitung*, 27 November.

Wickham, C.
1987   'Heimatdichter as "Nestbeschmutzer"', in H.W. Seliger (ed.), *The Concept of Heimat in Contemporary German Literature*. Munich: iudicium, pp. 183-97.

Würzburger, L.
1985   Letter. *Profil* 50.

Zeller, C.
1933   *Der Vogelhändler: Operette in drei Akten*. Cologne: Bosworth and Co.

Beyond Postmodernism:
The Late Work of Peter Handke

Fritz Wefelmeyer

In a speech in 1984 Peter Handke made the following comments on contemporary literature:

> Ich habe die starke Empfindung, daß das Formen, das Fassenwollen, kurz, das Schreiben in der Menschheit blüht wie je, oder: kurz vor der Blüte steht—wie je. Oft ist mir bei meiner eigenen Arbeit ein Mann aus der Bibel in den Sinn gekommen, den ich mir dann als den Patron für uns Schriftsteller, oder überhaupt für die Künstler, dachte. Man möge ruhig darüber lachen: es ist Johannes der Täufer. So wie er meinte, nach ihm käme der Größere, so empfinde auch ich immer, es nicht zu schaffen, doch einer, oder nicht bloß einer, würde auftreten, nicht nach mir, sondern vielleicht schon jetzt, und schreibend sagen, was der Fall ist: ein-facher, dringlicher, erlösend (Handke 1984).

What is striking in this extract are the images of the organic, of blossoming, of being in flower, with which Handke describes the act of writing. These images are in fact typical of the Handke of the 1980s because they indicate the way in which his attitude towards the question of form has changed. In contrast to his emphasis in earlier years, literary forms are now associated with the natural forces, which are invested with spiritual power. Indeed, in a further striking image, Handke goes as far as to compare the literary work with the sun, in that both possess the power to illuminate: 'Also mein Buch—vielleicht ist das nur ein Traum—das ist in meiner Vorstellung verbunden mit dem Bild der Sonne. Also die Seiten, die Lettern, auch die Farben des Papiers' (1990: 44).

The organic images are also interesting for another reason: they are a demonstration of Handke's view of the figure of John the Baptist, who is seen as the herald of a new power of form—

sunlike, blossoming, redemptive—which transcends all other powers. In the same way, Handke suggests, the writer can be seen as a forerunner, as someone who prepares the way. Yet is the avant-garde which Handke invokes with the figure of John the Baptist the avant-garde of modernism? Can this figure be said to stand for aesthetic innovations which break literary conventions and disappoint habitual responses? Even if one sees John the Baptist as a herald or forerunner, one hesitates to apply the category of modernism to this biblical figure. So can he be said to stand for premodernism, or better, postmodernism (Anz 1990: 9)? Or is this use of the biblical figure nothing more than an example of 'der real existierende Wahnsinn Peter Handkes', as a fellow writer put it, with sympathy but little understanding (Widmer 1986: 13)? Worse things still have been said of Handke by critics. Yet it is not untypical for his literary career that he himself should be a kind of herald of future trends to his contemporaries. For example, as far as his use of religious images and language is concerned, Botho Strauß has already followed his lead in his essay 'Der Aufstand gegen die sekundäre Welt'.

Peter Handke has always appeared to be somewhat ahead of the 'Zeitgeist', something which has earned him criticism and even scorn. Two examples will suffice to demonstrate this. He was, for instance, reproached with losing himself in formalistic and aesthetic experiments at a time when the student movement of 1968 was in full swing and much emphasis was being placed on social change through art. Handke had indeed distanced himself from Brechtian and Sartrean 'littérature engagée' at that time and appeared to be more interested in Ludwig Wittgenstein's philosophical model of language-games than in Marx's *Kapital* (cf. Blattmann 1984: 33-41). In other words, he was seeking a new form of writing at a time when others were preoccupied with content, especially of a political nature. Such was the case with, for example, Hans Magnus Enzensberger and Peter Schneider. However, it must be said that many of Handke's contemporaries followed suit in the 1970s. Following the reception of Russian and Czech formalism and a reading of Roland Barthes's insights into the way form mediates content, aesthetic experiences were no longer dismissed as peripheral and esoteric.

By then, however, Handke had already moved on, which brings me to my second example. After *Die Hornissen, Publikumsbeschimpfung* and *Kaspar*, came, at the beginning of the 1970s, *Der kurze Brief zum langen Abschied* and *Wunschloses Unglück*, texts which were seen as belonging to what became known as the new subjectivity or 'neue Innerlichkeit'. Some critics did not like this either: they claimed that Handke, along with others, was 'auf larmoyante Weise' turning back on himself: 'Eine Generation...findet in den Klagen Trost, und in dem artifiziellen Dunkel, auf dem die Autoren operieren, ihre Erleuchtung' (W.M. Lüdke, quoted in Blattmann 1984: 142).

When we move forward to the 1980s, however, the situation has changed again: political activism is now long since over and Handke's critics have become admirers and followers, if somewhat hesitant ones. W.M. Lüdke, for example, is among their number in his essay 'Am Ursprung liegt das Ziel'. Does this mean that Handke's message has got through? Other critics now point to a continuity between *Der kurze Brief zum langen Abschied* and, say, *Die Wiederholung*, written in the mid-1980s. In their opinion the link between the two periods is the religious, mystical, visionary element in Handke's writing, combined with a strong concentration on the act of narrating and the subjectivity of the narrator. As one critic even said on the cover of her book on Handke: 'Handke repräsentiert die zeitgenössische, postmoderne Subjektivität als Reflex mystischer Erfahrung' (Wagner-Egelhaaf 1989). Perhaps this then was the message of John the Baptist: that one should indulge in the free play of the signifier, liberate oneself from the demands of objectivity and enjoy the pleasures of pure subjectivity in the vast warehouse of signs (cf. Jameson 1986: 70-72). In other words, that one should enter into the world of the postmodern.

There were indeed many indications that Handke might be moving in this direction. One particular example is his reference in *Die Lehre der Sainte-Victoire* to the concept of analogy, that tempting refuge of poststructuralism:

Und so kam wieder die Lust auf das Eine in Allem. Ich wußte
ja: Der Zusammenhang ist möglich. Jeder einzelne Augenblick
meines Lebens geht mit jedem anderen zusammen—ohne
Hilfsglieder. Es existiert eine unmittelbare Verbindung: ich
muß sie nur freiphantasieren. Und zugleich kam die wohl-
bekannte Beengung: denn ich wußte auch, daß die *Analogien*
sich nicht leichthin ergeben durften; sie waren, Gegenteil von
dem täglichen Durcheinander im Kopf, nach heißen
Erschütterungen die goldenen Früchte der Phantasie (1980: 79).

Michel Foucault, for example, has praised analogy and has
shown in *The Order of Things* how Renaissance authors like
Aldrovandi make no qualitative distinction between the exact
observation of natural phenomena and the recording of
fantastic relationships between different phenomena. This is
because, for Aldrovandi and his contemporaries, nature was like
a vast script on which a commentary had to be written:

But the reason for this was not that they preferred the
authority of men to the precision of an unprejudiced eye, but
that nature, in itself, is an unbroken tissue of words and signs,
of accounts and characters, of discourse and forms. When one
is faced with the task of writing an animal's *history*, it is useless
and impossible to choose between the profession of naturalist
and that of compiler: one has to collect together into one and
the same form of knowledge all that has been *seen* and *heard*,
all that has been *recounted*, either by nature or by men, by the
language of the world, by tradition, or by the poets (Foucault
1970: 39-40).

In Aldrovandi the world and the commentary on it constitute,
according to Foucault, a complex net of substantial analogy-
relationships in which the knower and his object are closely
bound up and associated in the act of knowing. As such it offered
a complete contrast to the post-Renaissance world with its
attempt to fix the relationship between sign and nature and
thereby to bring the latter under the control of science. This has
been described by Peter Bürger as follows:

Während mit der Einsetzung einer binären Auffassung von
sprachlichen Zeichen die Natur sich zum Objekt verfestigt,
wären in der 'vorklassischen Sprachauffassung' die Welt und
das Wissen gleichermaßen sprachlichen Wesens, womit an die
Stelle des Subjekt-Objekt-Bezuges ein unendliches Reden trete,
der Wellenbewegung vergleichbar (Bürger 1987: 118).

We shall see later that there is indeed a similarity to Handke here. Foucault's critique of the dominance of scientific discourse and his interest in literary forms have made him a spokesman of postmodernism. He was the first to draw attention to the importance of analogy which has since been closely associated with postmodernism.

One might at this point wonder why the expression postmodernism and not modernism is being used. Literary modernism too can be understood, at least partly, as the attempt to dissolve and liquefy through the practice of art the rigid, petrified viewpoint referred to by Bürger. In this context one need only think of Bertolt Brecht's 'alienation effect' or the concept of de-automatization or defamiliarization as developed by Russian Formalism. Yet one could perhaps say that the concept of postmodernism expresses still more trenchantly than the concept of modernism the idea that there no longer exists a reliable connection between stylistic or linguistic forms, true statements about reality, and a coherent, responsible and authentic self. In particular, the way and extent to which the idea of a self has been questioned marks a departure from modernism. Authenticity and true self-expression are dismissed as concepts that are the heritage of metaphysics and enlightenment rationality. Philosophical reason and scientific rationality are part of a power structure that defines meaning and norms. In postmodernism, by contrast, meaning depends on contexts, and contexts are interchangeable. Different artistic styles and forms can be cited arbitrarily, as there is no universal authority which can act as a point of reference.

There may still be a nostalgia in postmodernism for the world of Aldrovandi and for substantial analogy (see p. 48) relationships, in which the individual feels intellectually and artistically at one with the world. For someone like Foucault, however, what is most interesting about the world of Aldrovandi is that it offers an alternative model to the concept of reality and absolute claims of modern scientific thought and rationality. This rationality wants to subject nature and man; its aim is, according to Foucault, a comprehensive power over all aspects of life. In other words, what is decisive here for him is liberation from a particular concept of reality rather than a genuine interest in a new, harmonious cosmology, in which, as in the case of Aldrovandi, subject and object are one.

Here already a difference becomes apparent between postmodernism and Handke, in that Handke takes analogy seriously, even if not in such a way that one could speak of an Aldrovandi revival. The description, or as Handke says, 'das Freiphantasieren' of an analogous relationship between two or more objects or events leads to an experience of the spiritual bond ('geistiges Band') uniting them. Analogy in Handke becomes a spiritual experience ('Geisterfahrung'). The spiritual link which is formed between them is also the proper dwelling place of the writer, as the title of one of Handke's books makes clear: *Aber ich lebe nur von den Zwischenräumen*. Spiritual experience, however, seems to be a closed book to postmodernism. Indeed, it could sometimes be said that postmodernism deliberately turns its back on this type of experience by following in the footsteps of Nietzsche and Heidegger and immediately dismissing it as so much metaphysics (see Derrida 1987). In this respect one can see that Handke does not share the preoccupations, aims or limitations of postmodernism. Handke goes beyond postmodernism, in that he draws on sources and follows paths that are alien to it and yet which might look towards the future.

In *La condition postmoderne* Jean-Francois Lyotard announces the end of the interpretative systems of Western thought and science which aim at unity and freedom from contradiction. Instead these systems are now simply seen as 'grand narratives'. The renunciation of all claims to a single truth paves the way for a multitude of language-games. According to Lyotard, behind these games there is no longer any single unifying meaning or metalanguage which would make it possible to translate these language-games into one another. Present-day knowledge is no longer to be found in philosophers' heads, so to speak, but, for example, on floppy disks. Knowledge, stripped of any philosophical pretensions, is now stored in databanks as information, and power belongs to those who own these databanks.

Indeed, this social trend goes hand in hand with an epistemological modesty, or, one might say, with a new freedom on the part of the philosophers who used to feel obliged to pursue metaphysical knowledge. If everything is now a matter of language-games, then the relationship between knowledge and reality is no longer of interest. What is of interest, however, is above all the wish to make the best of the game; in other words, to produce 'good stories'. This leads in turn to new criteria of judgment, which are now aesthetic, since stories can be either good or bad, boring or exciting, complete or incomplete, pleasing or unsuccessful and so on. Furthermore, if the intellectual language-game is above all interesting as a story, then attention is focused on the way in which intellectual knowledge or discourse is formulated and expressed.

For example, all the objects of historical knowledge, such as historical documents, dates, accounts and so forth, appear in the form of stories or are accompanied by explanatory stories, however short. History, as Hayden White argues in *Tropics of Discourse*, is dependent on the way it is told. This postmodern thinker draws attention to the rhetorical qualities of a story, for with stories—so the thesis goes—effects are aimed at, which means that power is exercised. The selection of subjects for a story (of, for example, particular historical events) is equally dependent either on power interests or on arbitrary points of view, because there is no longer a reasoning power based on truth which can validate or justify any particular selection. Furthermore, since the question as to the proper subject of a story cannot be definitively answered, there is no reason to assume that the subject itself (e.g. historical events, documents, experiences) requires a particular narrative form in order to be fully understood. Neither does it create any obligation or necessity to be continued in a narrative form.

Here we see an important difference between postmodernism and Peter Handke, because he is interested precisely in continuing history as a narrative: 'euer Arbeiten soll ein Wirken sein—gebt etwas weiter' (1982: 122). Particularly in the stories written in the 1980s he tries to demonstrate the necessity of the act of storytelling out of the personal history of the storytellers or the subject of the stories. One can see, for example, how stories such as *Die Wiederholung* and *Die Lehre der Sainte-Victoire* justify themselves in the act of narrating. It is only through the story that the storytellers are able to perceive the history of their lives, of their friends or relatives, of their people or a particular landscape as a single continuous whole. Not infrequently the storytellers can only continue with their own lives after they have told their story. Much the same could be said of Handke's other characters.

Handke's stories reject the somewhat naive claim of postmodernism that one can never step outside the relativity of the story as language-game. Such an attitude is naive because it is without any understanding of what actually takes place in a story. Certainly every story is a language-game, as Handke himself explicitly stresses (cf. 1990: 84). Reference has already been made to his interest in Wittgenstein's language-game model. What is interesting about a game, however, is that, in order to function as a game, it must have rules or a form. These forms are related to the realm of experience of Handke's storytellers or main protagonists. They could be said to perform two functions: firstly, they create a space, or, as Handke puts it, a 'Leere', in which the experienced world of the storyteller can be presented; secondly, they present the experience as part of a larger whole. However, experience itself is not chaos, but is formed, and the story has to do justice to the 'original form', that is the form which the experience originally took. In other words, the story is, as Handke insists, a form which 'realizes' the form of the experience.

Experience appears as a form, as a kind of letter or character which is not yet, however, a complete reality. It is waiting for the connecting bond of the story to bring it into a sequential order so that a legible and meaningful text is created. The story is a game which orders and connects signs in such a way as to make their significance graspable. At the same time the story ensures that the signs do not merge into each other or overlap with one another and thereby become illegible. The story creates 'Zwischenräume', not only between characters but also between words, sentences, paragraphs and so on. It can be described as playful in so far as it only has meaning in itself and refuses to obey the conventions and laws which determine practical everyday behaviour. The task of the language-game is to put the meaning of experience into a larger context; in doing so it is not, however, bound by the laws and concepts which determine the physical world. It plays with realities in order to realize and present the meaning of experiences.

Postmodern talk of the relativity of language-games, which admits of no independent criteria of truth and only considers the question of power interests to be relevant, can thus be seen to be inappropriate. The language-game must, as I have said, do justice to the experience by attempting to articulate its meaning. Just as every single character exists intact alongside other characters in the word, so the language-game of the story must bring the different experiences together into a cohesive whole, thereby articulating them. The postmodern concept of freedom—'anything goes'—which aims to emancipate literary forms from moral values and conditions of truth overlooks the fact that the freedom of the game is only intended to render an invention possible ('ein Erfinden') which is also a rediscovery ('ein Wiederfinden') of the original experience. Every story is, as another of Handke's titles indicates, a 'Wiederholung' (1986: 233).

This repetition is, however, nothing other than the insight into the true and necessary meaning of the experiences. The task of the language-game of the story is to show not only what the experiences actually are but also what value these have for other experiences in the concrete history of a person (Handke 1989: 68-70). In the postmodern novel experiences remain mere signs which follow an order which takes no real account of them. The postmodern author 'plays' with the experiences with the aim of creating an order which constantly forces the reader to seek meaning, while at the same time withholding that meaning. The postmodern story is a never-ending succession of mirrors from which neither the storyteller nor the reader can escape. Umberto Eco's novels are a demonstration of this (cf. de Lauretis 1986: 251-69). Handke's stories, however, release the narrator and the reader from the past by repeating it as a comprehensible text to which future experiences can be linked. With Handke the narrated past makes possible a narratable future. Postmodern literature, on the other hand, places emphasis on the story as an intellectual game, albeit often of a sophisticated and entertaining nature.

Moreover, postmodernism has rejected the whole concept of reason and the reasoning subject as outdated metaphysical ballast (cf. Cadava *et al.* 1991). As a result, in the postmodern story there is no longer any pressing need for a subject with transcendental power. The author is reduced to the historical person, to an organizer of material, and this historical person is him- or herself also just a text which sets in motion the different anthropological, psychological, sociological and other language-games that interpret this text. What is important is the play with signs and meanings, to prolong the reader's interpretative activity. The reader and the act of reading are as important as the author, if not more important.

Hanns-Josef Ortheil, a writer who describes himself as postmodern, has said,

> Die postmoderne Literatur ist die Literatur des kybernetischen Zeitalters. Sie verabschiedet nicht die ästhetischen Projekte der Moderne, sondern verfügt über diese als Modelle, die in Spiele höherer Ordnungen überführt werden können. Dabei treten an die Stelle vom Autor oder Erzähler ausgewiesener Welt-bilder, Strukturen, die dem Leser die entscheidende Arbeit zumuten. Der Leser wird zum intellektuellen Komplizen des Autors, das zentrale Medium der Komplizenschaft ist der Roman, als Vergewisserung über die noch möglichen Spielarten, der Welt zu begegnen (quoted in Hensel 1987).

Nothing could be further from Handke's intentions. It is true that in his case too the author does not present 'approved world views'; however, the text is far from being just a 'structure'. There is no question at all of what Ortheil calls 'Komplizenschaft' in Handke's works. The basic model is not that of a detective story (much favoured by postmodern writers), as Ortheil seems to suggest by his use of the terms 'Komplize' and 'Komplizenschaft'. The text is not a secret or puzzle which is endlessly deciphered or decoded. There is no question of playing 'hunt the meaning'. It is rather, as I have said, a question of finding a meaningful form which not only preserves experience but also articulates it. The reader has to recognize or 'realize' that form. This is a task which is indeed shared with the author who made a similar effort when he attempted to give form to his material and experience.

Of course Handke's narrators and protagonists are also acquainted with the 'indeterminable' ('das Unbestimmbare'), that 'Struktur' which eludes definitive signification. Indeed, it is the indeterminable which in one explicit case leads the narrator in *Die Wiederholung* to new experiences and the realization of form (p. 135). The indeterminable does not, however, have the effect of making the subject, the self of the narrator or protagonist, dissolve; on the contrary, it allows the self to become aware of itself, to discover its own 'I'. An extract from *Die Wiederholung* may clarify this. On his journey through Slovenia the narrator comes across a series of illegible human signs which make it possible for him to free the landscape he is experiencing from an identification with its historical and geo-political boundaries (namely part of what used to be Yugoslavia or the former Austrian Empire etc.). By virtue of their illegibility, these signs no longer define the landscape but rather create a space for other signs and experiences which can finally open up and reveal different aspects of that landscape:

> Aber vieldeutig erschien dann schon das PETROL-Schild einer Tankstelle, welches, durch das Geäst eines Baumes gesehen, an ein, nur im Traum erlebtes, China erinnerte, und eine gleichermaßen fremdartige Sinaiwüste öffnete sich hinter den Hochhausblöcken mit dem Anblick eines staubigen Fernbusses, von dessen Frontseite, wo die Walze mit den Zielangaben verrutscht war und genau in der Mitte zwischen zwei unleserlichen Ortsnamen stand, im Vorbeifahren das Fragment einer hebräischen Schriftrolle mir in die Augen sprang—ja, *in die Augen sprang*: denn das Sich-Öffnen der Landschaft rund um das Schriftbild war begleitet von einem Erschrecken (Handke 1986: 134).

The indeterminable can thus be said to be a stepping stone to a clearer determination or definition. It also throws light on the nature of illegible signs and their relationship to the recognizing human 'I'. Illegible signs are directed back upon themselves; they gather up and focus the power of recognition and understanding which would normally be used to read them. In this respect they resemble the 'blind window', that is, the imitation window set against the wall, which the narrator encounters:

> Seine Wirkung kam aus dem fehlenden Üblichen, dem
> Abwesenden: dem Undurchlässigen. Kraft der in ihm
> gebündelten Unbestimmbarkeit strahlte es meinen Blick
> zurück, und in mir hörte alles Stimmengewirr und Durch-
> einanderreden auf: Mein ganzes Wesen verstummte und las
> (p. 134).

The 'blind window' draws attention to the fact that it is mere
appearance ('Schein'). It can only, however, appear, if there is
light from the sun ('im Schein der Sonne'). Here Handke plays
with the double meaning of 'Schein': both appearance and light.
The sunlight is the necessary counterpart to the epistemological
activity carried out by the narrating and experiencing 'I'.
Without sunlight a recognition of the outside world is
impossible.

When the signs, because of their illegibility, draw attention to
themselves, to their appearance, rather than simply providing
access to the signified, then the 'I' can become aware of itself
(Handke 1986: 140-41). It is not the outward light of the sun but
the inner light (the epistemological 'I', its reading and
recognizing activity) which is reflected in the illegible signs, just
as the sun is reflected in the blind window. The illegible signs call
up, for instance, experiences which are stored in the self's
memory. This makes the self realize that it is actively involved in
the process of knowing and identifying. What the sun is for
physical objects, signs are for the signified: a light in which
things can appear ('erscheinen').

Language signs, of course, originate, metaphorically
speaking, in the inner sun, the human 'I'. If objects are to appear
in signs, in the light of the inner sun, this inner light must
correspond to the outer one in order for objects to be properly
comprehended. An object is only fully comprehended if mind and
senses have worked together and come to the same conclusion.
If one takes this fact into account, a number of otherwise
obscure statements made by Handke become clear, as for
instance the mysterious remark from *Aber ich lebe nur von den
Zwischenräumen*:

> Das Buch ist immer noch für mich die Verkörperung der
> Sonne, irgendwie kommt mir das vor. Die Buchstaben, die
> Wörter sind für mich so... die Sonne der Welt, also damit...
> hat man...hat man der Sonne gerecht zu werden. Ich schlag

auch nur ein Buch auf und vertief mich darin und erfreu mich
dran und richt mich dran auf und krieg davon Augen und
Ohren eingesetzt, wenn... wenn... wenn... die Sätze von der
Sonne geführt werden (p. 42).

Inner, mental activity brings together things which are
transmitted to the senses *eternally* by light; our inner light—that
is, our reasoning, form-giving powers—then connects these
impressions to a greater whole. With Handke the indeterminable leads, on the one hand, to an understanding of how the
inner world of the 'I' and the outer world of the senses are
related to each other and, on the other hand, to an understanding of how the world appears in language and how the
individual grasps the world in language. The indeterminable is
therefore not an end in itself, as it is in postmodernism, but leads
to a deeper, richer and more conscious understanding of the
world and the self.

Let us now look more closely at the role of language in the
process of understanding the world. Every single character in
the alphabet has a material shape and concrete form. This form
must be perceived before the meaning of a letter or a
combination of letters can be understood. This process applies
not only to human language. Signs, as physical shapes, can be
found in nature as well and belong to a different, although
kindred, language. To be able to read these signs, however, one
needs practice. It is such practice that Handke's novel *Die
Wiederholung* offers its readers. We see here how the language
of nature can be understood by someone who is prepared to
read it. The first-person narrator of *Die Wiederholung* experiences this when he recognizes the first letter of an alphabet one
morning in the silhouette of a grazing horse. He goes on to
discover, to decipher a whole alphabet of letters in nature:

In mich aufgenommen hatte ich die Einzelheiten des Tals
auch zuvor, nun aber schienen sie mir in ihrer Buchstäblich-
keit, eine im nachhinein, mit dem grasrupfenden Pferd als
dem Anfangsbuchstaben, sich aneinanderfügende Lettern-
reihe, als Zusammenhang. Schrift... Und zweierlei Träger der
Welt unterschied ich da: den Erdboden, welcher das Pferd trug,
und den Entzifferer, der diese Dinge geschultert hatte, in der
Form ihrer Merkmale und Zeichen. Ich spürte auch leibhaftig

die Schultern, wie sie sich verbreiteten…so als werde die
Erdenschwere, durch die Entzifferung, aufgehoben in eine
Luftschrift, oder in ein frei dahinfließendes einziges Wort aus
lauter Selbstlauten, wie es sich z.B. findet in dem lateinischen
Ausdruck Eoae, übersetzbar mit *Zur Zeit der Eos, Zur Zeit der
Morgenröte* oder einfach *Des Morgens* (pp. 114-15).

The alphabet the narrator has discovered in nature is now
transformed into a script in which is expressed the way in which
the narrator's 'I' experiences the natural alphabet. As he himself
puts it, the narrator transforms the deciphered text of nature
into a script which once again has a concrete external form, such
as *Eoae*. This form, however, derives from the 'I'. Yet the
so-called 'Erdenschrift' and 'Luftschrift' have in common the
fact that, as material signs, they are shaped into forms which
can be perceived by our senses. Obviously, nature itself, natural
phenomena, appear in shapes and forms. According to the
process of analogy which has already been mentioned, these
phenomena can be treated as letters or signs and then narrated.
They constitute a natural sign language that can be read by the
artist.

However, the forms that the artist uses sometimes have to
take on a new quality or indeed change when they try to present
natural forms. The language, for example, in which one
describes a landscape must follow the material forms exactly, be
closely linked with them and change or be further developed
accordingly. Just as there is a form in which one letter follows
another (e.g. *Eoae*), one word another, one sentence another, in
which one draws the next along with it, gently but firmly,
without force yet coherently, so too there is a form in nature. If
nature does indeed have the quality of letters or signs, then it
also has the form which can bring these together and create
meaning.

If human beings are prepared to read in the 'book of nature',
then nature itself will give them the appropriate yardstick (cf.
Handke 1982: 122). Traditionally this image of the 'book of
nature' has led to the idea of a divine creator or force, or simply
to the spirit ('Geist') which is at work in nature. In this idea the
spirit in human beings, their spiritual or mental activity, is
associated with the spirit of nature: the human mind, when
reading the 'book of nature' discovers in its letters or characters,

that is, in its material forms and shapes, the very spirit which created and joined these letters and still works upon them. Indeed the human mind is able to read the 'book of nature' because it is of the same spirit as its creator. In reading it the human mind is united with the spirit at work in nature:

> Ja, es gilt: dem langsamen Blick, wenn dieser zugleich ein Aufblicken ist, lächeln aus den Dingen die Antlitze der Götter... Leute von jetzt: entdeckt, entgegengehend, einander als Götter—als Raumaushalter, Raumerhalter. Wollt es, werdet es, seid es—und führt euch nicht auf als die Hunde, bei deren Anblick sofort die Phantasie erstirbt. Menschen, götterflüchtige Götter: Schafft den großen Satz (Handke 1982: 125).

It can therefore be seen that in Handke the discovery of a natural sign language, the language of nature, leads to the concept of 'Geist'. This concept of 'Geist' or of form, which is how Handke prefers to express it, places him in a tradition which could not be further from postmodernism. Jakob Böhme, Paracelsus, Spinoza, Goethe and Emerson, German idealism after Kant, English and German Romantics, all these are among his forerunners. According to this tradition, human beings form a spiritual unity and totality with their history and with nature. The human mind is both capable of grasping this totality and of completing it.

For Handke the task of the artist, of the storyteller, consists in finding forms which derive from the concrete relationship between human beings, on the one hand, and history and nature, on the other. At the same time the artist must produce and present these forms. Indeed, one could say that these forms demonstrate their own necessity by showing that, without them, a relationship with history and with nature would be arbitrary: 'Phantasie heißt ja nicht *Alice im Wunderland* oder *der Flüchtling versteckt sich in den Unterröcken der Großmutter*, sondern: an der richtigen Stelle den Fluß fließen, den Wind wehen, den Himmel blauen zu lassen' (Handke 1983: 93).

The act of storytelling consists in being able to read forms in history and nature which in turn can actually make these readable. Every successful reading is therefore a detection of forms and a confirmation of previous readings. The method of story-telling is one of repetition ('Wiederholung') which transforms existing forms into a greater whole, thus integrating them and giving them a new, broader meaning. A story does not simply repeat the past but turns it into a present which creates a link with our future experiences and actions. It is in a forward-looking process of repetition, which on principle remains open-ended, that the narrative forms are—paradoxically enough—finally justified.

Handke's novels demonstrate how much individuals long for these forms and how dependent they are on them in order to be able to continue their lives. It is from this desire for form that the categorical imperative of the storytelling derives: act in such a way that the actions can be narrated. The 'I' which awakens through its contact with history and nature is required to organize its actions into form, consciously and responsibly. It is at this point that Handke finally and definitively takes his leave of postmodernism. At the centre of the story with Handke remains the narrating, thinking 'I'. This is a long way from a decentred subjectivity, from the poststructuralist abolition of the subject:

> Es gibt zum einen das schweigende, das ruhige Ich, und zum zweiten das auf dieses einredende, andere *Ich*... Dieses Gerede-Ich, mit nichts beschäftigt als das ruhige Ich anzureden, sieht keinen Baum, hört kein Rauschen, spürt keine Wurzel unter den Füßen—es redet nur immer...während das ruhige Ich, wenn es endlich einmal das mephistophelische Ich los wird, ganz Auge, Ohr, Nase, Haut—Natur wird... Und dann gibt es eines, das die beiden gegensätzlichen Ich umschließt und die Gegensätze im guten aufhebt: das innehaltende, verlangsamende, phantasierende, ausdrückliche Denken...das phantasierende (umphantasierende) Ich ist mein Schreiber (Handke 1983: 84).

In this 'I' Handke discovers the possibility of forming a community with others, a possibility which exists precisely because the 'I' has the power, through forms, to create and bring together. The 'I' can give another 'I' the space in which to present and develop itself. Indeed, it could be compared to a letter which needs the distance between itself and the other letters, the other 'Is', in order to make itself readable, to give itself meaning. As is the case with the letters of a word, however, the meaning of the 'I' can only be understood when the various individual 'Is', these living letters, are brought together in a word, in a text. Handke shows that, although the individual 'I' has meaning, this meaning can only be properly understood in association with others. Human beings have the task of finding the appropriate form which can link all the 'Is' and, without doing them violence, make them speak.

Postmodernism is not interested in the 'I' which it sees as a chimera from the age of metaphysics and transcendental philosophy. Rather, it is concerned with liberating discourse from the restrictions of scientific rationality and the technological domination of nature. In postmodernism language-games must flow freely and not come under the influence of metaphysical concepts and political power interests. It has no answer, however, to the question as to how the liberated individual, in the world of free-floating signs, can grasp his or her existence as part of a larger whole that embraces other individuals. Yet, this whole can only be created out of the individual's powers of form. Here too it is unlikely that postmodernism will be of much help.

WORKS CITED

Anz, T.
  1990   'Im Zeichen der *Postmoderne*. Über die deutschsprachige Literatur der achtziger Jahre'. *Mitteilungen des Deutschen Germanistenverbandes* 2, pp. 4-11.
Blattmann, C.
  1984   *Suche nach Zusammenhang: Handkes Werk als Prozeß*. Vienna: Braumiller.
Bürger, P.
  1987   'Die Wiederkehr der Analogie', in C. Bürger and P. Bürger (eds.), *Postmoderne: Alltag, Allegorie und Avantgarde*. Frankfurt: Suhrkamp, pp. 114-21.
Cadava, E., P. Connor and J.-L. Nancy
  1991   *Who Comes after the Subject?* London: Routledge.
Derrida, J.
  1987   *De l'esprit: Heidegger et la question*. Paris: Editions Galilée.
Foucault, M.
  1970   *The Order of Things*. London: Tavistock.
Handke, P.
  1980   *Die Lehre der Sainte-Victoire*. Frankfurt: Suhrkamp.

1982   'Über die Dörfer'. *Spectaculum* 36, pp. 81-126.
1983   *Phantasien der Wiederholung*. Frankfurt: Suhrkamp.
1984   'Gegenreden und Rühmen'. *Die Zeit*, 29 June.
1986   *Die Wiederholung*. Frankfurt: Suhrkamp.
1989   *Versuch über die Müdigkeit*. Frankfurt: Suhrkamp.
1990   *Aber ich lebe nur von den Zwischenräumen: Ein Gespräch, geführt von Herbert Gamper*. Frankfurt: Suhrkamp.

Hensel, G.
1987   'Bluff dich durch die Postmoderne!' *Frankfurter Allgemeine Zeitung*, 6 June.

Huyssen, A., and K.R. Scherpe (eds.)
1986   *Postmoderne: Zeichen eines kulturellen Wandels*. Reinbek: Rowohlt.

Jameson, F.
1986   'Zur Logik der Kultur im Spätkapitalismus', in Huyssen and Scherpe 1986: 45-102.

Lauretis, T. de
1986   'Das Rätsel der Lösung—Umberto Ecos *Der Name der Rose* als postmoderner Roman', in Huyssen and Scherpe 1986: 252-69.

Lüdke, W.M.
1985   'Am Ursprung liegt das Ziel', in G. Melzer and J. Tükel (eds.), *Peter Handke: Die Arbeit am Glück*. Königstein: Athenäum, pp. 82-96.

Lyotard, J.-F.
1979   *La condition postmoderne: Rapport sur le savoir*. Paris: Gallimard.

Strauß, B.
1990   'Der Aufstand gegen die sekundäre Welt'. *Die Zeit*, 22 June.

Wagner-Egelhaaf, M.
1989   *Mystik der Moderne: Die visionäre Ästhetik der deutschen Literatur im 20. Jahrhundert*. Stuttgart: Metzler.

Widmer, Urs.
1986   'Der liebste Dichter'. *Literaturmagazin* 17, p. 13.

White, H.
1978   *Tropics of Discourse*. Baltimore: Johns Hopkins University Press.

'Die Wahrheit ist zwar konkret, aber sie läßt mit sich reden':
The Later Fictions of Andreas Okopenko

John J. White

As a poet turned prose writer, Andreas Okopenko has become
something of a literary paradox over the past couple of decades.
On the one hand, he is probably best-known, when at all,[1] as the
author of two notoriously unconventional 'Lexikon-Romane'
(*Lexikon einer sentimentalen Reise zum Exporteurtreffen in
Druden*, 1970, and *Meteoriten*, 1976), as well as a string of
fictions with rather complex narrative structures, the best
undoubtedly being the title story in the collection *Die Belege
des Michael Cetus* (1967). On the other hand, for all his
experimental eccentricities he is also a writer who evidently sets
great store by what he proudly calls his 'Wirklichkeits-
leidenschaft' and his concern for 'die Welt der *ungebrochenen
Erscheinungen*' (1970: 16). Hence, he in many respects appears
as an unashamedly old-fashioned realist, or to use the word he
prefers in his poetological *Vier Aufsätze,* a 'Konkretionist'
(pp. 51, 54, 64). Yet at the same time, while declaring himself a
'Gegenstands-Fan' (1970: 81), he admits to an obsession with
the mystically epiphanous experience of phenomena, for which
he uses the private term 'das Fluidische'.[2] The result of these

1. Revealingly, when Sten Nadolny included some general
speculations about the possibility of a novel written in lexicon form in
the second of his 1990 'Münchener Poetik-Vorlesungen', he had to be
informed by a member of the audience that Okopenko had written such
a work twenty years before, though when publishing this information,
he was still not able to spell the author's name correctly. See Nadolny
1990: 46-48, 60.
2. On this subject, referred to as the 'F-Erlebnis' in *Lexikon*, the first
essay, 'Fluidum. Bericht von einer außerordentlichen Erlebnisart'
(Okopenko 1979: 5-42), is particularly informative: about Okopenko's

various concerns is a series of highly personal amalgams of closely observed surfaces, often presented within complex collage structures, and a form of intensely subjectivist writing, a style bearing witness to acknowledged debts both to the *nouveau roman* and to Arno Schmidt (cf. 1970: 57-58, 193; 1979: 79). This interplay between realism and formal experimentation, but also surface description and 'das Fluidische', assumes various forms at different stages of Okopenko's career. Arguably, 'das Fluidische' has played less of a role in his fiction since the first lexicon novel; in general, the subjective dimension has moved more in the direction of quasi-autobiographical writings and sententiously presented social critical elements.

Okopenko has always been a self-confessed enemy of 'das Österreichelnde' in its various manifestations, from contemporary 'Mundartdichtung' to thematic parochialism:

> es hängt ja nicht an jeder Hausmauer das Holloderoh, steigt nicht aus jedem Schornstein der Radetzkymarsch... Ein Schuß Felix Austria—und selbst Kierkegaard würde eine gewisse Gemütlichkeit bekommen; die Würze ist nämlich sehr penetrant (1970: 179).

And yet, despite his suspicion of writers who choose to wear their Austrian credentials on their sleeves, Okopenko has, with novels like *Meteoriten* and *Kindernazi*, nevertheless become an invaluable recorder of both his native Austrian environment and many of his country's crimes and misdemeanours, from the problematic post-Anschluss period through to recent times. Moreover, despite being a writer whose work is firmly set in the context of postwar Austrian experimental literature (it has repeatedly been compared with Oswald Wiener's *die verbesserung von mitteleuropa*, 1969, Konrad Bayer's *Der Kopf des Vitus Bering*, 1965, and Gerhard Roth's *die autobiographie des albert einstein*, 1972), Okopenko still remains, as various parodies in *Der Akazienfresser* (1973) and the first lexicon novel reveal, an entrenched enemy—some would say, a disingenuously hostile

intentions, if not his achievements. At one point, Okopenko remarks 'Joyce sprach—wahrscheinlich das Fluidum meinend—von "Epiphanien"' (p. 21).

adversary—of the linguistically experimental avant-gardism of many of his contemporaries. Yet Okopenko's early association with the experimental magazine *Neue Wege* and, together with Hans Carl Artmann, his work in the cabaret group 'der keller', and the kind of material he fostered in the *publikationen einer wiener gruppe junger autoren*, not to mention his affiliation to the Grazer Autorenversammlung,[3] do not always really square with his later attempts at dissociating himself from the experimentalism of much contemporary Austrian writing.

Possibly in order to deflect attention from this, in his eyes, frivolous pedigree and to sidestep some of his debts to the Wiener Gruppe and Grazer Gruppe writers who have so clearly influenced him (even though he has later qualified this influence: 1979: 82-83), Okopenko singles out the more whimsical Ernst Jandl for one of his main programmatic attacks in *Lexicon*:

> Jandl—weil es ihm um die Sprache geht—glaubt, die Konstanz des Protokollführers plus die Variabilität des Protokollierten ergeben eine Konstanz. Ich—weil es mir um die Sache geht—glaube, die Konstanz des Protokollführers plus die Variabilität des Protokollierten ergeben eine Variabilität. So, wie die Konstanz des Fahrenden plus die Variabilität der Fahrpunkte eine Variabilität, genannt Fahrtvergnügen, ergeben. Nach Jandl wäre nur noch die Fahrt aus der eigenen Haut vergnüglich (p. 94).

Or, more crisply: 'Vom Manierismus unterscheidet mich hier wie überall, daß es mir um die Sache geht und nicht um den Radius meiner Pfauenräder' (p. 12). It may not be possible to relate all of these features convincingly to one another within the scope of the present account of Okopenko's more recent work (I shall be deliberately passing over the vexed issue of 'das Fluidische', for example). But I can only hope that they will emerge as less at odds with one another than they might at first appear to be.

At one point in his first lexicon novel of 1970, in what appears to be a surprisingly uncharacteristic move given his repeated categorical rejection of self-indulgent 'Sprachspiel' literature, Okopenko sketches out the possibility of various language-games that could be played with film titles. What is heralded as

3. For further details, see Okopenko 1967: 279-304; and Janetzki 1978.

the novel's 'Filmtitelspiel 1' invites readers to assemble current film titles and arrange them in pairs for comic contrastive effects: 'Man verkaufe ein Vokabelheft und treibe Titel der laufenden Kinoprogramme zu leidlich passenden Paaren' (1970: 81). We are given pertinent 'Beispiele aus Raum Wien/Zeit der Exportreise' (pp. 81-82). In other words, the game, like the entire journey to a meeting at Druden in the Wachau, which is the subject of this novel, becomes the vehicle for a great deal of lighthearted satire on the social mores of the specific time and the chosen region of Austria.

The following collocations should suffice to give the spirit of Okopenko's proposed game:

> Der verkaufte Großvater/Nackt jeden Abend
> Tödliche Tiefen/Die Wirtin von der Lahn
> Wenn am Sonntagabend die Dorfmusik spielt/
> Versuchs doch mal mit meiner Frau!
> Hochzeitsnacht vor Zeugen/Nur noch 72 Stunden
> Das Insektenweib/DDT
> Brennt Paris?/Knusprige Leichen mit Sex-Appeal (1970: 82)

And so on and, one might add, with a vengeance. In fact, the exercise clearly extends beyond the circumscribed scope required to score an easy satirical point or to function as an invitation to a variation on the game of consequences.

We are then invited to move on and play 'Filmtitelspiel 2' (pp. 83-85): this time by *inventing* titles relating to specific semantic fields. For example, one instruction ('Tu den Teufel in den Titel') generates such gems as 'Das Teufelsweib von Texas', 'Hölle auf Okinawa' and 'Samuru—Tochter des Satans'. Subsequently, 'Tu den Tierfang in den Titel' produces, *inter alia*, '100 Bandidos in der Falle', 'Frauen als Köder für CD7' and 'Kommissar X: Jagd auf Unbekannt'. 'Tu Todesarten in den Titel' similarly spawns a series of comic titles, including 'Hängen sollst du in Wyoming', 'Für eine Handvoll Blei', 'Pulverdampf ist kein Parfum' and 'Der Tiger parfumiert sich mit Dynamit' (the last seems to be the result of a crossed wire with one of the other games!). After regaling us with about 150 examples, by which time any potential satire has surely lost its edge, Okopenko once more threatens a 'Filmtitelspiel 3', about which, however, the following revealing remark is then made:

'Wer Wert darauf legt, daß dieser Roman naturalistisch ausfalle, überdehne das Verfahren nicht maßlos. Wer keinen Wert auf getreue Proportionen legt, schließe hier ruhig eine ganze Dissertation ein' (1970: 85). Here lies the essential clue to the function of this seemingly self-indulgent four-page entry. Okopenko has been deliberately overpressing the point with his linguistic game in order to prepare for this eventual caveat. For we are obviously assumed to be hoping—along with the work's author—'daß der Roman naturalistisch ausfalle'; hence an excess of verbal play is set up here as an Aunt Sally. Experiment in the service of realism, social satire and the mystical 'das Fluidische' are the work's watchwords, in other words, not verbal play and formal experimentation for their own sakes— this would lead to 'ungetreue Proportionen'. Or, as the narrator puts it right at the beginning of *Lexikon*:

> *Das ist Welt!*...ich will Ihnen keinen *sentimentalen Exporteur im Glaskasten* vorführen, sondern eine kleine Reise, ein Mikromodell Welt, gruppiert um den sentimentalen Exporteur, der ihr Bestandteil ist, wie sie sein Bestandteil ist (p. 6).

The question is: how can such an essentially mimetic aesthetic be effectively reconciled with the artifice of two full-scale 'Lexikon-Romane'? Or even of a novel like the later *Kindernazi*, roughly based on the diary paradigm, but this time applied in reverse chronological order (with entries running from the end of the war back to its beginning), and with, as a corollary, a complex interaction between various figures of the period and hindsight perspectives? Is Okopenko (despite various statements to the contrary) not in effect trying to square the circle, or, more specifically, attempting to have the best of three fashionable worlds—self-conscious formal experiment, intense subjective experience and satire-based social criticism? That at least two out of these three disparate elements are capable of being reconciled can be seen from the experimentally formulated political satires of the early Arno Schmidt like *Das steinerne Herz* (1956), *Die Gelehrtenrepublik* (1957) and *KAFF* (1960) or Peter Handke's more mystical works from *Die Wiederholung* (1986) to the current series of 'Versuche', above all the *Versuch über den geglückten Tag* (1991). But in trying to bring together formal experiment, politically committed social criticism *and* the mysticism referred to by the term 'das Fluidische', Okopenko clearly makes quite severe demands on his fiction.

In order to pursue some of these issues at a more detailed level, I should like to focus in particular on certain features of the 1970 *Lexikon einer sentimentalen Reise zum Exporteurtreffen in Druden*, to my mind, Okopenko's most successful work to date (see Haslinger 1971), and then to offer some related perspectives on his two principal later writings, *Meteoriten* (1976) and *Kindernazi* (1984).

As the word 'Lexikon' in the title implies, the reading-process demanded by Okopenko's first lexicon novel is more fragmented and decidedly less linear than was the case even with his earlier 'Protokollmethode', for example in the case of *Die Belege des Michael Cetus*. After an initial tongue-in-cheek assurance to the reader that 'das Material ist alphabetisch geordnet, damit Sie es mühelos auffinden', Okopenko is at pains to stress that it is nevertheless the reader's task to translate the work's permutational possibilities into a novel. 'Dieses Buch hat eine Gebrauchsanweisung, denn es wäre hübsch, wenn Sie sich aus ihm einen Roman basteln wollten' (1970: 5). Not only are we supplied with spaces in which to write our own comments, insert photographs of our own choice or add our own hand-drawn illustrations, we are also encouraged to recognize that the very act of deciding upon a reading sequence is uniquely text-creating, for it involves us in certain fundamental choices about whether to adhere slavishly to the alphabetical sequence, to dip in randomly or to follow up suggested individual cross-references. 'Wie im Lexikon haben Sie die Freiheit, jeden Hinweispfeil zu beherzigen oder zu übergehen' (p. 5); ours is the privilege (presented as a 'democratic' one) of instruction-guided 'aleatorische Textverwertung' (p. 7). 'Daß die Sentimentale Reise ein Möglichkeitsroman ist, wurde nun ausgesprochen. Er ist ein Mobile, wie man es von der Decke herabhängen hat, damit es in jedem Luftzittern mitlebt und wechselt' (p. 6). To which Okopenko adds in a rather defensive parenthesis: 'Bauer + Jelinek haben die aleatorische Textverwertung übrigens unabhängig von mir "erfunden"' (p. 7). He seems unaware of the aleatory principle followed by many of the Austrian and

West German 'Neues Hörspiel' dramatists at this time or of such permutational works of fiction as Marc Saporta's loose-leaf 'shufflable' novel *Composition No. 1* (1963) or its English equivalent, B.S. Johnson's *The Unfortunates* (1969). Formally the result, both here and in the later *Meteoriten*, largely resembles a cross between Peter O. Chotjewitz's *Die Insel* (1969), Julio Cortázar's *Hopscotch* (1967) and Milorad Pavić's *Dictionary of the Khazars* (1988), largely works with which Okopenko could not at the time be expected to have been familiar; but it is executed in a more complex and encyclopaedic vein than in any of these other three authors' works.

The guiding rationale behind both the original lexicon novel of 1970 and Okopenko's subsequent *Meteoriten* (1976) is the premise that both the chaos and the subjectivized version of reality that the requisite aleatory reading produces do in fact faithfully reflect the quality of life itself.

> Sie brauchen nur kreuz und quer durch mein Lexikon zu lesen, so wie Sie sich ja auch an Ihren Feldwebel, Ihre erste Flaschenmilch und Ihr künftiges Zimmer im Altersheim durcheinander erinnern können. *Das ist Welt.* In vor-geschriebener Reihenfolge vorgeschriebene Blicke zu werfen, ist hingegen klassische Lektüre oder vortauwetterlicher Ost-Tourismus. Ich will Sie—versuchen wir es einmal—aus der *Lektüre* in die *Welt* befreien (1970: 6).

That fictions of this kind are possible without being underpinned by analogous claims about reflecting the fortuitousness of the world can be seen from Dubravka Ugrešić's *Patchwork Story* (1981) where the reader is invited to 'start writing with scissors and paste'—in William Burroughs fashion—in order to construct a personal work. Here, the technique's raison d'être remains in the area of aesthetic play, rather than deriving from some quasi-mimetic principle.

Now, one might be forgiven for expecting a writer who views the world as haphazard and who associates randomly clustered bits of text with reality's 'chaos' *not* to organize his novel according to a superimposed alphabetical principle. Yet the sheer wilfulness of structuring discretely observed phenomena, collaged quotations, synchronically presented recollections, anecdotes and *obiter dicta* according to which letter of the alphabet chosen head nouns (and sometimes even other parts of speech) begin with, in fact serves to underline the capriciousness of any such disposition. *Meteoriten* refers to 'Knäuel' of information acquiring no more than a mere 'äußere Ordnung' (p. 12) by this means. In any case, Okopenko's ordering method generally entails somewhat arbitrarily selected lexical items. Thus, on the first couple of pages we move from 'Aberdeen' and 'Achselhöhle' to 'Affirmative Dichtung' and 'Arcimboldi', and among later groupings are such sequences as 'Auflockerungen 1-7', 'Katzen 1-5', 'Küssen 1-6', including a Richter scale of kisses from 1 to 9.99, and a gazetteer of 'Städtchen 1-15'. Moreover, whereas real lexica impose a rigorous factual (rather than experiential) taxonomic order upon reality, both of Okopenko's 'Lexikon-Romane' are more subjective, and at times even idiosyncratic, in their selective coverage; and they employ more anaphora in evoking the world cumulatively than one would ever expect to find in a lexicon, with the economy of its abstract definitions and condensed information.

Although the novel's blurb started a fashion when it referred to the work's 'articles', the individual entries are more heterogeneous and less reminiscent of a lexicon than such a term suggests. Some are what the author refers to in his 'Gebrauchsanweisung' as 'Mini-Essays', others are based on anecdotal material; there are also self-contained *Märchen*, inventories, reflections and dialogues, as well as the kind of ingredients that one thinks of as genuine lexicon material. In fact, the first lexicon novel is characterized as much by what distinguishes it from a lexicon proper as by what the two forms have in common. The very presence of Okopenko's 'Gebrauchsanweisung' tellingly highlights the fact that he is operating with no more than a loosely deployed lexicon principle. True, 'Wie im Lexikon' the material is ordered alphabetically, and there are admittedly 'Hinweispfeile' to help us plan a journey comparable to that of the hero J. on his way along the Danube to the Wachau, to the 'Exporteurtreffen in Druden' on 22 June 1968. But this still does not prevent the raw material of the work from constituting far more that of a novel than a lexicon, *even before the reader's engagement has constructed something specific out of the permutations*. Let me itemize (albeit non-alphabetically) some of the key respects in which *Lexikon* differs from a lexicon proper.

1. *Subjectivity*. Throughout the first lexicon novel we repeatedly hear Okopenko and the other characters from among its large cast speaking in their own voices: either pontificating about political and literary issues, satirizing their environment or recalling past faces, places and episodes. The frequency with which I have already been able to cite remarks from the work's narrator, clearly speaking *pro domo* as his author's mouthpiece, is one of the more obvious instances of this personalizing technique. Clearly, a real lexicon lacks any such character-oriented, subjective dimension, and (as a corollary) it also maintains a consistency of register, whereas Okopenko's novel rejoices in a whole kaleidoscope of material from a variety of stylistic sources and speaks indirectly through many voices.

2. *Use*. No matter what path we take through it, *Lexikon*'s eventual effects depend on the assumption that we will ultimately cover the work's entire ground, even if we do not read it systematically from 'Aberdeen' to 'Zz'. This is obviously conceived as a very different kind of (aesthetic) reception from the way most of us consult a lexicon.

3. *Dramatis personae*. By contrast to a lexicon's concept- and word-orientation, *Lexikon* has a colourful cast of characters (and the fact that the majority of their names are alphabetically inspired, from André Anarchique and Encore Edibelbek to Quenta Quebec and Xaver Yermit Zeisig, does not detract from the fact that they are sufficiently delineated to constitute fictional rather than lexical material). It is *their* stories—and the loose skeletal plot of a Danube journey (echoed in Handke's notion of 'Handlung' as an 'Eselsbrücke'!)—that serve to offer a predominantly fictive foundation to the lexicon format.

4. *Referentiality*. Okopenko's novel abounds in accounts of landscapes, people and incidents, objects and activities, mini-essays and historical and sociological details. It does not merely define concepts or words, it evokes reality or, more accurately, creates a surrogate world. Its deployment of satire in the service of 'Zeitkritik' is one example of such referentiality; another is its

sense of creating a setting for J.'s journey. The section entitled
'Landschaft' is programmatic in this respect:

> Ich empfehle die Wiederzurkenntnisnahme der Landschaft.
> Ich empfehle hierzu die Übung *beider* Standortbezüge:
> * des tragischen (Rilkes 'Gegenüber')
> * des harmonischen (Whitmans 'Inmitten')
> dem Subjekt-Mitobjekt-Charakter des Menschen entsprechend.
> Wiederaufnahme diplomatischer Beziehungen zur Landschaft,
> Steigerung dieses Klimawandels zur Make-Love-Not-War-
> Revolution im Umgang mit ursprünglicher und bemenschter
> Natur, Immanenzfrömmigkeit vor Bachwindung, Dottergelb,
> Roßapfel—und kein Kubikmillimeter mindererfreuliches
> Psychedelicum ist für den *high*sten Persönlichkeitsumschub
> mehr nötig (p. 154).

5. *Representativeness.* Despite the work's manifest eccentricities, there is one central respect in which Okopenko does not
intend his lexicon account of a contemporary Austrian journey
to be too quirkily parochial, in spite of the goal of an 'Exporteurtreffen in Druden' and in spite of the limited perspective
afforded by his chosen protagonist, the 'Chemiekaufmann' J.
The journey, like a lexicon, has to some extent to offer a
representative compendium of life at the time.

Under the heading '*Joyce*', Okopenko raises the question of
the relationship of his *tranche de vie* method in *Lexikon* to that
of James Joyce in *Ulysses*. 'Ist der Tag, der meine sentimentale
Reise einschließt', he asks, 'ein Abklatsch des Bloom-Tages?
Nein. Meine Sekunden sind nicht die Sekunden des Denkkon-
tinuums, sondern Blick- und Blindsekunden eines Weltmodell-
Diskontinuums' (p. 132). Given the multi-perspectival quality
of *Ulysses* (dominated by Bloom's, Dedalus's and Molly's
perspectives, but related not only to these), it may seem strange
to refer to Joyce's work as '*ein* Denkkontinuum', but nevertheless Okopenko's remark does help highlight a fundamental
difference. That is to say, the unifying principle in *Ulysses* is a
psychological one, the world is the world perceived by specific
characters. In Okopenko's first lexicon novel, the lexicon format
is intended to imply a relatively autonomous 'Weltmodell', a
constructed world, rather than an experienced world (which
may be another way of saying that J.'s Danube journey is less
central to the novel's presentation of reality than the title

implies). The same could be said of Okopenko's later 'cornucopian text': *Meteoriten*. In both works a 'Weltmodell-Diskontinuum', *one* based much more squarely on a lexical journey than on a boat-trip, *the other* on meteorite-like fragments of Austria's history 'zwischen Zweitem und Drittem Weltkrieg', (*Meteoriten*, dust jacket text), results in a collage essentially lacking the guiding focalizer principle that holds the various parts of Joyce's *Ulysses* together. And when I remarked earlier on the fact that the novel *Kindernazi* was only loosely based on the diary paradigm, it was a similar feature that I had in mind. For despite the reproduction of a photograph of a diminutive Okopenko in Hitler Youth uniform on the dust jacket and despite the whole series of recognizable parallels between the Okopenkos' family circumstances during the war and what *Kindernazi* describes, the novel is by no means simply the author's diary for the time. Not only is the style of narration too adult, but too many other figures dictate the narrative perspective of individual episodes. Again, the 'Diskontinuum' is not a 'Denkdiskontinuum', and there is no single diary persona holding all of the material together: we are once more closer to the 'Weltmodell' approach, this time presented largely through the family microcosm rather than that of a specific journey or meteor-like narrative fragments.

Adolf Haslinger concluded his excellent analysis of the first lexicon novel with the suggestion that Okopenko was 'ein Künstler der Kleinform' (Haslinger 1971: 80). The various collections of earlier poems (*Grüner November*, *Seltsame Tage*, *Orte wechselnden Unbehagens*), and the short stories in *Die Belege des Michael Cetus* and the 'Thrillgeschichten' of *Warnung vor Ypsilon* (1974) would have borne out such a view even before the publication of the author's two most recent novels. Now having, with *Meteoriten*, a further lexicon novel to his credit, as well as with *Kindernazi*, a loosely-structured narrative consisting of 62 'Episoden' each relating to a specific date during the period between April 1939 and 1 April 1945, Okopenko can only have reinforced his image as a writer interested in the representatively fragmentary and episodic. In *Meteoriten* the material is episodic enough to be digested in various orders, and even *Kindernazi* consists of episodes sufficiently autonomous to be narrated in reverse order without too much violation being done to any sense of teleology or family history.

For someone who once (paraphrasing Herbert Cysarz) observed, 'es gibt *nur* Neues unter der Sonne' (1970: 68) to produce more than one 'Lexikon-Roman' may seem a surprising thing to do. But the two works do, despite their surface generic affinity, differ markedly, and in terms of radicality the subsequent *Meteoriten* is even more fragmentary than its predecessor.

In a preamble to his second lexicon novel, Okopenko remarks, 'eventuelle Leser meines *Lexikon-Romans*, vielleicht von damals her neurotisiert im Gebrauch meiner Bücher, seien dahin beruhigt, daß die *Meteoriten* vollends ohne Spielregel lesbar sind' (1976: 12). We are supplied with no cross-references this time, there is no course to be steered (or avoided) between a journey novel and a zig-zagging lexical foray and there is far more randomness to the individual entries, despite the fact that they are again alphabetically ordered. Although there is a central figure called 'I' (the letter of the alphabet, not the first-person pronoun), we are assured that we shall never learn very much about him:

> Kaum wird hervorgehen, wer I war. Er wird nicht in seine Biographie, in seine sozialen Koordinaten eingewindelt vorliegen. Dieses Buch soll nicht Zeitgeschichte noch Stadtchronik noch Entwicklungsroman sein (darum: nur gedämpftes Ich, gebremste Kontinuität). Es soll einen wehleidigen *Sound* geben von der Zeit, die wir Überlebenden durchleben durften (1976: 14).

The 'sound' of these times is registered (as in the first lexicon novel) by a spectrum of heterogeneous methods, including the quotation of revealing small ads from the 'Nullpunkt' days ('Couch: Niebenutzt gegen bißl Mehl', p. 13), frequent recourse to authorial commentary ('Wie traurig...die Radioschlager, in denen man sich montags wieder auf den Sonntag freut', p. 33), recorded snatches of overheard conversation ('Buffet Grinzing. "Glauben Sie, vertragt mein Hund Westfälerschinken?"', p. 32), self-contained anecdotes, fairy tales, montaged documents such as programmes, magazine correspondence, gutter-press headlines ('Ein Dutzend Ermordete zu Würsten und Pasteten verarbeitet') and mini-biographies characteristic of the period ('Erstesmal im Jeep gesessen... Jetzt bin ich ein Ami-Girl', p. 107) The counterpointing (even at individual sentence level) of Austria's early postwar years, ambiguously half-defeated, half-liberated, with a largely damning panorama of more recent decades creates an overriding sense of lost opportunities. As is perhaps befitting for a novel presented as being set between the end of World War Two and the beginning of World War Three, there is now less concern with landscape than in the first lexicon novel and far more bitterness about human behaviour. Often attacks are delivered *ex cathedra*, usually in the form of dogmatic critical assertion: 'An manchen Leuten sind nur die Kleider intelligent' (p. 53); 'Die übelste Form der Geschlechts-krankheit sind die Schlagertexte' (p. 53); 'Es fällt auf, daß gerade die widerlichsten Männer und Frauen Sprachrohr ihres Geschlechts sein wollen' (p. 54); 'Die Geschlechter verdienen einander' (p. 54). Elsewhere, the mere act of quoting from another source becomes a gesture of social indictment: 'Die Mißhandlungen in diesem Film sind echt (nicht konstruiert) und nur geeignet für *absolut erwachsene* Menschen!' (p. 91); 'Mary Quant, Befreierin der MÄDCHEN aus Tradition' (p. 163); 'Helfen Sie mit, daß Wien so bleibt' (p. 115). Or, in a more extended passage:

> ENGLANDS OBERHENKER IN GRAZ. Albert Pierrepoint, Englands Oberhenker, kam gestern in Graz an. Er wird acht Todesurteile an Personen vollziehen, welche vom britischen Militärgericht verurteilt wurden. Außerdem will er österreichische Amtspersonen über die heute in England geübte Hinrichtungsmethode instruieren. Der Grund für seine Anwesenheit ist der Mangel an erfahrenen österreichischen Henkern (p. 81).

This occurs, it should be noted, in a novel with numerous references to Mauthausen. Elsewhere there are instances—possibly the above passage, more probably the following example—where one may suspect, indeed even hope, that Okopenko's method is not strictly that of documentary collage:

> Wer die Kleinigkeit von 1225 Schilling dafür ausgeben will, kann sich sein eigenes Dachau aus Selbstbauteilen

schicken lassen. Mit Wachturm, Zaun, Baracken, Stacheldraht
und Bewachern. Krematorium und Gaskammer wurden
weggelassen (p. 95).

Indeed, every so often, just as the reader is beginning to feel
Okopenko has allowed himself the luxury of taking on rather
soft social targets (a charge not without relevance to some part
of the original lexicon novel), there comes a hard-hitting
juxtaposition, as in the 'Vision' entry: '*Vision*. Jemandem in die
Straßenbahn hinaufhelfen, wenn er zurückfällt. Jemanden in
den Verbrennungsofen hineindrücken, wenn er heraus möchte'
(p. 214) or '*Omi*! Ja? Du bist überflüssig' (p. 161). As such
examples suggest, there is, in fact, a much more pressing sense
of modern Austria's 'unbewältigte Vergangenheit' in
Meteoriten than was to be found in the first lexicon novel, and
this theme is going to become even more central in *Kindernazi*.
Moreover, Okopenko's satire on the Austrian bourgeoisie's
Gemütlichkeit and parochialism is counterbalanced by the
political thrust of many of his entries. The novel begins with the
couplet: 'Lieber Gott, ich danke Dir für alles,/inklusive Molotow
und Dulles' (p. 5). And although not presented in chronological
order, many of the entries refer to what is going on beyond
Austria's borders, largely with little detectable impact on its
inhabitants. We hear of the distant Korean War (p. 208) and,
nearer home, the Hungarian Uprising (p. 137). We learn that
'Präsident Ford hat die amerikanische Bevölkerung aufgerufen,
Vietnam zu vergessen' (p. 97) and that at one stage 'die
Vernichtung der gesamten Erdbevölkerung 400 Milliarden
Dollar kostet' (p. 98). However, the only time that the Austrians
seem unduly ruffled by international events is when their
country is threatened by the 'Einmarschmongolen' at the end of
the War (p. 13) or when Americans are taking away their girls as
GI brides.

On the whole, Okopenko's *Meteoriten* has something of a
time capsule feel to it: as if its author had become much more
resigned in his attempt at documenting the foibles of a world
that will find its way to a Third World War. This perhaps
explains the palpable change in tone between the exuberance
and sheer love of reality to be found in the first lexicon novel—
coitus prolongatus is the work's own description of its

relationship to the world (p. 222)—and *Meteoriten*'s tendency towards a more politically motivated waspishness. And it is this same sense of imminent crisis, or of a world gone sour in recent decades, that might also account for the different focus in Okopenko's next novel, *Kindernazi* (1984), as it turns, breaking taboos at a well-timed moment,[4] to re-examine some of Okopenko's own personal memories of childhood in Nazi Austria and family recollections of the period.

Kindernazi was one of the earliest of a whole series of pieces of subjectivist fiction—including Alfred Andersch's *Der Vater eines Mörders* (1980), Max von der Grün's *Wie war das eigentlich?* (1979), Ludwig Harig's *Ordnung ist das ganze Leben* (1986) and *Weh dem, der aus der Reihe tanzt* (1990), Manfred Bieler's *Still wie die Nacht* (1989) and Günter de Bruyn's *Zwischenbilanz* (1992)—works in which writers explored their early years, quite often paying attention to the role they had played in the Hitler Youth movement. (An official Austrian visit from the Reich Youth Leader Baldur von Schirach is one proudly remembered incident in *Kindernazi*.) Okopenko's novel, though, has one major formal twist that distinguishes it from the other works on the subject. It begins at the end, with the collapse of Austria, and works its way backwards to the moment when the (Okopenko) family first arrive in Austria to become 'Reichsdeutsche' ('hier in Wien wirst du dich anpassen müssen', the child is told). But at the beginning of the novel, that is right at the end of the 'Großdeutsches Reich', he hears a very different piece of advice:

> Heute darfst du noch ein Nazi sein, sagt Papa, und weinen über euern Zusammenbruch... Aber jetzt Schluß, kommandiert Papa: Anatol! Hitler hat den Krieg verloren, verstanden? Wir müssen uns jetzt umstellen. Sei jetzt ein vernünftiger Mann. Stell dir vor, du warst ein großer Star, ein Kinderstar, und jetzt bist du ein Mann und deine Rolle ist aus. Tilki, jetzt darfst kein Nazi mehr sein, sagt Mama sehr schlaff (p. 7).

As this introductory entry for 1 April 1945 already indicates, we are not dealing with a diary in any strict sense. Lengthy

---

4. On Austrian literature's relatively late breaking of certain taboos concerning the period after the Anschluss, see Wigmore, 1991.

conversations are being reported verbatim, the style is that of epic narration—sometimes from other perspectives, not just the young Okopenko's—and (at a more general organizational level) the episodes remain too selective for one to feel that this is a chronicler's recording of day-by-day experiences.

From the Russians' entry into the 'Frontstadt Wien' in the spring of 1945, *Kindernazi* retraces the months and years to the beginnings of the country's new life as part of a new enlarged Reich. In lieu of a 'Weltmodell-Diskontinuum', we have more of a 'Weltkrieg-Diskontinuum', seen mainly through a child's eyes but also refracted via the adult Okopenko's attempt at recapturing the mood and details of this relatively naive period while at the same time revealing an awareness of where it was all leading. Various skeletons in Austria's historical cupboard were already visible in both *Lexikon* and *Meteoriten* but now through a series of images of school and 'Kinderverschickungs-lager', experiences with the 'Jungvolk 'and politicized family scenes, Okopenko adds his own contribution to the 'Neue Subjektivität' approach to 'Vergangenheitsbewältigung'.

The progression from defeat, via hoping against hope that there will still be a final victory, to the initial moment where the family comes to a Vienna that has just experienced the euphoria of Anschluss, gives the work a highly critical edge. For the naive mood of the early war years is invariably seen against the detailed description of where things were to lead.

Most disturbing are often the small insights into daily life under 'Austrofaschismus'. 'Ein Neuer aus Jöllenbeck, Westfalen, hielt mich Österreicher für einen Rheinländer, ich war sehr stolz' (1984: 32), the young boy records. Or: 'wenn wir Lieder aus dem Reich nicht können, läßt uns der (KVL-Lagerleiter) einen Strafausmarsch machen' (p. 54). We are given details of one boy's 'Paradeaufsatz' at school ('Stalingrad mahnt!', p. 61); and hear of the shop 'wegen Preistreiberei geschlossen' (p. 81) at the time of the Normandy landings. As we move back from the end of the war to the early years of unification with Germany, we find people entertaining fresh dreams: of a life in new colonies 'in kommendem deutschen Schwarzland' (p. 85). In general, the Austrian people reveal a new globally inspired confidence: 'mit den Japanern und der "Festung Europa" an unserer Seite werden wir sie schon alle kleinkriegen' (p. 92).

The dust cover text says to the prospective reader of *Kindernazi*:

> Sie wundern sich, daß dieser Stoff hier gegen die Chronologie erzählt wird, also von 1945 rückwärts bis 1939? Das ist in der Tat ungewöhnlich, aber es könnte doch sein, daß man so eher begreift, was damals geschehen ist, als wenn man noch einmal dem ach so bekannten Ablauf bis zur Katastrophe folgt. Sie bezweifeln dennoch, daß man das Rad der Geschichte zurückdrehen kann? Da haben Sie natürlich recht, wohl aber kann man die Spur, die dieses Rad hinterlassen hat, Schritt für Schritt zurückverfolgen, Episode für Episode, von denen jede einzelne sich mit der Kraft der Erinnerung gegen die Zeitflucht stemmt. Sie finden, das klingt ein wenig kompliziert? Nicht komplizierter, als die Wirklichkeit damals war, damals und natürlich auch heute.

The further we go back in time, the younger are many of the people who voice the recorded jingoistic utterances. Thus, it is in a schoolchild's essay on the exhibition 'Das Sowjetparadies... das politisch aufklärend wirken soll' that we hear, 'wie alle anständigen Insassen der Festung Europa werden (wir) dieses verbrecherische Judenkrebsgeschwür von der Landkarte fegen und das wahre, deutsche Paradies schaffen... Wir schaffen, was Napoleon nicht geschafft hat' (pp. 106-107). Or, after having asked his father what Dachau was, the central figure nevertheless feels moved to conclude a section betraying his puzzlement with the declaration: 'ich gleite begeistert in die Moral und die Siegesfolge des Blitzkrieges' (p. 118).

A comparison with the method of reversing chronology also employed by Martin Amis in *Time's Arrow* (1991) will serve to bring out the relatively controlled nature of Okopenko's method in *Kindernazi*. Whereas no reader encountering Amis's character in New York in our own times could predict where a reversal of time's arrow would be taking us as the novel reverses through history, the family Okopenko depicted at the time of Austria's collapse in 1945 has a much more typical and therefore predictable prehistory. The reader is taken back through patterns of common experience, and as a result there is a sense of uncovering an inevitable course from Anschluss to defeat. The effects in Amis's novel are local and often very

disturbing: for example, his extermination camps create Jews
rather than destroying them, and the whole process of the
holocaust is estranged by its component events being presented
in reverse order. Even at the level of the individual sentence,
familiar history becomes surreal in *Time's Arrow*. In *Kindernazi*,
on the other hand, the individual sections are not re-ordered
sentence by sentence in this way; the reversal of time's arrow
only occurs on the macroscopic scale as the entries are arranged
back to front but not changed individually. For the reader, the
effect is less destabilizing. Admittedly, hindsight knowledge will
tell us in any case that the Anschluss will eventually end in
tragedy, so by reversing the order of his material Okopenko has
arguably simply made more explicit what would have been
implicit in the reading process in any case, even if events in the
family's history had been narrated in conventional chronological order. On one level, the effect is of reaching back nostal-
gically to happier times in the family's fortunes, but a narrative
irony continually makes it clear that such happiness, which
increases as the text unfolds, is the product of political naivety.

Okopenko has always been a critic of certain features of
Austrian political and social life, in the earlier works usually
seeing parallels between past and present. But *Kindernazi* has a
more specific, personal focus: that of a child growing up during
the period of the Second World War and, despite some uncomfortable questions, generally being taken in by the mood of the
time. Its credentials are those of a highly personal confession.

In a *Lexikon* entry, 'Ortsbestimmung', Okopenko once tried—
not without a modicum of self-indulgent hyperbole—to assess
his own place within Austrian literature:

> Weil ich nicht blasiert sondern begeistert (→ Begeisterung),
> nicht 'innersprachlich' sondern 'gegenständlich' (→ Realismus),
> nicht zitatbetont sondern erlebnisbetont (→ Freiheit, die ich
> meine) schreibe, weil mich Landschaften (!) und Zweier-
> beziehungen (!) emovieren, Zweierbeziehungen sogar übern
> elementaren→Sex hinaus, habe ich mich in eine Harakiri-
> Position begeben. Achgott, die Avantgarde will mich nicht,
> und achgott, in der konservativen Dichtung hab ich schon gar
> nichts verloren (pp. 198-99).

He here (in 1970) makes this so-called 'Harakiri-Position' sound like the predicament of someone with his back to the wall. I would suggest that since then, rather than a position from which to commit literary suicide, he has invariably made it into his unique strength.

WORKS CITED

Haslinger, A.
1971   'Vereinzelung und Integration. Okopenkos *Lexikon*, ein Beitrag zum modernen österreichischen Roman', in G. Weiss und K. Zelewitz (eds.), *Peripherie und Zentrum. Studien zur österreichischen Literatur: Festschrift für Adalbert Schmidt*. Salzburg: Bergland, pp. 55-85.

Janetzki, U.
1978   'Andreas Okopenko', in H.L. Arnold (ed.), *Kritisches Lexikon zur deutschsprachigen Gegenwartsliteratur*. Munich: Edition Text und Kritik.

Nadolny, S.
1990   *Das Erzählen und die guten Absichten*. Munich: Piper.

Okopenko, A.
1957   *Grüner November*. Munich: Piper.
1963   *Seltsame Tage*. Esslingen: Bechtle.
1967   'Der Fall "Neue Wege"', in O. Breicha and G. Fritsch (eds.), *Aufforderung zum Mißtrauen*. Salzburg: Residenz Verlag, pp. 279-304.
1970   *Lexikon einer sentimentalen Reise zum Exporteurtreffen in Druden*. Salzburg: Residenz.
1971   *Orte wechselnden Unbehagens*. Salzburg: Residenz.
1973   *Der Akazienfresser: Parodien, Hommagen, Wellenritte*. Salzburg: Residenz.
1974   *Warnung vor Ypsilon: Thrill-Geschichten*. Salzburg: Residenz.
1976   *Meteoriten*. Salzburg: Residenz.
1979   *Vier Aufsätze: Ortsbestimmung einer Einsamkeit*. Salzburg: Residenz.
1984   *Kindernazi*. Salzburg: Residenz.

Wigmore, J.
1991   ' "Vergangenheitsbewältigung" in Austria. The Personal and the Political in *Alle unsere Spiele* by Erika Mitterer and *Februarschatten* by Elisabeth Reichart'. *German Life and Letters* 44, pp. 477-87.

Erich Fried—German, Jew, British and Socialist: The Composite Identity of an Austrian Emigré

Axel Goodbody

Erich Fried was born in Vienna in 1921, as the only child in an assimilated middle-class Jewish family. He emigrated to Britain in August 1938, after his father, caught in a clumsy attempt to move money belonging to Jewish friends out of the country, had died at the hands of Nazi interrogators. His maternal grandmother, who had brought him up, was subsequently to perish in Auschwitz. During the war, Fried published his first poetry in London, including two slim volumes with the titles *Deutschland* and *Österreich* (reprinted in *Frühe Gedichte*, 1986). He chose to continue to live in London until his death in 1988, after becoming a British citizen during the war, but, from the early fifties, concentrated his literary and political activity in the Federal Republic of Germany. For some thirty years, links with the country of his birth seemed almost non-existent. However, Fried, who consistently described Austria as 'Heimat', or, more precisely, 'meine engere Heimat', became increasingly involved in Austrian affairs in the last decade of his life. He resumed Austrian citizenship in 1980 (while retaining his British passport), was awarded a series of Austrian state prizes, published a number of books in Austria, and took a prominent part in the campaign against Kurt Waldheim.

The question whether his youth in Vienna and this late homecoming qualify Fried as an Austrian writer led me to reflect on the other dimensions of his personality and what part they may have played in his writing. His identity was formed by childhood memories of Austria, but equally by his experience as a Jew, by residence in Britain and familiarity with British culture, by friendship with writers and the appreciation of his work in West Germany, and not least by his Marxism. It is hoped that the following observations on German, Austrian, Jewish and socialist concerns at the various stages of his life, on related themes in his work, and on his links with German, Austrian, English and Jewish cultural tradition, may throw some light on his motivation as a writer and his stylistic development.

Britain, Germany and Austria as Spheres of Activity and Themes in Fried's Work

Arriving in London five months after the Anschluss, aged seventeen, Fried was determined to become a writer, to investigate the origins of fascism and war, and to avenge his father's death by combating racism and social injustice in every form. He escaped internment, apparently because he aroused the sympathy of the (Jewish) police officers sent to arrest him (Kaukoreit 1984, Reinhold 1988). He soon became involved in both German and Austrian refugee organisations. These included the Jewish Refugees Committee, Young Austria (the youth organisation of the Austrian Centre), and the Freier Deutscher Kulturbund. Drawn himself to Trotskyism, he sympathized with the communists who were the driving force in the last two of these organizations, and for a time he was an active guest at Freie Deutsche Jugend meetings, and a member of the Austrian Kommunistischer Jugendverband which formed the core of Young Austria, as well as a candidate for membership in the Austrian Communist Party. He took an active part in the many cultural activities sponsored by these organizations, acting in sketches, reciting and reading in the literary evenings which played such an important role in émigré life, and writing texts of his own for them. It was here that he formed friendships with writers such as the poets Joseph Kalmer and Hans Schmeier, and met the socialist nature poet Theodor Kramer, the novelist Robert Neumann and the economic historian Jürgen Kuczynski (see Fried 1982b: 8-13)

His first poems were published in London émigré journals such as *Zeitspiegel, Jugend voran* and *Die Zeitung*, and in anthologies such as the Freie Deutsche Kulturbund publication *Die Vertriebenen. Dichtung der Emigration: 37 Poems by*

Refugee Authors from Austria, Czechoslovakia and Germany (FDKB: London, 1941). In 1942 he was admitted as guest member to the Austrian PEN, which acted as publisher for the volume *Deutschland* in 1944. Antifascist pathos, but also detachment, and the ability to identify with the enemy which was to become a characteristic of Fried and to give rise to countless misunderstandings, are expressed in these poems, for instance 'Einigen Gefallenen' (1986a: 43) and 'Der Richter' (1986A: 53). The poems in his subsequent volume *Österreich* are more intimate, presenting Austria, and particularly Vienna, as an object of nostalgia, although this is tempered with political and social realism. 'Es muß sein. *Zu den Fliegerangriffen auf Wien*' (1986a: 68) expresses his sorrow at the destruction of Vienna, but at the same time recognition of its necessity. Fried's homelessness was soon compounded by a new dimension: estrangement from his Austrian fellow émigrés over the question of Austrian participation in war guilt. Just old enough to remember the Bloody Friday of 1927 and the crushing of the socialist rising in 1934, he had experienced the systematic abolition of Austrian democratic institutions at school during the thirties. In 'An Österreich' he writes of Austria's guilt:

> Nicht Liebe wär's, von deiner Schuld zu schweigen…
> Du sollst einst nicht nur mit dem Finger zeigen:
> Den argen Nachbar straft, der mir gebot!
> Zu deiner Schuld mußt du dich selbst bekennen
> und im Gericht den eignen Namen nennen (1986a: 78).

In the immediate postwar years, Fried was able to place poems in British, German, Swiss and Austrian journals. These included the re-education digest *Neue Auslese* and the journals *Blick in die Welt*, for which he worked as editor from 1950–51, and *Zeitung*, both of which had been initiated by the British Central Office for Information, but enjoyed considerable editorial autonomy, as well as *Am Goldenen Tor*, edited by Alfred Döblin, the Munich-based *Literarische Revue*, and Otto Basil's *Plan* in Vienna. Though short-lived, *Plan* provided an important forum for a new generation of young Austrians (Aichinger, Bachmann, Celan, Jandl), and made a significant contribution towards the development of a new cultural programme with Aichinger's 'Aufruf zum Mißtrauen' in 1946.

Despite Basil's initiative and the efforts of men such as Hans Weigel and the communist Viktor Matejka to integrate Austrian émigrés in the newly emerging cultural scene in Austria (see Fried 1987b: 17-18, 79), Fried did not return from London.

The reasons for this he has repeatedly stated: on the one hand it was difficult to accept that Nazis responsible for crimes such as his father's brutal interrogation should be allowed to live comfortable lives in Germany and Austria, and forget the past. On the other, and perhaps more significantly, the cold war would have made it impossible for him to avoid choosing between Stalinism and anti-Communism, and while he no longer felt he could return to Austria to build up the country *with* the communists, he had too much respect for them to wish to do so *against* them. Austria held little attraction for the émigré in the early fifties, with its conservative political climate, and the re-establishment of traditional cultural values, motivated by the desire to emphasize Austrian national identity and distinguish it from German culture. Fried was deeply sceptical about such efforts, and has stressed the attraction of the Federal Republic of Germany for Austrian writers for many years after the war:

> Das literarische Leben in der Bundesrepublik bot viel mehr Möglichkeiten als das meiner engeren Heimat Österreich und setzte sich—vielleicht dadurch—auch mit Kunst- und Zeitproblemen ernsthafter auseinander. Deshalb kamen viele österreichischen Schriftsteller nach Deutschland, das auch für mich Schwerpunkt meiner Wirksamkeit wurde. Da ich aber nie deutscher Staatsbürger war, zögerte ich, London ganz zu verlassen (1988a: 159).

Fried considered moving to the north of the Federal Republic (Berlin or Hamburg). Through the exiled Germanist Werner Milch he had established contact with Elisabeth Langgässer, who wrote to the publisher Eugen Claassen in 1948 in support of Fried's poem cycle 'Landlos'. Claassen visited Fried in London and assisted him in finding translation contracts. However, plans to publish a volume of Fried's poems had to be temporarily shelved on Claassen's death. As the fifties drew on, new reasons for Fried's hesitation regarding a move to Germany emerged: the restoration under Adenauer, the ban on the KPD and rearmament.

This did not prevent Fried either from spending time in Germany or from becoming involved in public debate on politics, society and culture there. From 1953 on he made regular visits to West Germany, and soon also to the GDR, Austria and Switzerland: by 1980 he was spending four or five months a year outside Britain. He found support and friendship among those West German writers who shared his critical humanism and undogmatic socialism. The Gruppe 47, with which he had contacts from the late 1950s and of which he was a member between 1963 and its demise in 1967, effectively brought him out of emigration. Fried's subsequent involvement in West German politics was such that for decades there was hardly a major issue of public interest in which he was not personally involved. He attacked nationalism, anti-Semitism and the anachronistic *Ostpolitik* of the Adenauer government, and took a prominent part in public protest in the sixties and seventies against the Vietnam war, in Easter marches against rearmament, the Student Movement, and opposition to the witch-hunt on terrorists (he knew and admired Ulrike Meinhof). He gave countless public readings and appeared on radio and television. After the publication of *und Vietnam und*, and again in the late seventies, his writing was surrounded by controversy: a Bremen senator called for his books to be burned, the CDU included him in their infamous 'Dokumentation über Zitate zum Terrorismus', his work was described as 'Mörderpoesie' in the *FAZ* and he was dismissed as a 'Verschwörungsneurotiker' in *Die Zeit*, while his poems were removed from Bavarian schoolbooks. By the eighties he had become an elder statesman of the left, campaigning in the Peace Movement, on ecological issues and on behalf of repentant terrorists.

There was, however, a gap of almost three decades before he developed a similar intensity of involvement in Austrian affairs. He only returned to Austria in 1962, when he visited Vienna at the invitation of the Austrian Gesellschaft für Literatur. The changing climate in the 1970s, when the Kreisky government encouraged a review of the past, facilitated a belated reintegration of Austrian émigrés. The founding of the Grazer Autorenversammlung in 1973 also provided Austrian culture with a focus with which Fried could identify politically. From

1980 on he was present at Austrian symposia and congresses every year, for instance addressing an audience of over two thousand in Vienna in April 1985, together with the psychologist Erwin Ringel, on Austria's past, the origins of authoritarian patterns of behaviour, poetry and efforts for peace. The result of this event was the publication *Die da reden gegen Vernichtung* (Fried, Hrdlicka and Ringel). When the issue of the suppression of the past came to a head with Kurt Waldheim's candidacy for the Austrian presidency in 1986, Fried became a member of the Pro-Steyrer-Komitee, and contributed a series of polemical articles to the *Wochenpresse*. However, even in the eighties, Fried still spent more time in Germany than Austria, and Austrian issues play only a minor role in his creative writing. There are stories about his childhood in Vienna in the volume *Angst und Trost* and limericks and other critical pieces on Waldheim (e.g. 1987b: 225 or 1988b: 51), and other minor snipings such as an attack on the commercialisation of Salzburg (1988b: 60), but there is no volume of poems devoted to Austrian affairs to compare with those on Vietnam, Israel and the Federal Republic of Germany.

There were literary reasons as well as the political ones mentioned above for Fried's choice of Germany rather than Austria as a sphere of action in the fifties, sixties and seventies. Through his first success in Germany with translations of Dylan Thomas and other English writers in the early fifties, he established contact with publishers, radio and theatre. He contributed to journals such as *Texte und Zeichen* and *Akzente*, placed reviews and poems in *Die Zeit*, and was involved with the left-wing journal *Kürbiskern* for several years after its founding in 1966. The distinguished theatre director Kurt Hübner commissioned a translation of *A Midsummer Night's Dream* for the Bremen theatre in 1963. This was to be the first in a series of nearly thirty translations of Shakespeare's plays. Fried found publishers for his poems in Claassen (from 1958), Hanser (from 1964), and above all Wagenbach. His meeting with Klaus Wagenbach in the West Berlin Akademie der Künste in the winter of 1965 was the start of a lengthy friendship and cooperation. His growing public recognition was aided by a positive review of *Warngedichte* by Harald Hartung in

Frankfurter Hefte in 1966, and a vigorous defence of *und Vietnam und* by Peter Rühmkorf in *Der Spiegel* in 1967. Though the literary quality of the poems in *und Vietnam und* was hotly disputed at the time, Peter Härtling and Günter Grass being among Fried's harshest critics, it was through them that Fried became widely known, and they marked a significant development in the politicization of literature in the sixties.[1] Together with Martin Walser he was awarded the Fördergabe des Schillergedächtnispreises in Stuttgart in 1965, though his political activities were too controversial for this to be followed by other literary prizes for more than a decade.

In contrast Fried published little in Austria before the late seventies: a handful of articles and poems in the Salzburg journal *Literatur und Kritik* in 1966 and 1969, and in the left-wing Viennese *Tagebuch* in 1968 and 1971. His first Austrian book publications appeared in 1984–85 with a play and the volume *Von Bis nach Seit*, which collected unpublished and scattered poems written between 1945 and 1958. These were followed by *Die da reden gegen Vernichtung* in 1986, and the two collections of his speeches and articles *Nicht verdrängen nicht gewöhnen: Texte zu Österreich* (1987), and *Gedanken in und an Deutschland* (1988). Fried received the first mark of official recognition in Austria, the award of the newly created Würdigungspreis für Literatur of the Federal Ministry for Education and Art, in 1973, at a time when his political controversiality debarred him from such recognition in West Germany. It was followed in 1980 by the Preis für Literatur der Stadt Wien, and in 1986, on Fried's sixty-fifth birthday, by the Staatspreis für Verdienste um die österreichische Kultur im Ausland. This last reflects Fried's controversiality in Austria too, for although the poet's birthday was celebrated at a festive assembly with speeches from the politicians Bruno Kreisky and Fred Sinowatz, Austrian writers and artists including Hrdlicka, Qualtinger and Peter Turrini, and West and East German

1. Though in the seventies and eighties Fried turned to other publishers like the left-wing Verlag Association in Hamburg or the Bund Verlag in Cologne, probably because Wagenbach was reluctant to publish the pro-Palestinian poems of *Höre Israel!*, he continued nonetheless to publish an astonishing average of a volume a year with Wagenbach.

friends Hans Mayer, Wolf Biermann and Gerhard Wolf, the newly created award was in the nature of a consolation prize in view of the refusal of the more conservative members of the Kunstsenat to award him the Großer Österreichischer Staatspreis für Literatur.[2]

But such official awards reflect government policy rather than public recognition, and may not give a true picture of Fried's reception in Austria. Johann Holzner has argued that Fried was at first received very cautiously in Austria, his views on the Nazi past mistrusted, and his principled but undogmatic approach to controversial issues not appreciated before the late sixties (Holzner 1985: 166). Although political rehabilitation and tributes followed in the seventies, and some of his poems began to find their way into schoolbooks, his work, despite the academic and critical reception documented by Volker Kaukoreit's bibliography in *Text und Kritik*, had little impact on Austrian writing, at least up to the eighties.

Links with Austrian, English and Jewish Cultural Tradition

'Sprachkritik' or sceptical preoccupation with language has often been regarded as a distinctively Austrian tradition, coming to the fore in Nestroy's plays, Hofmannsthal's 'Brief des Lord Chandos', Wittgenstein's critical language philosophy, and Kraus's satirical analysis of language. It has been suggested that Austria's ethnic and linguistic diversity has contributed to the development of a tradition which emerges again in the fifties in the concrete poetry of the Wiener Gruppe. It seems plausible to argue a parallel here in Fried's phonetic and morphological experimentation, his revelation of links between apparently unrelated spheres of reference by means of carefully chosen similar-sounding words, or his scrutiny of words and sayings, constantly bringing fresh nuances of meaning to light (see

2. By now he was also receiving recognition in West Germany. In 1986 he was awarded the Ossietzky Medal of the International League for Human Rights in West Berlin, and in 1987 he received quasi-definitive recognition as a serious writer through the award of the Büchner Prize. Shortly before his death he was also made an honorary doctor of the University of Osnabrück.

Reinhold 1988: 582-83). In his novel *Ein Soldat und ein Mädchen* (1960) Fried explains what he calls the 'ernsthaftes Wortspiel' as a means whereby writers distance themselves from painful experience, and as 'eine Art Gegengewicht, wenn alles rund um einen her einstürzt' (1982b: 43-44). Manipulation of language, including punning, playing with and on words, already practised in one or two of the wartime poems, constitutes one of Fried's most consistent and distinctive literary techniques, used to expose social stereotypes and power structures in his poems from the volume *Warngedichte* (1964) onwards.

One of Fried's favourite conversational anecdotes reveals how Karl Kraus served as an early literary model. Together with his mother, he witnessed some of the events in Vienna on Bloody Friday in July 1927, when the Police President Schober ordered his men to fire on the demonstrating crowds, and 87 workers were killed. The posters which Kraus had put up throughout the city demanding Schober's resignation left a lasting impression on the child Fried through their elegant use of language: 'Johann Schober. Ich fordere Sie auf, abzutreten', whereby 'ab' was printed immediately below 'auf'. In 1941 Fried dedicated a sonnet to Kraus, expressing his admiration for the older writer's probity, energy and exposure of adversaries through their own words in the lines:

> Und so hast du uns Form und Spott gelehrt
> und schliffst uns scharf zur Schneide das Gewissen...
> und rühmend kann man dieses von dir sagen:
> An ihren Worten hast du sie erkannt,
> mit ihren Worten hast du sie geschlagen. (1991: 63).

Kraus did not, however, exercise a discernible stylistic influence on Fried, nor indeed did the Austrian émigrés Theodor Kramer and Joseph Kalmer, from whom Fried learnt the handiwork of poetry in London. Among his Austrian contemporaries showing an experimental approach to language Fried seems to have been closest to Ernst Jandl, with whom he shared both political affinity (Jandl joined the Sozialistische Partei Österreichs in 1951) and strong ties with Britain. Jandl was a prisoner of war in Britain for ten months, lived in London for periods in the fifties and sixties, and has written in English and translated English poetry.[3]

Links between Fried's characteristic use of language and a specifically Austrian tradition are at best tenuous and less important than his familiarity with England and English literature. In the 'Nachwort' to *Gedichte* (1958), Fried acknowledges the influence on his work of both English poetry and, in a more general way, how the English think and feel:

> Ich weiß mich nicht nur von der modernen englischen Lyrik und einzelnen älteren englischen Dichtern beeinflußt, sondern vor allem von der Art und Weise, wie man in England—in jedem Land anders—mit Gedanken und Gefühlen umgeht, wie man sie gestaltet oder verschweigt, gegen sie oder mit ihnen lebt (1958: 108).

English is close enough to and distant enough from German for its literary movements and experiments to provide him with 'Möglichkeiten zur Erweiterung des Sagbaren'. His poems belong to a 'zweite Generation deutscher Lyrik auf englischem Boden', less concerned with the themes of emigration, loneliness and injustice than those of older émigrés, and increasingly shaped and enriched in expression by elements derived from the English linguistic and cultural environment (1958: 108-109).

In *Ein Soldat und ein Mädchen* Fried is quite specific as to the nature of his debt to English literature. Three passages in the novel, ostensibly the writing of a Jewish émigré whose papers Fried is editing, are characterized by 'das Kunstmittel der Aussage durch Montage von Wortklangassoziationen' (see 'Nachwort zur ersten Auflage', p. 232). I illustrate from the first of these, entitled 'Die Nacht', which describes the traumatic central happening in the novel. The Jewish émigré, serving in Germany as a GI in 1945, has consented to spend the night with a Nazi girl in her cell, on the eve of her execution for her actions in a concentration camp, fulfilling her last wish to sleep with him:

> Nagt dann die Sorge noch an denen, die nackt sind? Und was morgen würgt, wirkt es schon in dieser Nacht; schont es sie

---

3. As evidence of Fried's interest in Jandl, see 1987: 25, 48, and two poems devoted to Jandl in the eighties (1987b: 169-70).

nicht? Ist nicht die Todeszelle die letzte Zelle des Lebens, eine
Stelle der Stille im Wirbelwind des Verwehens, an der sich das
Entzweite wieder vereint und der Verwaiste und das Verrohte
weiß und rot wird? (p. 45).

The narrator and fictitious editor draws attention to this
technique, using the émigré's own phrase 'ernsthaftes Wortspiel'
(p. 43), and later describes it as a forging of links between
concepts on the basis of phonetic similarities (p. 54). Its origins,
he asserts, lie in contemporary English literature: 'Er [the
émigré] hat das anscheinend aus der neueren Literatur seiner
zweiten Heimat übernommen, aber bis an die Grenzen des
Möglichen weitergeführt' (pp. 43-44, cf. p. 151). Such a seemingly
unequivocal statement prompts one to ask what effect British
exile had on Fried's writing, what English writers exercised a
tangible influence on him, and whether this was a lasting one.

In interviews Fried has spoken of the disadvantages as well as
the advantages for the writer in exile: above all the danger of an
impoverishment of language cut off from the sources of
enrichment and change. The émigré's language all too easily
becomes stiff and dry in the attempt to prevent English language
expressions encroaching on German. However, everyday
contact with a foreign language and culture can equally open
one's eyes to the distortion of consciousness inherent in one's
native linguistic convention. Fried's fascination with the shape
and sound of German words—he speaks of 'Spracherotik'
(1985: 6)—undoubtedly reflects a de-automatization of expression in German in the English-speaking environment. While
quite capable of writing in English, at least after he had lived in
London for a few years, he seems to have done so only
reluctantly. Curiously, his first book publication was a sixteen-
page brochure entitled *They Fight in the Dark: The Story of
Austria's Youth*, published by Young Austria in 1944. He appears
not to have written poems in English, although he collaborated
on occasion with translators, for instance his fellow exile Georg
Rapp, in the volume *On Pain of Seeing*. [4]

4. See the text on the flyleaf of this collection, which contains 54
poems selected and arranged by Fried, from the volumes *Warngedichte,
und Vietnam und*, *Anfechtungen* and *Zeitfragen*. I am indebted to
Professor J. Ritchie for drawing my attention to this publication.

More significant for Fried than reading any works of English literature was at first the opportunity to read, as librarian at the Austrian Centre, German political theorists, novelists and poets such as Marx and Rosa Luxemburg, Freud, Feuchtwanger and Kafka, Brecht, Toller and the Expressionists. Fried has repeatedly said that England does not possess an assimilative culture. Nevertheless, the poems he wrote in London in the war years already reveal his familiarity with various aspects of British culture. These range from deference to Shakespeare in the poems 'Botschaft an Macbeth' and 'Hamlet an Fortinbras' (1986a: 47-48) to adaptation of the nursery rhyme 'Oranges and Lemons' in 'Wiener Glockenspiel' (1986a: 89)—in much the same way as he had adapted the German children's games 'Die goldene Brücke' and 'Der Plumpsack' in 'Der Terror sagt sein Sprüchlein auf' and 'Münchner Ringelreihn' (1986a: 18-19).[5] In poems written in the late forties and early fifties some English place names and words appear. A few later poems examine the peculiarities of English words: 'Dog Drol' (1984: 52) and 'Englischer Gruß' (1974: 47). Fried also incorporates translations of poems from English and English mottos in several volumes.

One likely stylistic influence from English literature on Fried is the poetry of Dylan Thomas, whose major works Fried translated from about 1950 onwards. In the 'Nachwort' of his translation of Thomas's selected poetry, published in 1967, Fried expresses his admiration for the Welshman's skilful handling of poetic structure, his use of assonance, rhyme and half-rhyme, and the associative links between similar-sounding words, introducing a surrealist touch and appealing to the subconscious. Where he writes of 'Wortspiel' and 'assoziative Querverbindungen ähnlich klingender Worte' (1991: 70) we may divine techniques assimilated in his own writing through translation, as for instance in the following poem, entitled 'Botschaft':

Professor J. Ritchie for drawing my attention to this publication.
   5. See also 'Die Meilen nach Babylon', written in 1956, in Fried 1986b: 110.

Taut auf der Stirn dein Tod
tu deinem Kind dich kund
nimm einen Mond in den Mund
steig durch das Beet ins Boot

Hüllt Charons Bart an Bord
sacht dein Gesicht
fürcht vor der Nacht dich nicht
wart auf kein Sterbenswort (1958: 19)

Assonance, internal rhyme, and in particular the partial rhyme found here, in which vowels may be approximate or quite different (in other instances even the rhymed consonants are similar rather than identical) are reminiscent of Dylan Thomas's diction.

Because he first achieved recognition in Germany through his translations of Dylan Thomas, Fried felt it necessary to make the point in the 'Nachwort' to *Gedichte* that not every feature in his writing which was unusual in German poetry was attributable to Thomas's influence. However, far from citing German poets such as Arp and Schwitters as his models, he referred to other English writers:

In Wirklichkeit aber haben mich schon vorhandene Ähnlichkeiten der Auffassung, gemeinsame Einflüsse und Interessen (z.B. Bewunderung für Hopkins, Joyce, Owen, cummings) zu ihm [i.e. Dylan Thomas] hingezogen (1958: 109).

What links these writers is precisely their pioneering use of partial rhyme to forge often surprising links of meaning. This is reflected in Fried's extensive use of alliteration and assonance in the 1950s, teasing out unexpected nuances of meaning, as in the following:

Der mein Gewand
gewinnt
von dem bin ich wund

Nun fährt er mit einem Ruck
in meinen Rock
und blickt nicht mehr zurück
('Gebet für den Zenturio', 1985: 37)

Auf hohen Horsten hängt mir des Himmels Haut,
voll blauen Bluts: aus ältestem Adelsstamm,
    und stammelnd steig ich über Strauchwerk,
    streb ich die steinigen Halden aufwärts
    ('Bergung des Herzens', 1985: 75)

The programmatic poem 'Logos' initially subscribes to Luther's word fundamentalism, only to modify this by means of the 'ernsthaftes Wortspiel'. Fried's focus on individual words rather than imagery, which distinguishes such poems from most of what was being written in German at the time, is situated in a tight framework of parallelism:

> Das Wort ist mein Schwert
> und das Wort beschwert mich
>
> Das Wort ist mein Schild
> und das Wort schilt mich
>
> Das Wort ist fest
> und das Wort ist lose
>
> Das Wort ist mein Fest
> und das Wort ist mein Los (1985: 31)

The use of such disciplined sequences (cf. 'Zeitenge', 1985: 56) often combined with chiasmus, forming a climax, or more often taking an argument to its logical but absurd conclusion, together with the manipulation and adaptation of individual words, points forward to the 'Warngedichte' of the 1960s, in which Fried was to bring the poetic techniques mastered in the fifties to bear on more accessible subject matter.

In her book on Fried as translator of modern English poetry, Angelika Heimann warns against exaggerating the impact of Fried's extensive work as translator (of Shakespeare, Dylan Thomas, e.e. cummings, Sylvia Plath, T.S. Eliot, J.M. Synge and others), and argues that Fried did not allow his translating to impinge unduly on his creative writing. She acknowledges the influence of modern English poetry in Fried's word manipulation, alliteration and assonance, but writes equally of the German Baroque poems to which Fried was introduced in London by Werner Milch, and of the importance for him of Rilke's 'Sonette an Orpheus' and Georg Jünger's 'Lob der Vokale' (Heimann 1987: 55, 58-59; see also Fried 1979: 269-72).

By the sixties, in any case, English literature had become of secondary importance for Fried. Among the writers with whom he now expresses sympathy and identification are his Austrian contemporaries Ingeborg Bachmann and Paul Celan. These poets, 'beide Selbst halb und halb Exildichter', as Fried puts it, have made a more fruitful contribution to German literature in the postwar period than that of *Kahlschlaglyrik* (1988a: 159).

In his obituary on Bachmann and in articles written in the eighties Fried relates how he learnt of Bachmann's deep depression when she visited London in 1967—by then he had already known her for some years—and pays tribute to her sensitivity, and the scope and realism of her writing. However it is to Celan that he is most closely linked by their experience of the holocaust among their closest relatives and their common motivation for writing.[6] Celan, whose 'Todesfuge' had been published in the first number of *Plan*, met Fried in the late forties, visited him several times in London and gave readings at his home. It would be hard to imagine two poets whose approach to writing appears more different, and Fried takes issue with what he interprets as traces of disregard for humanity in Celan's poems, as well as his tendency towards silence and hermeticism. But Celan's writing, like *Ein Soldat und ein Mädchen* and many of Fried's poems, reflects expulsion, destruction and self-doubt. Fried differs from Celan in the complexity of his feelings regarding the Nazis, many of whom, as he knew from his schooldays, were 'normal' people (see Liebelt 1986: 46), and in his determination to be fair to opponents, for instance in his comments on anti-Semitic writers such as Ernst Jünger and Ezra Pound, or his controversial protest against excessive sentences for prominent neo-Nazis in the Federal Republic. Coming from a family in which observance of Jewish custom was a matter of tradition rather than faith, Fried held Christian ethics in deep respect (see 1988a: 138 and 1991: 52). Whereas Jewish themes, for instance Old Testament stories, are alluded to throughout his work, there are also many references to Christian motifs. Though he alludes to the Jewish liturgy and Jewish culture in several poems, such as 'Eli' (1985: 68-69), 'Wer weiß etwas von einem (Echod mi Jodea)'

6. See 'Als deutschsprachiger Jude Deutschland heute sehen', in Fried 1988a: 195-212. For Fried's assessment of Celan see 1979: 281-82. The half dozen poems he devoted to Celan in the seventies and eighties reveal respect and qualified affinity. For discussion of Fried's relationship towards Celan, see also Holzner 1986, 'Die Worte sind gefallen'; and Goltschnigg 1988.

(1958: 89), and 'Höre, Israel!' (1983: 55-61), there is little evidence of formal influence on his poetry. Nonetheless, the anti-Zionism which became one of Fried's central concerns after the Six-Day War of 1967, and Fried's support for the Palestinians, which brought him attacks in the media and death threats from the Jewish Defence League, show his identification with the Israelis. His polemical attacks on the injustice they were responsible for in his eyes reflect his view of their moral potential (see Zeller 1986).

The Parameters of Fried's Pursuit of Detachment and Justice

Fried argues in the introduction to his first volume of poems, *Deutschland*, that it is easier for him as an Austrian to write on the subject of German guilt, that his degree of detachment permits a more balanced judgment:

> Ich bin Österreicher. Deutschland habe ich nur auf der Durchreise nach England gesehen. Deutsche habe ich bei der Besetzung meiner Heimat als Feinde, in der Emigration als Freunde kennengelernt. Vielleicht konnte ich diese Gedichte schreiben, weil ich jener innigeren Bindung entbehre, die nahe Angehörige angesichts tragischer Ereignisse verstummen läßt (1986a: 13).

Fried's Austrianness may also explain in part his detachment from the cold war antagonism between the two German states after 1949. 'Fachausdrücke', one of three poems which he contributed to the anthology *Deutsche Teilung: Ein Lyrik-Lesebuch* in 1966, lampoons the West and East German preoccupation with mutual denigration:

> In Frabi ists guter Ton
> vom 'bösen Friba' zu sprechen
> In Friba darf man nur sagen
> 'das sogenannte Frabi'
>
> Wenn Fribaner oder Frabiner
> vom künftigen Einswerden reden
> und ein Fremder glaubt es liegt beiden
> das gleiche am Herzen

dann verstehen Frabiner darunter
den Sieg der Frabinisierung
und Fribaner erhoffen
die große Fribanisation (pp. 129-30)

Fried's speeches throughout the sixties and seventies show a determination to balance criticism of socialist countries with exposure of injustice in Western ones, for instance when he compares treatment of the dissident Robert Havemann by the East German authorities with that of Peter Brückner in the Federal Republic (1988a: 167).

Fried's position regarding East Germany and the Eastern European states was, however, less motivated by Austrian neutrality than by his ideological standpoint. Deeply impressed as a schoolboy by the Social Democratic principles of his teacher Franz Ederer, and 'converted' to Marxism in 1938, he had first hesitated in London to join the Austrian Kommunistischer Jugendverband, then joined, in the belief that he could work for reform of its failings from inside, only to leave it early in 1944 when the suicide of his friend Hans Schmeier made clear to him the untenable position of any free-thinking individual in the party. Like his friend the Austrian communist Ernst Fischer, he adopted an uncomfortable position of undogmatic socialism between the various parties. Until he resigned from the BBC in 1968, because he felt its programmes were becoming a relic of cold war days, he conducted a 'Zweifrontenkampf' in his broadcasts against Stalinism and cold war anti-communism. On Fried's occasional visits to the GDR he was greeted as 'der Engländer', familiar to many from his early morning broadcasts, and respected for his detachment and balance (see Biermann 1990: 177).

Fried repeatedly cites informed public opinion in England as an instance when censuring German politicians from the late sixties on, and refers to the absence in Britain of the German and Austrian tendency to hysteria in certain political situations. On the other hand, he never tried to become English and only felt British when confronted with disparaging remarks about the English in Germany. He once spoke of the inevitability of his involvement in German rather than English literature, where the issues of the past and its possible repetition are of less importance, and writers are not fired by the thought 'That mustn't ever happen again' (1987b: 242). Considering he was a member of the British Labour Party for many years, his direct involvement in British politics was minimal.

The question of identity, as Ursula Reinhold remarks, is a central one in Fried's work (Reinhold 1988: 581). Hanjo Kesting writes of his threefold homelessness: as an Austrian in Germany, as a German in exile, and as a Jew in the world—he might have added as a supporter of the Palestinians among the Jews—and sums up: 'Vier Länder und keine Heimat' (Kesting 1982: 40). The clash between Jewish and German/Austrian allegiances is revealed as traumatic in his study of the psychological intricacies of guilt in *Ein Soldat und ein Mädchen*. Fried's search for identity in the 1950s was further complicated by living in Britain, and his partial identification with English culture.

But for his family in London, Fried might well have returned to Austria before he died. As he grew older, and turned to childhood memories in the face of death (he fought cancer for seven years), his emotional bond with the country of his birth became stronger:

> Ich fühle mich, was meine Heimat betrifft, als Österreicher... Die Landschaften, die ich als Kind gesehen habe, und die sich gar nicht so wesentlich verändert haben—das ist meine Heimat. Und diese Heimat hat mich geprägt. Ich bin sehr froh, daß ich jetzt auch meine österreichische Staatsbürgerschaft wieder habe (Liebelt 1986: 46-47).

However, Austrianness was only one factor, and indeed perhaps a subordinate one, in Fried's make-up as an émigré, as 'bibelfester jüdischer Agnostiker' (Zeller 1986: 128) and unaligned Marxist, who unrepentantly supported a non-dogmatic form of socialism which embraced anarchism and respected the findings of psychology.[7] His determination from the earliest days to oppose injustice and dishonesty, to promote humanity, tolerance and democracy in a world of human

---

7. See Fried *et al.* 1986: 182-83, 188, and the poems 'Brief nach Moskau' (1987a: 36), 'Diskussionsbasis' (1987a: 48), 'Warnung' (1988b: 32) and 'Weil ich lebe' (1988b: 56).

suffering, lies and alienation made him an anarchistic outsider from any interest group. His boyhood rebellion against his father's strictness and conservatism, coupled with determination to compensate for his physical clumsiness (he suffered from a muscular disorder), found expression in precocious reading and the cultivation of a phenomenal memory for phrases and passages as a child, as well as unusually early political awareness and identification with the victims of injustice.[8] These personal factors go some way towards explaining a desire to become involved in German politics which was quite unusual for a Jewish émigré.

WORKS CITED

Biermann, W.
    1990   'und Erich Fried und', in H. Stein (ed.), *Klartexte im Getümmel: 13 Jahren im Westen. Von der Ausbürgerung zur November-Revolution.* Cologne: Kiepenheuer und Witsch.
Morawietz, K. (ed.)
    1966   *Deutsche Teilung: Ein Lyrik-Lesebuch.* Wiesbaden: Limes.
Fried, E.
    1958   *Gedichte.* Hamburg: Claassen.
    1964a   'Ein Versuch, Farbe zu bekennen', in H. Kesten (ed.), *Ich lebe nicht in der Bundesrepublik.* Munich: List, pp. 43-48.
    1964b   *Warngedichte.* Munich: Hanser.
    1967   *und Vietnam und.* Berlin: Wagenbach.
    1969   *On Pain of Seeing: Poems by Erich Fried.* Poetry Europe Series 11. London: Rapp & Whiting.
    1974   *Gegengift: 49 Gedichte und ein Zyklus.* Berlin: Wagenbach.
    1979   'Lesen und Schreiben während des Exils. Interview mit Anke Winckler', in L. Winckler, *Antifaschistische Literatur. III. Prosaformen.* Königstein/Taunus: Scriptor, pp. 269-84.
    1982a   'Anläufe und Anfechtungen. Gespräch mit Erich Fried', in H. Kesting, *Dichter ohne Vaterland: Gespräche und Aufsätze zur Literatur.* Berlin: Dietz, pp. 24-38.
    1982b   *Ein Soldat und ein Mädchen: Roman.* Düsseldorf: Claassen, 2nd edn.
    1983a   *Angst und Trost: Erzählungen und Gedichte über Juden und Nazis.* Frankfurt: Alibaba.
    1983b   *Höre, Israel! Gedichte und Fußnoten.* Frankfurt/Main: Syndikat.
    1984   *Zeitfragen und Überlegungen: 80 Gedichte, sowie ein Zyklus.* Berlin: Wagenbach.

8. See Lampe 1989: chs. 2, 3; Wolff 1986: 41-42, 82.

1985   *Von Bis nach Seit: Gedichte aus den Jahren 1945–1958*. Vienna: Promedia.
1986a   *Frühe Gedichte*. Düsseldorf: Claassen.
1986b   *Reich der Steine: Zyklische Gedichte*. Frankfurt/Main: Fischer.
1987a   *Am Rande unserer Lebenszeit*. Berlin: Wagenbach.
1987b   *Nicht verdrängen nicht gewöhnen: Texte zum Thema Österreich*. Ed. M. Lewin. Vienna: Europaverlag.
1988a   *Gedanken in und an Deutschland: Essays und Reden*. Ed. M. Lewin. Vienna: Europaverlag.
1988b   *Unverwundenes: Liebe, Trauer, Widersprüche. Gedichte*. Berlin: Wagenbach.
1991   *Einer singt aus der Zeit gegen die Zeit. Erich Fried 1921–1988: Materialien und Texte zu Leben und Werk*. Ed. V. Kaukoreit and H. Vahl. Darmstadt: Jürgen Häusser.

Fried, E., with A. Hrdlicka and E. Ringel
1986   *Die da reden gegen Vernichtung: Psychologie, bildende Kunst und Dichtung gegen den Krieg*. Vienna: Europaverlag.

Goltschnigg, D.
1988   'Intertextuelle Traditionsbezüge im Medium des Zitats am Beispiel von Erich Frieds lyrischem Dialog mit Paul Celan', in G. Labroisse and G.P. Knapp (eds.), *Literarische Tradition Heute: Deutschsprachige Gegenwartsliteratur in ihrem Verhältnis zur Tradition*. Amsterdam: Rodopi, pp. 27-59.

Heimann, A.
1987   *'Bless Thee! Thou art Translated!: Erich Fried als Übersetzer moderner englischsprachiger Lyrik*. Münchener Studien zur neueren englischen Literatur, 4. Amsterdam: Grüner.

Holzner, J.
1985   'Divergente Formen der Vergangenheitsbewältigung: das literarische Werk Erich Frieds und seine Rezeption in Österreich', in D.G. Daviau and L.M. Fischer (eds.), *Exil: Wirkung und Wertung. Ausgewählte Beiträge zum 5. Symposium über deutsche und österreichische Exilliteratur*. Columbia, SC: Camden House, pp. 161-72.

1986   'Die Worte sind gefallen. Notizen zu Paul Celan und Erich Fried', in H.L. Arnold (ed.), *Text und Kritik* 91, pp. 33-42.

Kaiser, K.
1990   'Gespräch mit Erich Fried. Exil in Großbritannien. Kalmer, Schmeier und andere'. *Zwischenwelt. Jahrbuch der Theodor Kramer Gesellschaft*, 1, pp. 80-90.

Kaukoreit, V.
1981   'Der Weg eines bunten Getüms. Eine vorläufige Biographie des Dichters Erich Fried'. *Freibeuter* 7, pp. 20-23.
1984   'Erich Fried im Londoner Exil'. *Die Horen* 134, pp. 59-72.

1986   'Auswahlbibliographie', in H.L. Arnold (ed.), *Text und Kritik* 91, pp. 112-32.

Kaukoreit, V., and M. Töteberg
1985   'Erich Fried', in *Kritisches Lexikon der deutschsprachigen Gegenwartsliteratur*. Munich: Edition Text und Kritik.

Kesting, H.
1982   'Gedichte ohne Vaterland. Der Lyriker Erich Fried', in *Dichter ohne Vaterland: Gespräche und Aufsätze zur Literatur*. Berlin: Dietz. pp. 39-51.

Lampe, G.
1989   *'Ich will mich erinnern an alles was man vergißt': Erich Fried. Biographie und Werk*. Cologne: Bund.

Liebelt, L.
1986   'Wir müssen gegen die totale Verlustchance arbeiten. Gespräch mit Erich Fried', in Wolff 1986: 40-56.

Reinhold, U.
1988   'Erich Fried', in H. Haase *et al.* (eds.), *Österreichische Literatur des zwanzigsten Jahrhunderts: Einzeldarstellungen*. Berlin: Volk & Wissen, pp. 581-604.

Wolff, R., (ed.)
1986   *Erich Fried: Gespräche und Kritiken*. Bonn: Bouvier.

Zeller, M.
1986   'Im Zeichen des ewigen Juden. Zur Konkretion des politischen Engagements in der Lyrik Erich Frieds', in Wolff 1986: 94-148.

The Search for Wholeness:
The Novels of Matthias Mander

Michael Mitchell

Matthias Mander was born in Graz in 1933 and came to wider notice in 1979 with the publication of his first novel, *Der Kasuar*, which was accompanied in the following year by a collection of short stories, *Das Tuch der Geiger*. He has since published two further large-scale novels, *Wüstungen* (1985), and *Der Sog* (1989). Mander is not a full-time writer, but has another, 'regular' profession—indeed, two others (in *Der Kasuar* a computer programmer who is also a poet remarks, 'hauptberuflich Literatur machen kann man nur, wenn man lügt; man kann sie nur als Nebenberuf ehrlich betreiben' [p. 53]). Mander occupies a senior managerial position with the firm of Waagner-Biró AG, for whom he has worked since 1952. He entered the firm as an accountant but appears to have become increasingly involved with computerization. An integrated computer system for business planning that he designed won a prize at an international competition in London in 1976, for example. In addition to this, he has teaching posts at the Vienna Wirtschaftsuniversität and at the Institut für Unternehmungsführung of Innsbruck University. It is an impressive career and one that leads one to assume that the industrious and conscientious figures that play an important role in his novels are, at least in those qualities, reflections of the author.

With his inside knowledge of the business world and involvement with computer systems, Mander is well qualified to be the chronicler of the 1980s which some reviewers celebrate him as; the dust jacket of *Wüstungen*, for example, proclaims it to be 'eine Realienkunde der achtziger Jahre'. In all three novels the characters are occupied with questions of business, finance and technology, and the central characters are, or have been, in senior managerial posts: Rausak (*Der Kasuar*) is 'Prokurist', Zwigott (*Wüstungen*) was 'Disponent' before going to teach in a 'Handelsakademie', Vorhofer (*Der Sog*) is Deputy Managing Director of a large industrial concern. Apart from these, the range of figures spreads right across industry and related areas: there are engineers, technicians, scientists, government and trade union officials, foremen, stores supervisors, secretaries, computer specialists. His novels are certainly unusual, if not unique, in Austrian literature in portraying the world of industry at all levels and from the inside.

Although I am not aware that Mander uses the expression, one could describe the three novels as a trilogy. This is because in the background of each looms the shape of 'Erz-Blech-Chemie', a huge (fictitious) industrial conglomerate for which most of the figures work. The EBC, as it is generally referred to, exhibits many features of the gigantic industrial and commercial concerns which dominate the world today: for example, the intrigues and in-fighting among senior management; the struggle for international contracts including the moral problems created by the use of slush funds; the closing down of factories and the commercial, political and human considerations involved. Such organizations—and their culture—are international, but the EBC does reveal specifically Austrian features as well. One of Rausak's first responsible tasks, as was Mander's, is concerned with the Austrian take-over of factories from the Soviet USIA (a Russian acronym for the Administration of Soviet Property in Austria) after the State Treaty. The dependence on exports, the close and complex interrelationship between business and government and the importance of party membership for one's career are also features which characterize the EBC as Austrian. The EBC is not a portrait of Waagner-Biró. In its huge scale, multiple activities and close connection with the state it seems to reflect the holding company for Austria's nationalized industries, the Östereichische Industrieverwaltungs-Aktiengesellschaft, or ÖIAG.

The portrayal of modern industrial society is a striking feature, but Mander's novels are not 'Romane der Arbeitswelt', nor examples of a new genre, the 'Managerroman'. The concerns of the novels and their characters are much wider-ranging: current political events, environmental and social concerns appear, as well as other interests of the many figures from archaeology, biology, geology and chemistry, to music, art, religion and even do-it-yourself housebuilding. But, on the other hand, the world of business and industry is not merely background. Mander is interested in the whole person, so that the whole of a character's interests can inform the novel, but he recognizes, in a way that is unusual in Western literature, that work is the substratum of our existence. For the characters in these novels, work is as important a part of their lives as their personal relationships and other private interests. It appears on all levels, from the individual perspective to the macroeconomic level of governmental decisions and the international trade cycle.

The wide range of material incorporated in the novels is important for their linguistic texture. Most of the characters are specialists in their own, usually scientific or technical, sphere, and they use the language of that sphere with a rigour that makes few concessions to the non-specialist. The result is a language that is demanding on the reader but one, surprisingly, that is not a mishmash of technical jargon, but a modern poetic language of great power. Its precision is the essential prerequisite for its expressiveness on the metaphorical level.

The connection between work and the individual personality operates in two complementary directions. On the one hand, the individual characters try to integrate their professional activities into their personal lives; on the other, they want their work, their effect on the public domain, to correspond to their inner beliefs, that is, they want to see their ethical principles realized in their work. Both of these aspects can be illustrated in a figure who tries to realize an absolute congruence of inner and outer reality and whom the inevitable failure destroys. This is the bank manager, Siegl (*Wüstungen*), whose life has become divided into two almost hermetically-sealed parts. On his way to work a gradual transformation from husband and father to bank manager takes place: he polishes his shoes, shaves, puts on his tie, sometimes even has to stop to sew on shirt buttons. But, more importantly, the transformation is an inner one as well:

Im Augenblick seiner Einfahrt in die Stadt Gänserndorf...der
Öffnung der Glastür zu seinem Geldinstitut, [fiel] die
Verstrickung in Kinderpflege, Wohnungserhaltung, Hausbau,
Geldsorgen und Eheführung mit seiner tschechischen Frau
Eva vom ihm ab, zugleich [begann] ein eigenständiges
Kopfleben (pp. 263-64).

But the division is not the cliché of the rich personal life that is
unfulfilled in the arid surroundings of an institution devoted
entirely to money. Both sides have their satisfactions and their
problems, but it is in fact the breakdown of Siegl's relationship
with his wife which so drains him that he has to divide his life up
in order to survive.

Siegl is a devout Christian who tries to apply the moral
precepts of his belief in his life. He is a conscientious character,
too conscientious for his own good, 'ein Mann von Ordnung, ja
Reinheit', one of the other characters comments, 'seine Urteile
folgen den Zehn Geboten, der Bankordnung, dem Bilanzrecht'
(p. 288). Putting the Ten Commandments on the same level as
banking regulations is almost comically grotesque, but each in its
own sphere is an authority that Siegl accepts. His problem is
that he refuses to keep them in separate spheres, but wants to
mould immediate, practical reality according to the eternal
verities. An example of this is his response to the revelation that
funds which have been deposited in his bank and which he has
invested, come from a group of arms smugglers. Although
completely innocent of any involvement in the crime, or even of
knowledge of the provenance of the money, he feels drawn into
a web of guilt by association which serves to increase his
depression.

Siegl's life is a failure, a double failure. On the one hand he
does not succeed in integrating his private and public life, and on
the other, he fails to realize his religious and moral ideals in
practical action. He is presented as an extreme, rather than an
ideal; his absolute demands are impossible to fulfil in reality,
and to insist on them is to provoke disaster. But he is still
presented as a positive figure: his failure is as much a comment
on the nature of society as on the rigidity of the idealist. His
gradual loss of control over himself and his life engages the
reader's sympathy and is one of the few narrative strands that
help to hold together the disparate material. His death by

electrocution is left a mystery (murder, suicide or an accident?), emphasizing that the clear-cut distinctions he sought in his life are not possible.

The search for wholeness, then, is one that is largely frustrated, unfulfilled. And yet it is necessary: to abandon the search is to reduce one's humanity. The search for internal and external fulfilment and for their integration into one whole must continue, even without the prospect of any final achievement.

In the main characters of the three novels three different approaches to life are explored, and I would like to look briefly at each in turn. Rausak, the central figure of *Der Kasuar*, tries to gather together his experience of life, order it and write it down for his children. The novel is not autobiographical in form, but a montage of anecdotes, memories, brief portraits, scraps of conversation, images and ideas arranged, in general, thematically. The material is organized in a complex structure which gives the book a depth and unity which Rausak's life, as he gradually comes to realize, does not possess (see Mitchell 1990).

Rausak's life was an attempt to achieve a kind of wholeness by remaining *open* to the demands of various aspects of reality, and it ends in half unconscious, half willing adaptation to the restrictions imposed by the socio-economic environment. This is reflected in the symbol of the cassowary (his name, Rausak, is, of course, 'Kasuar' spelled backwards): the cassowary is a flightless bird whose physical characteristics, especially the horny crest on the top of its head, represent an adaptation to a life spent crashing through the undergrowth. The memory of life in a wider, freer dimension remains, the bird is described as a 'starkes Landtier, dennoch eine Flugseele' (p. 419). In Rausak the 'airborne soul', though gradually disappearing in the three sections of the final part of the novel, is still there, vestigially, in the image with which the novel closes: 'Dolch aus Kasuar-knochen: späte, weitabliegende, doch nicht völlig entfremdete Erfüllung flugfähigen Röhrengebeins…allergeheimste, feder-leichte Wehr' (p. 419). Rausak's connection with his totemic animal and the one-sided adaptation it represents has a physical manifestation in the osteoma, a cancerous growth of the bone, inside his forehead which causes his death.

If *Der Kasuar* centres on an idealist who finds himself forced to adapt and restrict his expectations, the main figure in Mander's novel *Der Sog* has deliberately restricted his life to his professional function in order to achieve power and position. His name, too, is symbolic: Dr Urban Vorhofer is, as 'Vize-Präsident' of the EBC, in the temple forecourt of power. The main illustration of the way he has ruthlessly subordinated all aspects of his being to the achievement of power within the EBC is the story, which emerges from scraps of memory and short reflections, of his brief affair with an employee who has borne his child. Vorhofer has cut them both out of his life, seemingly afraid of any demands on his energies other than those of his position at the EBC. He is the counter-figure to Rausak and Siegl, the realist who has rejected the ideal of wholeness to make his life a neat but one-dimensional unity.

The actual narrative of *Der Sog* is the story of a descent through purgatory to a death which is also in some senses a rebirth. Arlet, the President of the EBC, has been assassinated, and Vorhofer has seen, scratched on the wall of the lift, the words 'VORHOFER ALS NÄCHSTER' (p. 5). After the staff Christmas party at the EBC headquarters in Vienna, he locks himself in the empty building over the holiday as the best way of avoiding his presumed assassin (it is characteristic that he should seek protection from the outside world within the EBC). The book is divided into eight chapters for the eight days from 24 to 31 December, each of which is spent on a different floor of the building, starting on the seventh and ending up on the ground floor. In this descent he is stripped naked, both physically and psychologically; he suffers what appears to be a heart attack and a lacerated stomach ulcer, faints then recovers and stumbles, rolls and crawls around the building in search of food, drink, warmth and comfort. He vomits blood and his bowels empty, so that his exit from the building on the morning of a new year, stripped, bloody and smeared in excrement is a kind of symbolic birth *inter faeces urinamque*. As he vows to become a real father to his child it becomes an emotional and moral rebirth; but it is too late for realization, and ends in physical death.

The texture of *Der Sog* is a rich weave of Vorhofer's perceptions, memories, reflections and obsessions which compensates for and fills out the rigid division of the chapters into one for each day and each floor. There is much about contemporary life, especially about the interconnected worlds of business and politics, but there are also complexes of images arising from his personal concerns which, having been repressed, often appear in nightmarish forms; in particular there is a group of images from the end of the war, revolving around a huge Nazi bunker dug into a hillside and a mare giving birth amid the bombs. The EBC building itself comes to have a symbolic function. It is a modern steel and glass structure and over the Christmas period one vertical and one horizontal row of lights is left on, representing a cross. This reflects the externalized Christianity of society which is publicly acknowledged but not taken to heart. It is significant that Vorhofer feels most exposed when he is in one of the rooms with a lighted window. On the final pages the phrase 'VORHOFER ALS NÄCHSTER' is repeated, gradually contracting—is it his death-rattle?—until all that is left are the letters CHRST: whether they refer to Christ or Christa, his lover, or both, they do hint at the possibility of a spiritual or emotional rebirth which his death does not allow him to realize.

The one figure in Mander's novels who most nearly approaches, and manages to maintain, a *juste milieu* is the main character of *Wüstungen*, Zwigott. *Wüstungen* is the record of a kind of sabbatical year. Zwigott has resigned from a senior position with the EBC in disgust at the way what he sees as the true function of the company—to supply human needs and provide employment—is constantly subordinated to the interests of power politics and personal advancement. He takes a teaching post at the Handelsakademie in Gänserndorf, but at the end of the year decides to return to the EBC, even though he knows that conditions will be no better than when he left. At the end of his 'sabbatical year' Zwigott re-enters 'the world' with a triple dedication: to the individuals who work for the EBC; to his young ward, the son of the dead bank manager Siegl; and to the priest whom he will accompany round his scattered Marchfeld parishes as organist: he has chosen a life of service, even if it is 'wissentliches Dienen in deviaten Systemen' (p. 16).

The 'Wüstungen' of the title are abandoned settlements in the Marchfeld in which Zwigott and a group of colleagues become interested; they go on expeditions to search for their sites, which are only recognizable by a few shards or the presence of particular groupings of plants. The old Marchfeld villages were exposed to invasion, wild animals, flood and frost, and when he decides to return to the EBC Zwigott sees himself as similarly exposed; not, of course, in his physical existence, but in the psychological and moral sphere. Zwigott returns because, as the colleague who persuades him to do so says:

> Das widersprüchliche, unvollkommene, oft ins Unrecht gesetzte, aber unvermeidliche Produktionssystem braucht Mitarbeiter, die diese Vorläufigkeit ertragen können... Sie bekommen von mir keine Gewißheit, außer der einen, daß Sie einsteigen müssen, wenn Sie ehrlich bleiben wollen (p. 251).

Wholeness is a dream, if a necessary dream. The most we can actually achieve in this world is to recognize that life is a makeshift business and be honest with ourselves. It is the inability to accept this that destroys the bank manager, Siegl.

Wholeness is not only presented through the main characters, but appears on many levels in the novels. In *Wüstungen*, for example, there is a complex of figures and images representing the possibility of a sudden qualitative change, of brief moments when the 'Vorläufigkeit' of existence seems overcome. This centres on a historical figure from the Marchfeld, Hans Kudlich, the 'Bauernbefreier' of 1848, on whom Zwigott is preparing a speech. Zwigott calls him a 'Synoptiker', that is someone who can break with conventional, hidebound ways of thinking and introduce a completely new view of the world at one stroke. There is a parallel to this in *Der Sog* in Vorhofer's work, originally his doctoral thesis, on the Russian Prime Minister and agrarian reformer Stolypin. Further examples come in *Wüstungen* when some of the Handelsakademie teachers visit the Marchfeld birthplace of Ernst Mach, whose vision of 'das unrettbare Ich' came in a sudden moment of illumination (p. 113). The village next to Mach's birthplace was the first in Austria to carry out the consolidation of agricultural holdings, modernizing the old strip system, a change Zwigott feels is as important in agriculture and food supply as Mach's vision for physics and philosophy.

Another excursion, this time a class visit to a Marchfeld oil-well, provides a different example: an innovation in drilling techniques is explained whereby the direction of boring can be changed not by trying to twist the rods, but by uncoupling them and starting in a new direction from the bottom of the pipe. This is the impulse for an argument amongst the teachers as to whether a social version of such a complete change in direction, what one of them calls the 'Abkopplung von Zwangsfolgen' (p. 141), would be possible. Some of them quote the examples of Kudlich, Mach and agrarian reform given above, whilst a pessimist counterbalances them with a list of the main events of the current year (1982): the Iran–Iraq War; the Falklands War; the murder of the Israeli ambassador in London and war in the Lebanon; the massacre of Palestinians in the refugee camps; the US passing the largest military budget of all time. The overall picture in the three novels, of a world of war, famine, injustice, rising crime and unemployment, seems to confirm the pessimistic view, which the positive images of Hans Kudlich, Ernst Mach, land reform and the drilling innovation cannot offset in any quantitative sense. But they do remain as signs of human potentiality, as what, in the course of the argument, one character calls, 'Metapher...für den möglichen Überstieg in ein anderes menschliches Verhalten' (p. 143).

In all three novels the main character is used as a lens through which to focus on a much broader segment of society. In *Der Kasuar* and *Der Sog* this broader segment is the world of the EBC. In *Wüstungen* the industrial combine is left in the background; the broader picture is of the Marchfeld, the region around Gänserndorf where Zwigott works after leaving the company.

Zwigott observes and explores his new environment and his perspective is enlarged by material gathered by the German teacher for her 'Marchfeldroman'. This project is a collective novel on which she has persuaded many of the staff and students of the Handelsakademie to collaborate. Disparate contributions on the region are fed into a computer programmed to analyse, sort, group, rearrange and redistribute them according to various schemes. Although *Wüstungen* is not that 'Marchfeldroman' (no more than *Der Kasuar* is entirely congruent with Rausak's material), something suggesting a total picture of the area begins to emerge in the variety of aspects that are touched on in the novel: the immediacy of the landscape as physical impression and as atmosphere creating a sense of the *genius loci* is underpinned by information on the palaeontology, geology and meteorology of the area, its history from Roman times to Napoleon, its place names, its churches, the development of industry and agriculture; at one point it is even seen in its strategic importance in the military planning of East and West. The Marchfeld is small and compact and manageable enough to be seen in something approaching its totality, and this enables Mander to use it as a microcosm of a nation and, beyond that, of the developed world.

This totality is not, of course, a neat unity with no loose ends. It *suggests* connections without restricting them to one precise relationship. We cannot know the totality of effect one particular cause may have, therefore none of our actions is final; they are all makeshift responses to a developing situation. An example in *Wüstungen* is the Marchfeld Canal project: it is an attempt to make good the effects of the regulation of the Danube at the end of the last century which was undertaken to solve the problem of flooding, but which led to the gradual lowering of the water table and the dessication of the land. It is not presented just as a solution to one specific problem, but appears in a wide variety of contexts, technical, agricultural, geological, political, historical, topographical, even spiritual: the drying-out has affected the foundations of a church, and Siegl compares the dessication of the Marchfeld 'mit der seelischen Austrocknung seiner Bewohner' (p. 359). The picture of the Marchfeld in *Wüstungen* is not one that is in any quantitative respect complete, but it is one that gives us a sense of the region as a whole and as a living organism.

There is a further dimension to the question of wholeness in these novels, and that is the aesthetic dimension. As well as being exemplified by the novels, the question of aesthetic form is a theme of *Der Kasuar* and *Wüstungen*. In *Wüstungen* Zwigott, although originally unwilling, agrees to contribute to the

'Marchfeldroman', but his continuing scepticism towards literature means that both literary form and the relationship between literature and the world are recurring and legitimate themes in *Wüstungen*. One of the things that irritates Zwigott about literature is what the German teacher calls its 'erzwungene Unfertigkeit, Widersprüchlichkeit' (p. 86), transposing Zwigott's expression of his dissatisfaction at his work in the EBC: 'Diese lebenverdrängende, unbehebbare Unfertigkeit' (p. 86). Zwigott's training as an accountant has given him something of a 'balance-sheet mentality': he would like everything to work out neatly. A better understanding of the contradictory relationship between art and life (though never a complete acceptance of it) is one thing that Zwigott learns during his year at the Handelsakademie, and it is something that helps him avoid the rigidity of absolute demands that his friend Siegl suffered from, and accept the 'Vorläufigkeit' of the world of the industrial combine and, by extension, of life in general.

In *Der Kasuar* Rausak is attempting to give shape to his experience as he writes it down for his children. He wants both his life and his record of it to reflect a deeper unity of various different levels. In a limited area, cost accounting for example, Rausak can program a computer to generate such a 'multidimensional model' of reality: 'alle sachlichen Einflußgrößen könnten gewichtet und zu einem vieldimensionalen Modell verknüpft werden, auf dem Varianten durchzuspielen sind' (pp. 145-46). But, in a similar way to Zwigott, he finds that this is impossible in the wider sphere of his own life: 'sein Mythos vielflächiger, tief geschichteter, ineinanderwirkender Lebensebenen war nicht durchhaltbar' (p. 405).

But Rausak's failure is not Mander's failure. The thematization of literary creation is not an excuse for the author's inability to give his own novel a satisfying unity; nor is it an ironic attempt in the manner of Thomas Mann to create distance. It is one further aspect of the theme of wholeness, adding to and at the same time emphasizing the complexity of interrelationship within the novels, which do succeed in weaving many disparate threads into an integrated whole. It is not a restrictive whole, in which all contradictions are neatly resolved, but one which is large enough to include loose ends, such as was illustrated with the example of the Marchfeld or the mystery of Siegl's death.

The key structural question, both in the thematic discussions and in the form of the novels, is the jump from the additive nature of the material to a multi-layered unity. All three novels illustrate this in that all have a basic structure which reveals the piecemeal, additive nature of the material gathered. *Wüstungen* and *Der Sog* have this in an extreme form in the choice of the calendar as a structural base, in *Der Kasuar* it comes from the way Rausak orders his material into thematic units. But all three have a richness of interrelationship on the material, thematic, metaphorical and symbolic level which overcomes the rigidity of what in *Wüstungen* Mander calls the 'Chronik der äußeren Geschehnisse' (the heading of the contents page, p. 5). The breakthrough from the additive listing of fact and event to the truth behind appearances is described in one of the reflections on Rausak's 'memoirs':

> Was sind Rausaks Aufzeichnungen? Ein Er-zählen, im Tonfall und Sinn wie errechnen, ermessen, erarbeiten, erwandern, erklettern, ertrotzen, Faktum an Faktum, Datum an Datum, ohne Wölbung, Gipfelung, Erlösung: sammeln, schlichten, in großer Zahl so aufgelistet, daß Gesetze erkennbar werden müßten, wenn in der Wirklichkeit Gesetze herrschten (1979: 202).

As the subjunctive of the final clauses suggests, Rausak himself does not achieve the breakthrough that he was trying to 'force' by collecting and ordering his life's experience. But as a novel, *Der Kasuar* has an overall *aesthetic* structure, the 'laws' of which emerge from the various 'facts' and 'data'. That is, in their aesthetic structure the novels rise above the compartmentalization of life their characters suffer under, and this acts as a symbol of man's potential, though unrealizable, universality. Aesthetic form has a moral force in Mander's novels. Aesthetic wholeness is a sign that the moral and emotional wholeness we search after but can never fully realize is not entirely an illusion.

Universality was a concern of a writer who clearly served as an example to Mander: Heimito von Doderer (he is mentioned in *Der Kasuar*). Doderer said 'der Mensch ist universal gemeint, wenn auch nicht nach allen Seiten fähig, so doch von allen Seiten ansprechbar' (Doderer 1964: 18). A large-scale aesthetic structure which adds a deeper dimension to the themes and material is also a feature of Doderer's major novels. Mander is very much a conservative in the Austrian tradition in his insistent belief in the value of the individual and in the value and feasibility of aesthetic creation. The philosophy of 'Dienen', of a service which accepts the provisional whilst believing in the absolute, even if we can never know it with certainty, makes him heir to another Austrian icon, Adalbert Stifter. Most of Mander's characters are motivated in part by religious belief, vague in some, very precise in others. Although one suspects the author may share this belief, in the novels it is situated within the figures, not on the narratorial level. For the reader God is a symbol of the wholeness they are searching for. 'Gott ist, insofern er gesucht wird' (1989: 337): the importance of wholeness lies in the search, not in any presumed achievement.

WORKS CITED

Doderer, H. von
    1964   *Tangenten: Tagebuch eines Schriftstellers 1940–1950*. Munich: Biederstein.

Mander, M.
    1979   *Der Kasuar*. Graz: Styria.
    1980   *Das Tuch der Geiger*. Graz: Styria.
    1985   *Wüstungen*. Graz: Styria.
    1989   *Der Sog*. Graz: Styria.

Mitchell, M.
    1990   'The Tradition of the "Big" Novel in Austria: Sebestyén, Vasovec, Mander'. *Modern Austrian Literature* 23, 3/4, pp. 1-15.

'Auch Schweigen kann Verrat sein.'
Coming to Terms with Women's History:
Elisabeth Reichart's *Februarschatten* and *Komm über den See*

Juliet Wigmore

The newfound attention paid to women's history in recent years, particularly by feminist historians, has been marked by increasingly refined approaches. Nowhere is this more apparent than in the discussions of the role of women during the Third Reich, which has formed part of the wider controversy surrounding the reassessment of that period of history. Although the discussion has focused largely on Germany, rather than specifically on Austria, many of the ideas which have emerged about the position of women at that time are equally applicable to the period following the Anschluss in Austria. In the literary context, where ethical issues are at stake, this is certainly the case.

It is a well-known fact that Austrians have been accused of a long-standing failure to face up to their involvement in the Nazi period, an attitude which to many people seemed to be epitomized by their determination to elect Kurt Waldheim President in 1986 despite the doubts surrounding his role during the Second World War. At the same time, some of the harshest critics of Austrian attitudes towards this topic have included certain leading writers, such as Thomas Bernhard. Since about 1980 several women writers have also made a significant contribution to this debate, particularly in regard to Austrian complicity in the Nazi past, notably with works such as Elfriede Jelinek's *Burgtheater* (1982). A number of women writers have also addressed themselves specifically to the role played by women at that time. A prime example is Marie-Thérèse Kerschbaumer's *Der weibliche Name des Widerstands* (1980) which relates fictitious accounts, in the first person, of women who died under the Nazi regime because they represented various forms of opposition to the dictatorship. Those who might more conveniently be classed as 'victims' of the regime are treated by Kerschbaumer as forces of resistance to it, an approach which politicizes their role and contributes to raising consciousness about women's history. A similar question of how to interpret the role of the 'victims' of the Nazi period is central to the two novels by Elisabeth Reichart which will be discussed here.

Within the historical—as opposed to the literary—debate surrounding the nature of women's part in the Third Reich, discussion has focused on the extent to which women, as well as men, can be held responsible for the many types of atrocities committed at that time, despite the fact that in general women had less overt political power than men. Thus, the debate has developed chronologically from an initial assumption that women played only a minor role, to the investigation of women's participation in Nazi structures and more recently towards detailed examination of specific professional areas. Here the crucial question arises: to what extent did women actively promote, or even initiate, Nazi policy, as opposed to merely implementing decisions taken by men? In other words, the issue is whether women must be regarded as active perpetrators or alternatively as conforming mainly to a more traditionally 'feminine', passive role within the system (see Windaus-Walser 1988). These are by no means the only concerns of historians who have written about women's part in the Third Reich, but they are the issues which are the most relevant to Elisabeth Reichart's novels.[1] Apart from its obvious importance to the historical discussion, the raising of such ethical issues is essential to the literary treatment of women's involvement in the Third Reich.

In her book *Opfer und Täterinnen: Frauenbiographien des Nationalsozialismus*, Angelika Ebbinghaus has assembled

---

1. Less relevant to the present literary discussion but of great importance in recent historical debate, for instance, has been discussion of the relative importance of gender as compared with race and class. See for instance, Schmidt 1987: 50-65.

documentary evidence both of victims and, more provocatively, of women who promoted Nazi social policy (Ebbinghaus 1987). As she comments, 'Die Beziehung von Opfern und Täterinnen im Nationalsozialismus bildet ein Stück ausgeblendete Geschichte von Frauen' (p. 7). By showing how, precisely in the female-dominated fields of social work and the caring professions, a number of women made successful careers by perpetrating atrocities on other women, she contributes to creating a differentiated picture of women's activities at that time. She suggests that in certain cases women were indeed more assiduous than was strictly necessary and states, 'Frauen waren zwar meist in untergeordneter Position tätig, zeichneten sich aber durch hohe Arbeitsidentifikation und Pflichterfüllung aus' (p. 7). Ebbinghaus declares one of her aims to be to address herself to the tendency which she perceives among certain historians to classify women exclusively as victims of the system. She thus presents as inadequate any suggestion of the 'Gnade der weiblichen Geburt', treating it as being at least as problematic as Chancellor Kohl's remark about the 'Gnade der späten Geburt', on which it is based. Refusing to accept the truth about the part women played means underestimating their role in history, suppresses unpleasant facts and prevents people, and women in particular, from facing up to the possibility of guilt incurred.

While studies such as that by Ebbinghaus serve to distinguish a variety of different roles played by women, instead of being content with one collective idea of women as 'victims', the two novels by Elisabeth Reichart treat the intricate relationship between the roles of victim and persecutor and show that the distinction between the two is sometimes blurred. Indeed, the novelist suggests that they may represent two aspects of one and the same person, who played different roles at different times, or, indeed, who may understand her own actions within the historical context differently at different times in her own life. By focusing in her novels on the role of individual women, Reichart makes the issue of the 'victim' central. Ultimately it is of course not just a question for women, but, given that Austrians have tended to see their country as the 'victim' of German aggression, one that may be construed as applying to the Austrian attitude towards the Nazi past quite generally.

Elisabeth Reichart's novels are not concerned with the wider problems of racism or the preconditions or mentality which gave rise to fascism or to the Anschluss. Instead, they concern events of the past and their aftermath primarily in terms of the way they have affected the course of individuals' lives, while also raising issues for wider sections of Austrian society.

Februarschatten (1984) and *Komm über den See* (1988) both reflect a generation problem, presented largely in terms of female representatives. While the older generation experienced the horrors of the Nazi period directly, the younger woman in each case is struggling to understand her mother's generation and, in *Komm über den See*, her own mother's actions. Apart from this common underlying theme, however, the two novels are structured quite differently and are concerned with different aspects of the question. In *Februarschatten*, where the generation conflict emerges through a mother–daughter dyad, the narrator is the main protagonist, the mother figure, called Hilde. She tells the story of her early life, somewhat reluctantly, to her more politically radical daughter, Erika, who wants to write a novel about her mother's life but has realized that she knows too little. Hilde, who has always felt herself to be a victim of circumstances beyond her control, as well as of other people's cruelty and rejection, is here given the opportunity to speak for herself and tell her own version of events instead of being at the mercy of others. In doing so, she is forced to reconsider the rather easy and convenient role she has adopted as social victim. In laying claim to her own account of history, she first comes to admit responsibility for her own actions, including an act of betrayal, and having faced up to this aspect, she separates out the amorphous mass of her repressed memories which hitherto has not allowed her to distinguish between her dual role as both victim and oppressor. Eventually, her increasing consciousness about the part she played results in the dissipation of some of the fears which have plagued her since childhood, epitomized by her fear of the shadows on the wall at night, from which the novel takes its title.

Hilde's confusion between her status as victim on the one hand and as persecutor on the other is by no means unusual, as

Ebbinghaus's account of the real historical situation clearly illustrates. Thus Ebbinghaus comments on how, when put on trial after the end of the war, nurses were unable to accept responsibility for their misdeeds: 'Sie bedauerten immer nur sich selbst. Sie verharrten in der Rolle von Opfern, obwohl sie die Täterinnen waren' (Ebbinghaus 1987: 10). Ebbinghaus interprets this attitude as taking refuge in a traditional female role according to which women are seen as being incapable of brutality. Although Hilde's actions in the past are not directly comparable with these women's behaviour, the description of their attitude aptly characterizes the way she too views her own position at the outset. However, as she re-examines a crucial moment in her youth, she begins to face up to the guilt she has incurred and the subsequent fears she experienced and so gradually to come to terms with her culpability. This approach enables the reader too to reconsider the role of the self-styled victim: for when Hilde comes to accept some degree of responsibility for her present situation, as well as for the events of the past which gave rise to it, the simplistic aspect of her original self-designation as 'victim' is undermined, since she is clearly not untainted.[2]

The central episode which Hilde relates is based on an actual incident from the war, known as the 'Mühlviertler Hasenjagd' of 2 February 1945. Reichart's narrative is explicitly presented against the background of this historical event, as is indicated by a note at the end of the novel:

> historischer hintergrund
>
> die sogenannte
> MÜHLVIERTLER HASENJAGD
>
> in der nacht zum 2. februar 1945 brachen ca. 500 der 570 häftlinge aus der sonderbaracke 20 des KL MAUTHAUSEN aus.
>
> in der baracke waren vor allem sowjetische offiziere. bis heute wurden 17 überlebende eruiert.

---

2. A more extreme account of someone who, though genuinely a 'victim', felt guilty merely because she survived the holocaust can be seen in Grete Weil, *Meine Schwester Antigone* (1980).

> alle anderen wurden von den nationalsozialistischen und
> von bis dahin 'unpolitischen' mühlviertlern ermordet. wenige
> mühlviertler wagten zu helfen (Reichart 1989: 105).

Though only a child at the time, Hilde also became involved in
this action, which was presented to the local people, according
to her account, as a contribution to patriotism and as a
challenge to them to prove their loyalty to 'Germany'. Hilde's
efforts consisted in betraying a Russian fugitive whom her
brother was harbouring, an action which led presumably to the
man's death but also to her brother's committing suicide as an
immediate consequence. Hilde, however, never admits to this
betrayal in so many words: instead, the gaps in her narrative
allow the reader to interpret her account in this way.

Thus, Hilde's story suggests that no one, not even a child,
could escape complicity in the collective guilt. The motive for her
involvement in the manhunt, however, appears to reside in the
feelings of rejection that she experienced even prior to this
incident. While these feelings are partly the direct responsibility
of her parents, who never showed her any affection but
disciplined her harshly, they are also a consequence of the
general poverty experienced by the family as a whole together
with the group of people who lived in their vicinity. Thus, on the
one hand Hilde comes to the realization that she must indeed
bear individual responsibility for the guilt she incurred, with the
result that her original position as victim becomes untenable.
Nevertheless, on the other hand the reader comes to perceive
her as having been a victim of a prevalent form of social
deprivation and thereby gains insight into the broader context
of her guilt, which partly explains the villagers' actions, without
exonerating them.

When Hilde and her daughter revisit the village of her childhood, as part of the consciousness-raising exercise associated
with her piecing together her memory of the past, the behaviour
of the local people towards them suggests that they for their
part have not yet faced up to their guilt and responsibility in
relation to this episode. Instead they still look upon Hilde with
disapproval, reminding themselves of her guilt. She overhears
fragments of their conversation about her: 'daß die sich
hierhertraut...Unverschämtheit...Frechheit' (Reichart 1989: 82).

The narrative perspective precludes any objective assessment of whether Hilde incurred greater guilt than the other villagers. Yet their self-righteousness certainly suggests that Hilde has been treated as a scapegoat. She is in fact an exception, first in having left the village in search of a better life, and now in attempting to express her experiences and feelings and thus to inform the younger generation.

The author herself has suggested that it was this very suppression of information about the past which prompted her to write the novel. For although she grew up not far from the place where the Mühlviertler Hasenjagd occurred, she heard nothing about it for many years:

> Die 'Hasenjagd' geschah in der Gegend, in der ich aufgewachsen bin, beteiligt an ihr waren Menschen, denen ich auf der Straße begegnen konnte. Als ich von dem Vorgang erfuhr—da war ich kein Kind mehr—, wollte ich wissen, was für Leute das gewesen sind, die mit der Mistgabel auf wehrlose Menschen losgegangen sind (Reichart 1987: 131).

Like the rest of the villagers, Hilde has done her utmost to 'forget' this incident, but in adopting this attitude she has also failed to confront other painful issues in her life, and instead of accepting some measure of responsibility for them, she harbours resentment against others. She even resents her daughter, to whom she is telling the story, and her defensiveness in this respect, together with her reluctance to face the past, is graphically conveyed by the manner of narration. Much of her tale is fragmented and does not comprise a consistent narrative. It darts back and forth between past and present and is told partly in the first person and partly in the third person, reminding the reader of the presence of Erika, who is ostensibly recording her mother's words. The tension created between the more distant perspective represented by the third person narrative and the more intimate first person passages enables the reader to consider the role of the self-styled victim from a point of view that avoids being accusatory but comes across as a genuine attempt to uncover and understand the truth and the motivation for the despicable acts of the past. As Marianne Krumrey states in her review of the novel:

Diese Erzählweise offenbart die ganze Tragik eines Menschen,
der, obwohl ohnmächtig, schuldhaft in die Geschichte
verstrickt ist und der, gerade weil er Anstand und Mensch-
lichkeit besitzt, ein Leben lang darunter leidet... Nicht
späte Anklage ist hier beabsichtigt, aber gelungen ist ein
tiefes Eindringen in die Dialektik von Einzelschicksal und
Geschichte (Krumrey 1987: 185).

The topic of 'Ohnmacht' mentioned here is treated further in
Komm über den See. In *Februarschatten* Hilde succeeds in
gaining some control over her own life through addressing
herself to her own responsibility for her present suffering.
Unlike the people of her old village who continue to treat her as
a scapegoat for the guilt they share with her, her attitude begins
to change, as she ceases to lay the blame exclusively on others
and acknowledges her own part in creating her present
situation. As she describes her childhood, it also becomes clear to
the reader that she should not be perceived as wholly guilty: but
it is only through her confronting the past that the apportioning
of guilt and innocence can be made appropriately.

While *Februarschatten* uncovers the guilt of the self-styled
'victim' and prompts a re-examination of the relationship
between victim and persecutor, in *Komm über den See* the
author addresses herself to the subject of the Resistance in
Austria and, in particular, women's participation in the
movement. Despite the more positive expectations that this
topic might arouse, it is shown to be no less problematic, fraught
with guilt and resentment and scarcely less suppressed than the
despicable episode which is central to *Februarschatten*.

In *Komm über den See* again two narrative positions are
represented, but here their contributions are clearly separated.
The main chapters are narrated in the third person from the
point of view of Ruth, a woman in her mid-forties whose own
life position is at a turning point. Her professional interest in
history, as a newly qualified teacher of that subject, together
with a scanty knowledge of her mother's life—she died when
Ruth was seven—has prompted Ruth to conduct research into
women members of the Resistance, with whom her mother was
associated. Each main chapter is, however, prefaced by a short
section headed 'SIE' which is narrated partly in the first person
and partly in the third person, focusing on the past, particularly

the war years and the struggles of women in the Resistance movement. The identity of the second narrator is revealed only at the end of the tale: it is Anna Zach, an elderly woman who supported the Resistance and who, as the reader eventually learns, was betrayed by Ruth's mother under torture. Now an old woman, Anna is despised by the good citizens of Gmunden, the provincial town where the tale is set, for they evidently do not wish to be reminded of the uncomfortable past and regard Anna as a thorn in the flesh. As in *Februarschatten* two generations are thus represented, who piece together the past. In the later novel, however, a broader canvas of social attitudes is depicted. Anna Zach herself is in effect a substitute, in narrative terms, for Ruth's mother who never told her story, not simply because she died, but because of the general attitude which prevailed after the war. Moreover, Anna is at first as reluctant as Hilde in *Februarschatten* to speak about the past, although her reasons are different in certain important respects. Yet when she eventually does so, she too is shown to be an exception to the rule of silence that generally prevails.

The problem of speaking about the past, even when it concerns justifiable or even laudable actions, is attested by actual testimonies of women's participation in the Resistance. For instance, having related her account of her wartime activities, in the early 1980s, a former partisan, Johanna Sadolschek, known as Zala, ends with a bitter comment about present-day attitudes:

> Man schaut uns jetzt so an, als wärn wir Verbrecher, wir, die wir wirklich was dazugetan haben, daß Österreich die Freiheit hat, das kränkt einen schon. Wissens, da wird man von einigen Bandit gerufen und verworfen, von den Leuten beim Heimatdienst, den deutschnationalen, o ja, es gibt manche noch, und immer mehr und mehr...wir sind doch Antifaschisten, wir haben doch was für Österreich beigebracht, daß Österreich die Freiheit kriegt hat und unabhängig ist, die wollen das gar nit akzeptieren, kein einziges Mal hab ich ein Lob kriegt hier. Eher das Gegenteil (Berger 1985: 141).

This woman, like many others, recounts how she suffered in the cause of the Resistance, and she relates the general apathy towards the past to the political attitudes of the present. Thus, as such accounts from real-life suggest, in addressing this issue,

Reichart's novel itself constitutes a radical approach not only to the past but to a whole mindset prevalent in contemporary Austria.

Unlike *Februarschatten*, *Komm über den See* does not focus on one particular incident from the past but rather on the more general issue of the suppressing of knowledge about the past, even including the Resistance, which might otherwise be regarded as a cause for some pride and self-esteem. There is, furthermore, an implied parallel between the suppression of Austria's political past and the suppression of women's history in patriarchal society generally. As a history teacher, Ruth is aware that what is known of the past is selective and is largely a matter of who has been empowered to write down the accounts to which historians have access. Thus, she comments, thinking about her search for information about the women of the Resistance,

> Ich habe kaum etwas über Widerstandskämpferinnen gefunden, ihr Leben nur zwischen den Zeilen, keine hat zur Feder gegriffen, das Schreiben auch eine Geschlechterfrage, nach ihnen werde ich suchen (p. 92).

Her interest in reclaiming this aspect of women's history has indeed already brought down on her the patriarchally inspired scorn of her former husband, who, as she recalls, once shouted at her, 'Dein Interesse an diesen Frauen ist nicht normal!' (p. 39). Women's invisibility in this area of history is perhaps partly attributable to the division of labour which apparently prevailed in the Resistance movement as much as it did elsewhere. For although women acted as couriers and provided essential supplies, as is also indicated in the novel by Anna Zach's account, in many respects the usual societal expectations were upheld, as the following non-fictional account suggests:

> Zwar waren Frauen und Männer gleichermaßen an der Herstellung von Aufklärungsmaterial beteiligt, doch haben Frauen vor allem getippt, abgezogen und organisatorische Tätigkeiten im Zusammenhang mit der Transferierung, dem Vertrieb und dem Verstecken des Materials übernommen... Frauen tippten Artikel, die von Männern verfaßt wurden. Damit ist eine geschlechtsspezifische Arbeitsteilung

angesprochen, von der auch der Partisanenbereich nicht ausgenommen war...

Die Masse der Frauen hat vor allem die mühevolle Kleinarbeit, jene kaum registrierten, aber lebensnotwendigen Hilfstätigkeiten ausgeführt. Den Ruhm für spektakuläre Taten konnten zumeist Männer für sich verbuchen, während Frauen dafür sorgten, daß die Grundlage jeder Widerstandstätigkeit klappte (Berger 1985: 250).

Yet, as other accounts of these activities show, women too were imprisoned, tortured and in some cases executed as a result of their political stance: this aspect is reflected in the novel by the experiences of Anna Zach and the mothers of Ruth and another woman, called Martha.

While Ruth, the newly appointed history teacher, is aware that there is history all around her in her new home town of Gmunden, and not least evidence of persecution,[3] she realizes that the education system does not encourage children to look beyond the most banal facts about local history, and she remarks that 'die Spuren, denen sie nachgeht, für die meisten Kinder nicht einmal Spuren sind' (Reichart 1988: 92). A well-meaning colleague at the school where Ruth teaches explicitly warns her to avoid material that is potentially controversial or even subversive and, mistaking her for a teacher of German, advises her not to read literature by Brecht or other such troublemakers.

Facing up to the past and understanding one's own history, in the way Ruth attempts to, is shown to be crucial to the development of identity. Recently divorced and now embarking upon a new career at a relatively advanced age, Ruth's interest in the women of the Resistance is not merely an intellectual pursuit; it is also provoked by her awareness of being a woman at a turning point, under pressure and needing to establish a new identity for herself, as well as reflecting on her own past. In the story that she eventually hears from Anna Zach, she discovers historical antecedents in the form of women who were faced with a crisis situation, left alone by their menfolk, under political pressure and having to be utterly self-reliant in order to preserve themselves and those who were dependent upon them,

---

3. Such persecution, specifically of members of the Resistance in Gmunden is attested in Berger 1985: 238.

especially their comrades in the Resistance.

Yet Ruth's striving to establish a new identity for herself by looking to the historical past for models leads her to discover more about her own individual past than she had anticipated. Through Anna Zach she eventually receives confirmation of something she had gradually come to suspect: that in early childhood she was not 'Ruth' but was called 'Brigitta', a name she associates with the novel by Stifter. Her parents, she discovers, changed her name after her mother was arrested by the Gestapo, when she heard them threaten to torture her child. In this way they attempted to blot out the memory of this episode. Ruth is perplexed and now asks herself, 'Ist meine Mutter wirklich eine Verräterin? Hat sie Anna verraten? Hat sie mich verraten?' (p. 186). Her mother did indeed betray Anna in the conventional sense of the word, yet Ruth's feeling that she too has been betrayed is centred on the denial of her identity, which is clearly shown to be the effect of attempting to conceal the uncomfortable truth. The reason for refusing to face the past in this case is not merely a matter of rejecting incriminating evidence, as it is mainly in *Februarschatten*, but is motivated in Ruth's parents' case by the desire to avoid being reminded of the sense of powerlessness that they endured.

The issue of 'powerlessness', of 'Ohnmacht', is experienced by others too. It is broached in the first section narrated by the as yet anonymous 'SIE', who recalls how powerless she felt when she realized that not everybody responded to the fascist regime with the same animosity as she did. In an interview, Elisabeth Reichart has suggested that the powerlessness expressed in the novel is not to be treated as something wholly negative, unlike resignation, because it is only when people attempt to take action that they become aware of how powerless they are, whereas resignation means refusing even to make such an attempt. As she expresses it: 'Außerdem hängt Ohnmacht für mich mit wissender Sehnsucht zusammen; nur wer sich auseinandersetzt, spürt, wie begrenzt seine gesellschaftlichen Möglichkeiten sind' (Reichart 1987: 129). It is the sense of powerlessness incurred in the face of injustice which has made several characters in the novel resort to silence: by contrast, learning to speak again about events of the past, as Anna eventually does, has an empowering effect.

The powerlessness which causes people to suppress painful memories has also led to the betrayal which Ruth formulates to herself in the words: 'Auch Schweigen kann Verrat sein' (Reichart 1988: 181). Not only speaking and naming names can constitute a betrayal. So too is *not* speaking about the past a betrayal of the present and, in the case of the younger generation, of their education. Just as Ruth feels that her own identity has been betrayed, so she regards withholding the historical truth as tantamount to allowing younger generations to continue with a false sense of cultural and national identity. When the headmaster of the school where she teaches refuses to allow Anna Zach to be invited to address the children, Ruth herself realizes how easily the act of betrayal can occur: for she is almost persuaded to his point of view, by the headmaster's reasoned tones and her own need to retain her teaching post. Yet she realizes in time that refusing to allow Anna to tell her story would mean silencing her forever and thus betraying her again, just as Ruth's mother betrayed her, not only by revealing her name to the Gestapo, but by her subsequent refusal to answer Anna's letters or to account for her action.

Even Anna herself is not wholly innocent of suppressing the past. For as she eventually explains to Ruth, although she at first attempted to enlighten people about the appalling conditions in the concentration camp, when she found that nobody wanted to hear about it, she decided to be silent henceforth. This is why she now stubbornly resists Ruth's attempts to make her speak. The fact that she is now old and is one of the few survivors of her generation makes it all the more urgent that she should tell her story so that the younger generation is not denied this knowledge forever.

The need to educate the younger generation about the facts of the Resistance applies even to Ruth who is fundamentally willing to hear the truth about it. Yet from what she says early in the novel to Christian, a journalist whom she meets in Gmunden, it is evident that she too does not know the full story:

> Die Verantwortung für sich haben nur die Widerstands-
> kämpfer übernommen, und indem sie das taten, waren sie
> fähig, auch für andere verantwortlich zu sein—woher sonst

die vielen, die unter der ärgsten Folter niemanden verraten haben (p. 66).

Her own illusions about the Resistance in this respect are therefore also modified when she learns about her mother's betrayal from Anna Zach.

A further aspect of the complex relationship between silence and betrayal is reflected in the figures of Martha's mother and herself. Unlike Ruth's mother, Martha's mother, who likewise experienced internment in Ravensbrück, remained silent under torture. Yet while her silence in the past was clearly heroic, it occurs to Ruth that she too probably remained silent when asked about her experiences by Martha, if indeed Martha ever asked:

> Was war vorher: die Zelle, die Gestapo, die Folter, ihr Schweigen—immer? Und dann wieder die Haft und dann der Transport und dann Ravensbrück. Über all das kein Wort, sooft ich Martha auch fragte. Hat sie ihre Mutter danach gefragt, hat ihre Mutter geschwiegen, wie Martha geschwiegen hat? (p. 40)

Martha herself accuses Ruth of paying too much attention to the past and not enough to her, Martha, in the present. Yet it is clear that without a healthier attitude towards the past, society itself can never be healthy, as is also suggested by the fact that Martha is periodically confined to a psychiatric hospital. A more directly political implication of this attitude is mentioned by the journalist Christian, who has discovered that an eminent local political figure, a 'Volksvertreter', actually still celebrates 'Kristallnacht'. Yet, after months of research into this man's behaviour, Christian is finally prevented by the broadcasting authorities from using the material. Ruth reports his feelings about this matter in words loaded with cynicism about the liberal democracy:

> Und in seinem Fall und in vielen anderen Fäll nehme sich eben der freie ORF die Freiheit, auf die Arbeit eines freien Redakteurs über den Umgang eines freiheitlichen Politikers mit der nationalsozialistischen Vergangenheit freiwillig zu verzichten (p. 63).

Despite the danger of losing her job, Ruth decides that the past must be given a hearing: although this will take place between her and Anna in private, previous experience leaves her under no illusion that their meeting will remain unnoticed in this 'Nest', or that it will be without risk to her future. Not only does this meeting then result in confirmation of Ruth's own submerged identity, but by telling her story, Anna too is enabled to reclaim her identity—that of a woman who experienced both active participation in the Resistance and persecution and victimization as a consequence of it, as well as betrayal and rejection by her friend, Ruth's mother.

Like that of Hilde in *Februarschatten*, the tale Anna tells is fragmented, as she pieces it together, reactivating her memory: 'Vor jeder Erinnerung das Wissen: alle Sätze in dieses Gestern können nur Brücken zu Inseln sein, was sie verbinden, es bleibt für immer getrennt' (p. 7). Each of the sections headed 'SIE' is introduced by this sentence, or part of it, for at each repetition it is abbreviated by one clause until, in the final section, it is completely absent and Anna then speaks directly about the present. The impression thus created is that the past has become one with the present and that Anna Zach has ceased to put up defences against it, and has allowed it to surface. At this point she refers particularly to her feelings of resentment about the word 'Opfer', used to designate the women of the Resistance, because it relegates their achievements to a passive role: 'Nennt uns nicht Opfer! Ich kann dieses Wort nicht hören, es gehört mit zu den Vereinbarungen, die über uns getroffen wurden' (p. 153). Echoing the terminology of modern feminist thinking, she prefers to see herself as a 'survivor', emphasizing the strength of these women. In her tale she lays claim to having attempted to survive against all odds and to maintain human dignity: 'Wir waren es doch, die versuchten zu überleben, als Menschen zu überleben' (p. 153). Thus, although the perspective is quite different, the idea of treating women as 'victims' of the system is contradicted here as much as it is in *Februarschatten*. For not only is it morally unsound to conceal guilt by claiming victim status, as Hilde does, it is also unjust to women who attempted to play an active role in throwing off the oppressors.

The need to re-establish a true identity is reflected pointedly in Martha's comment about her own and Ruth's mother's appearance when they returned from the concentration camp: 'Sie haben uns unsere Mütter unkenntlich gemacht' (p. 25). The distortion that occurred was, the novel implies, not only physical. The author suggests indeed that the silence with which this episode has been treated constitutes a distortion of history, a distortion of women's history in particular, and that it represents self-delusion and a distortion of identity with regard to the present. In this way, Elisabeth Reichart both contributes to raising consciousness about the submerged Austrian past and at the same time lends women a central role in the issues invoked by it.

WORKS CITED

Berger, K., *et al.* (eds.)
    1985   *Der Himmel ist blau. Kann sein. Frauen im Widerstand. Österreich 1938–1945.* Vienna: Promedia.
Ebbinghaus, A., (ed.)
    1987   *Opfer und Täterinnen: Frauenbiographien des Nationalsozialismus*, II. Hamburg: Hamburger Stiftung für Sozialgeschichte des 20. Jahrhunderts.
Jelinek, E.
    1984   'Burgtheater', in *Theaterstücke*. Cologne: Prometh.
Kerschbaumer, M.-T.
    1980   *Der weibliche Name des Widerstands*. Olten: Walter.
Krumrey, M.
    1987   'Quälende Erinnerung'. *Neue deutsche Literatur* 35, 9, pp. 184-86.
Reichart, E.
    1987   'Elisabeth Reichart im Gespräch' (Arnim Roscher). *Neue deutsche Literatur* 35, 9, pp. 129-32.
    1988   *Komm über den See.* Frankfurt: Fischer.
    1989   *Februarschatten.* Frankfurt: Fischer (First published 1984).
Schmidt, D.
    1987   'Die peinlichen Verwandtschaften—Frauenforschung zum Nationalsozialismus', in H. Gerstenberger and D. Schmidt (eds.), *Normalität und Normalisierung*. Münster: Westfälisches Dampfboot.
Weil, G.
    1980   *Meine Schwester Antigone.* Zurich: Benziger.
Windaus-Walser, K.
    1988   'Gnade der weiblichen Geburt?'. *Feministische Studien* 1, pp. 102-15.

'Leiden als unvollständiger Akt der Rebellion': The Literature and Critical Analysis of Waltraud Anna Mitgutsch

Brian Keith-Smith

'Leiden als unvollständiger Akt der Rebellion' was Waltraud Anna Mitgutsch's response, in a letter to me in September 1990, to the question as to whether she could understand a positive value in suffering. A full awareness of this mainspring in her writings emerges when we first consider how she highlighted suffering in the works of Austrian and American poets in three major critical essays.

In her article 'Weltverlust in der zeitgenössischen Lyrik, exemplarisch dargestellt an Paul Celan und Sylvia Plath' (1977) she emphasizes the importance of the perspective of the writer or narrator figure. Celan's early experiences of death are revealed as the cause of his progress through 'Sprachzerfall' to 'Sprachreduktion' to complete 'Verstummen' in metaphors of suffering. Both he and Plath, Mitgutsch claims, base their poetry on formulations in the negative. For both, withdrawal of the so-called 'other'—the partner in dialogue (whether person or thing or event in nature)—isolates the lyrical self from the world. Mitgutsch identifies a tension between positive and negative metaphors and a dialectical principle in the work of both poets. This is accompanied by a fragmentation and disintegration of language, with a corresponding set of metaphors. The disintegrated self flounders with an intensity which 'die Distanz zwischen Dichter und lyrischem Ich aufzuheben droht und damit das lyrische Sprechen an den Rand des Verstummens bringt' (Mitgutsch 1977: 272).

In her article 'Die Rezeption des Expressionismus in der zeitgenössischen amerikanischen Lyrik' (1979) Mitgutsch traces

the search in the fifties and sixties for forms of expression that
go beyond rational consciousness and logical structures of
meaning to look at reality in a radically different way and
produce a new awareness of the world and of the self. In the
lyrics of Trakl, Rilke, Lorca and Neruda, the 'deep image' poets
found a language 'die die konkrete Außenwelt auf eine
Innenwelt transparent machte und beide Bereiche zu einer
surrealen Traumlandschaft verschmolz' (1979: 91). Closest to
the theme of suffering in this group was James Wright whose
'aura' effect in the poem 'The Jewel' defines the space around
things and the lyrical self:

> There is this cave
> in the air behind my body
> that nobody is going to touch:
> a cloister, a silence
> closing around a blossom of fire
>
> When I stand upright in the wind
> my bones turn to dark emeralds.
> (quoted in Mitgutsch 1979: 101)

In such poetry, Mitgutsch claims, the images become 'Chiffren
einer intersubjektiven Wirklichkeit' (p. 102), not total collapse as
with Georg Trakl, but an intensification of something
threatened and isolated. In W.S. Merwin's poetry (e.g. 'Late
Night in Autumn') the inner world absorbs the outer world and
transforms it into a visionary landscape of the soul, 'die
Schmerz in seinem Licht wandelt' (Mitgutsch 1979: 104).

The emphasis on perspective, disintegration of the self and the
interrelation of 'Außenwelt' and 'Innenwelt' is taken a step
further in the article 'Hermetic Languages as Subversion: The
Poetry of Christine Lavant', who, Mitgutsch claims, 'suffered
because she saw herself with the eyes of her society: from the
outside as an outsider'. Rejection of such conventions as
identity, hierarchical relationships, the dichotomy of inner and
outer worlds and other models resulted in a private system of
signs and meanings filling an emptiness around her, often
intuited as 'you'. A language of narcissistic identification results
(as in the poem 'Spindel im Mund'), and Lavant challenges the
'you' set up as an imaginary dialogue-partner (Mitgutsch 1984:
87-88). As Mitgutsch points out, Lavant's poetry 'revolves

around absence' (p. 94) of a real 'you'-figure and reveals an ambivalent attitude towards loneliness throughout. Isolation goes hand-in-hand with desperate resistance; autonomy is asserted in self-protective self-sufficiency. Her suffering is seen as 'always carried out on her female body' with its 'particular female vulnerability' (p. 100). Further to this, Mitgutsch insists,

> Rebellion increases her suffering and sharpens the desire for a freedom and an autonomy beyond the realms of the father, but the best she can hope for is dogged survival... Each step towards autonomy and freedom is purchased at the high price of isolation, guilt, imagined or real punishment, and self-doubt (p. 102).

With some of these critical views in mind it is productive to examine suffering and rebellion in Mitgutsch's narrative works. The opening section of her novel *Die Züchtigung* shows the transference from mother to daughter of hatred, largely caused by a traumatized childhood, marital problems and the fear of having unsuccessful, unruly children. Until she was fourteen the main narrator figure Vera suffers beatings from her mother that produce in her 'Lebensangst', yet at times she claims she was proud to have a well brought up and beaten child. By the end of the novel she becomes aware that mothers automatically pass on to their daughters their own fate, not least their rebelliousness. In as much as the narrator figure is remembering the intense experiences of her childhood, she is retrospectively caught up (again) in a love–hate relationship with her mother. The act of narration could become a way to break out of this involvement. However even in the final paragraph she is forced to recognize how dependent she is. The torture of physical chastisement now becomes a totally conscious psychological subservience. To narrate is to relive the past, but here this results in a transference of former feelings into an awareness that rebellion—whether by moving away to form her own life or later by narration—can perhaps never succeed. Vera's attitudes as a narrator alter according to the intensity of the recorded emotions. Because she can never achieve one stable perspective, her self never attains independent profile. This first novel has been praised for its taboo-breaking quality and powerful language, and reviewers have taken sections describing beatings to sum up its exceptional qualities, yet these descriptions only take up a few pages. Maria-Regina Kecht has written an interpretation of the mother–daughter relations in this novel, comparing and contrasting them with those in Elfriede Jelinek's *Die Klavierspielerin*. However, little attention has yet been paid to the concept of Vera's suffering as an incomplete form of rebellion against her mother's norms of cleanliness and asexuality.

Vera's mother Marie is an outsider in a society still observing nineteenth-century social divisions, a girl born from peasant stock whose marriage she hoped would compensate for the lovelessness and indignities of her childhood, for the shame that was forced on her at puberty by her mother, and for the sense of rejection when she was made to give up hopes of becoming a teacher and work on the farm, despite her extraordinarily high achievements at school. Marie had nothing in common with her brothers and sisters, had to watch her cat being tortured, cursed her brother who later died from typhus at the Russian front, and had to play the role of ugly sister to Fanni, which made Marie hate all other women and everything womanly in herself. At eighteen years of age she had become an old maid and a loner—qualities which helped her to accept a tree-feller ten years older than herself as her fiancé, who, as the first person in her life to show her real affection, at least sent her postcards from the front. He returned looking like death, but willing to marry her now when her youth was already past. Fatally, she identified her innocence with freedom, and clung to her lonely excursions into the surrounding countryside. Her wedding, because of its frugality and the downtrodden demeanour of the bridegroom, made her feel cheated as never before. The first night of her marriage was 'eine der größten Demütigungen ihres Lebens... eine mit körperlichem und seelischem Schmerz ertragene Einsamkeit. In diesem Bett begann der langsame Tod ihrer zwanzigjährigen Ehe' (Mitgutsch 1988a: 33). Precisely in Marie's need to define herself, exacerbated by her hopeless partnership with a husband who comes from a lower social class even than her own and never rises further than being a tram conductor, we see her first longings for independence. The true character of this and its consequences emerges in the way Vera, her daughter, records it retrospectively: 'Wenn wir versuchen, uns zu definieren, wenn uns andere mit Worten zu fassen suchen, greifen wir auf unsere Mütter zurück' (p. 133). In this most important section of the novel, Vera's ambivalent attitude towards her mother is expressed in three comments that suggest her awareness of the disintegrated character of her mother:

> Meine Mutter war eine Rebellin...sie hielt nichts von den herkömmlichen Rollenverstellungen, und während ich es sage, weiß ich, daß es nicht wahr ist, auch wenn sie mich nicht auf Küche und Haushalt gedrillt hat... Meine Mutter war eine große, stattliche Dame mit gutem, bürgerlichem Geschmack, eine perfekte Hausfrau mit überdurchschnittlicher Intelligenz, verschwiegen, korrekt im Verhalten, etwas arrogant... Aber meine Mutter ist eine Leerstelle, die sich mit Angst füllt, wenn ich meinen Blick auf sie richte, ich habe sie nie entziffern können, sie richtet sich hinter den Worten, die sie bannen sollen, auf, wächst wie ein Albdruck, und ich erstarre, während sie mich verschlingt (pp. 133-34).

In identifying her mother in three such different ways and as her 'Doppelgängerin' (p. 134), and in asking whether that gives her the right to beat her own child, Vera tries to proclaim her growing apparent independence from the system of family and social life under which she herself has suffered. However, her life, determined by paternal and maternal restrictions, cannot finally be transformed into one single independent mode of existence. A form of rebellion takes place each time the reflective first-person narrator tries to assert herself. Inasmuch as this is never fully achieved, the narrative becomes a fragmented demonstration of Vera's unbreakable ties back to her mother. The related themes of 'Angst' and 'Scham' serve not so much as consistently worked out leitmotifs in a linear structure, but rather as points of reference to which the narrator frequently returns. The narrative stance (first- and third-person, outer and inner events, affirmation and questioning, summing-up and lengthy exploration of one episode) frequently changes. An impression is thus given of a narrator seeking a consistent image of herself, an independent profile, which, however, is forever distorted, incomplete, almost a hideous reflection of self-destruction. The descriptions of Vera's mother quoted above and taken together might be seen as an extension of Mitgutsch's radical interpretation of the language used by the 'deep image' poets, of the narcissism in Christine Lavant's poetry, of the intense and finally self-destructive anger of Sylvia Plath or the suffering into silence of Paul Celan. From such landscapes of the soul the narrator tries to escape, until on the last page she confesses,

> Ich habe sie sechzehn Jahre lang immer von neuem begraben, sie ist immer wieder aufgestanden und ist mir nachgekommen... Ich bin sie und sage, du bist nichts wert, und versinke in Trauer um meinen Verlust, um meinen Ich-Verlust, um meinen Du-Verlust, um den Verlust der ganzen Liebe, die es auf der Welt gibt. Denn es gibt ja nur sie und mich (p. 246).

In her final perception of the situation, which sums up the main theme of suffering within the book's narrative process, Vera lists a trinity of modes of behaviour as the restrictions against which she has as yet struggled in vain: 'Sie herrscht, und ich diene, und wenn ich meinen ganzen Mut sammle und Widerstand leiste, gewinnt sie immer, im Namen des Gehorsams, der Vernunft und der Angst' (p. 246). Such an obviously prayer-structured phrase with which to end the novel might act as a form of bereavement therapy where one can face up to realities. Thus Vera has already claimed, 'Schmutzwäsche versteckt man vor Fremden, ich habe an ein Tabu gerührt, wir sind eine Nation geschlagener Kinder' (p. 123). By identifying obedience, reason and fear as her mother's levers of control over her (Vera's) potential independence, Vera faces up to important shibboleths of bourgeois society and presumably still hopes for time to seek a more authentic life in continuing to strive against their hegemony.

However, this Vera cannot do, because authenticity would mean, for instance, breaking with catch phrases and stereotyped attitudes passed on from one generation to the next such as 'Wer sein Kind liebt, züchtigt es', or 'Hochmut kommt vor dem Fall'. Her mother clings to them because Marie's sense of security was destroyed in her own youth. Mitgutsch sets such phrases ambiguously, either as a form of 'erlebte Rede', or as a remark recorded by the narrator almost as a model at the end of an episode but without comment. The reader is thus made aware of different perspectives on these home truths. Marie, Vera's mother, emerges as a rebel who has been formed by her necessary clinging to conformist views which in fact become a further reason for her suffering. Vera's views are heavily conditioned by her mother's involvement with the implications of such a phrase as 'Wer sein Kind liebt, züchtigt es' (p. 19). Vera is thereby subjected to an ever-changing uncertainty: can she trust her mother's use of such words as justification for her mother's and her own actions? Also, can she construct a sense of normality proceeding from and despite such insidious phrases? The phrases act as a means by which the narrator seems to achieve critical distance in as much as the reader recognizes that this has all been focalized internally and cannot be read as being intrinsically true. Furthermore, Vera identifies through such phrases links between chastisement, love and acceptance of inherited values. She begins to recognize them as a sign of the growth in double standards arising from her mother's destruction of self-esteem in her childhood, standards practised around her and preventing the healthy development of her inner world. She cannot gain an authentic response to life, for precisely the insights she has into her earlier life prevent this. Thus in retrospect she realizes, for instance, that by the age of eighteen she already felt an old maid. Similarly, her mother, she tells us, suffered anxiety that she might appear to others as a failed mother. To present the appearance of control and order to the outside world, Marie needs to beat out of her daughter Vera almost ritually all potential deviation from a supposed norm. In doing this, she not only molests Vera's inner world, but transfers anxiety, in particular that inspired by others, as the primary feature of mother–daughter dependence. This leads Vera to realize 'Ich hatte Angst vor den Leuten, weil ich die Angst meiner Mutter spürte' (p. 102), an example of transference working back in the next generation and preventing the development of the daughter's inner world.

Transference of a similar order, but in totally different circumstances, determines the story and structure of Mitgutsch's second novel *Das andere Gesicht*. Sonja, plagued with angst and watching life go past as a 'Zaungast', is a friend of Jana from childhood, an outsider living spontaneously off her

feelings and fantasies. Sonja's experiences are summed up on
the first page as 'Vorspiel, Vorleben, Übungsfahrt ins wirkliche
Leben, Vorbereitung'. Jana, a refugee, fascinates Sonja, for she
has inherited from her mother attacks of depression and from
her grandfather a sense of relaxed calm, a form of paradise
where 'alles war ohne Warum und ohne Ende' (Mitgutsch
1988b: 18). This is confirmed by her reflections in the mirror,
which also threaten her with increasing awareness of transience
and death.

This novel is constructed on alternating episodes narrated in
turn by Sonja and Jana. Sonja tells the story of their relationship
at first in 'Märchen' form to reproduce Jana's search for total
expansion away from the narrowness of one role and one form
of existence, an expansion she eventually believes to have found
in marrying an artist, Achim. In her rediscovery of paradise she
would become 'Geliebte, Mutter, Schwester und Kampf-
genossin' (p. 27)—each of these implying a different relationship
with an 'other' person or with the world. Such a vision of light
coming into her life (in keeping with W.S. Merwin's poems
quoted by Mitgutsch in her article) is destroyed, however, by
Achim who brings about the collapse of the brittle relationship
between the two women. This moves through a gamut of
feelings from Sonja's dependence and Jana's indifference to
mutual hatred. Both become aware of an emptiness around
them filled neither by relationship nor travel nor language. Each
builds round herself her special 'aura' comparable to that
evoked in James Wright's poem 'The Jewel'. Jana seeks her aura
through flight—from her background, from commitment, from
self-identification. In a scene to be almost repeated when she
take over a new flat with Achim and their son Daniel, Jana
comments on her mother's refusal to accept a new flat in words
that register her first act of rebellion: 'Damals begann das
Wegwollen, das Davonlaufen, das Fremdsein und Nichtdazu-
gehören, die Gefahr' (p. 69). This develops into withdrawal
from all reality with associated arousals of angst. Jana learns to
cut herself off from her mother's world: 'Jenseits der Grenze, in
meinem Reich, sprach man eine andere Sprache, nichts galt,
was den anderen unumstößliche Wahrheit war, und niemand
durchschaute meine Gesetze' (p. 73). Her willed self-isolation,

foreshadowed by Mitgutsch in her article on Christine Lavant, ends in her treatment in a clinic for nervous disorders, which is apparently successful; but Sonja's reactions are anxiety-ridden in the face of what she feels to be unreal, even uncontrollable. It requires a new friend and 'Ersatzmutter', Karin, to show her the way to the rediscovery of paradise: 'Selbstverleugnung, Hingabefähigkeit, Selbstaufopferung, Treue' (p. 101).

Jana and Sonja go on a series of exotic journeys, Jana to gain self-confidence, Sonja trying to emerge from her need for security and seeking to expand her self-consciousness. Shared experiences are used by Jana as a psychological bolster to defy her inadequacies, by Sonja as a support in her determination to prove that they can become at least 'Fremde...Gaffsüchtige, Voyeure' (p. 140) in the adventure of an alternative life style. The double-narrator technique focuses suffering and rebellion in both; it also reveals the characters' incomplete understanding of each other. The narrative process again shows up incompleteness: alienation and isolation appear more acute when the other person becomes an 'Außenwelt' to a corresponding 'Innenwelt'. The result is a narrative that parallels the 'surreale Traumwelt' which, according to Mitgutsch, the 'deep image' poets found in Trakl, Rilke, Lorca and Neruda. Even Achim is presented in a double focus by Jana who nurtures his image in her imagination, protecting it from the outside world: 'kein Verrat, den er mir antat, kein Schmerz, den er mir zufügte, konnte seine Schönheit verzerren' (p. 175).

This becomes the hidden turning point of the novel—the awareness, as in all three novels, of the theme of betrayal, of 'Verrat', by one of the central characters. From now on the formulations are predominantly of suffering and expressed in at least implied negatives. The closeness of the two women now becomes, according to Sonja, a nagging, unbridgeable distance. Jana's marriage kindles in Sonja the flame of jealousy. Sonja seizes her opportunity when, on a trip abroad, Achim leaves Jana and their son on the edge of town. Sonja and Achim consummate their affair in his temporary studio. The breakdown of interpersonal relationships aggravates the long-growing dissociation in both women of reflecting and reflected selves, a feature underlined by the structure of alternating narrator figures and by less immediate identification of the narrator figure at the beginning of each section. Jana has to live without the love she has now lost, Sonja has to seek a landscape 'ohne Orientierungspunkte...eine innere Landschaft mit Straßen ohne Anfang und Ende voll unbekannter Inseln' where every step is 'schon wieder im Dunkeln, eine Gratwanderung, ortlos' (p. 242). Where the women's relationship has already become a story of 'gescheiterter Annäherungen und einer fortschreitenden Entzweiung' (p. 179), Sonja now sees Achim, Jana and herself as three lonelinesses 'die einander nicht mehr sein konnten als Instrumente der Zerstörung aller Hoffnungen und Illusionen' (p. 180). The two women are bound to each other as rivals; Sonja becomes for Jana a despised part of herself taking revenge for the fact that she has never been regarded seriously, and she assumes a form of 'Über-Ich'. Sonja feels that Jana has crept into her self and estranged her from it to the point that Sonja no longer knows what to expect from life. The root cause of this mutual process of destruction lies in Achim. His relationship with Jana is further undermined by lack of parental responsibility towards their son Daniel which he covers up when the baby dies of a sudden fever, blaming Jana who was then solely in charge. The final image of the book is provided by Sonja's dream when she approaches a vision of Jana, only to discover that it is her own mirror image. As for Vera in *Die Züchtigung*, the process of transference, through suffering and despite rebellion, has become the deceptively enchanting experience of total interchange of personality. The 'I', the 'you' and love have, however, all been sacrificed.

Where *Die Züchtigung* showed above all the problems of being a daughter and *Das andere Gesicht* explored the love–hate relationship between two women, Mitgutsch's third novel *Ausgrenzung* focuses on the painful existence of a mother who desperately seeks help in trying to bring up her son Jakob who is eventually labelled as autistic. Marta, a lecturer married to an utterly selfish man, is at first accused by various medical professionals of showing insufficient love for her child. A struggle is triggered off between her desire for freedom to be herself and responsibility to cope on her own with an unpredictable, at times aggressive child. She is forced to make admissions that are only partly true, using formulae that explain away situations but which neither help them nor prevent an ever-increasing sense of failure and, still worse, encourage a process of self-isolation and destruction. This is registered in a style which, in setting up distance between the narrator and the central figure, prompts the narrator almost to justify Marta's feelings. Mitgutsch thereby again produces a double focus on essential statements. The first sentence with its invitation to joint consideration modified by a subjunctive produces a tone of alienation between doctor and 'patient' 'Und jetzt überlegen wir einmal, wo es begonnen haben könnte, sagte die *Ärztin*' (Mitgutsch 1989: 7). The patronizing attitude inherent in the falsely friendly tone is supported at once by Marta's feeling cold despite the April sunshine:

> Marta saß zusammengekauert in einem ledernen Armstuhl vor einem sauber ausgeräumtem Kamin, und es fror sie, obwohl die Aprilsonne durchs hohe Fenster schien. Vielleicht war es gar nicht die Kälte des Raums mit den grob verputzten Wänden, die dieses Zittern hervorrief (p. 7).

Such intensification of the feeling of estrangement through an accompanying physical reaction in a transference towards 'erlebte Rede' is one of Mitgutsch's frequently used stylistic devices. It is all the more effective, when, as here, the central character either does not interpret the physical reaction, or only hesitantly begins to comprehend the message implied. Marta's suffering is not just the physical effort of bringing up an exceptional child, it is also growing awareness of the slowing-down of her powers of understanding and the closing-down of opportunities to develop herself in contact with colleagues and friends. This manifests itself not only in the condition of her life but also in the style used to describe her inner world. Her reflections are at first conditioned by this need to explain herself, a form of anxiety (almost guilt) built up by the inhuman professionalism of the medical world. Treated as a case, she responds as a case: 'Ich war eine unzufriedene, depressive Mutter, ich war nicht fähig, von meinen Bedürfnissen abzusehen und dabei glücklich zu sein' (p. 59). Marta's sense of isolation breeds anxiety in her relationship with the world, with her husband, with her child and with her own self. This encourages her to ask self-searching questions, to try to telephone for advice from former friends who are now divorce lawyers and to express her wish to leave her husband. Yet each time she tries to assert herself she is either interrupted by the screams of her son, or by her friends' lack of interest. Mitgutsch thus spins a web around Marta that isolates her and focuses her attention on her son. She suffers from having to give up her career, loss of personal dialogue and of any existence independent of her role as a mother, leaving her with three wishes: for a healthy child, career success and freedom. This is paralleled by stylistic features that record her gradual subjection and internalization into an ever more uncertain self.

An early stage in this comes with her growing awareness that Jakob lacks dialogue and is surrounded by a 'leerer Graben' (p. 72), that he has lack of eye contact and even shuts himself off from the music that first brings him tears of sadness and joy. Marta is made even more aware of her own isolation and turns to self-defensive measures:

> Es war etwas Unsichtbares zwischen Jakob und allem, was ihn umgab. Oder war es das: Da war nichts Unsichtbares zwischen Jakob und seiner Umwelt, es war, als umgäbe ihn ein leerer Graben. Die 'leere Festung', dacht sie plötzlich, und glaubte, ihr Herzschlag, der ausgesetzt haben mußte, würde nie wieder einsetzen, ein völliger Stillstand, über den Hohlraum gespannt zwischen ihr und dem aufsteigenden Verdacht (p. 72).

Later she has to decide how much to propel Jakob into potentially embarrassing, even dangerous encounters with the outside world; but she also has to endure the pain she feels she has caused her husband Felix, despite the fact that he plays on this to his own advantage. She is encouraged to work on her guilt feelings while Jakob spends five days in a clinic, only to find him emerge having lost months of progress in communication. Jakob's playing with rhyming language is seen as a mockery of reason, and he is declared abnormal by a young doctor whose understanding is based on academic rather than practical knowledge. Marta's reaction to this marks a new stage—first of refusal to listen, then the realization that patient defiance might bring results. The abstract nouns of professional definition that close off but do not answer a problem are followed by clauses bearing verbs of action, only to be threatened by Jakob's own dissent in the face of so-called normal behaviour:

> Schließlich war es amtlich beglaubigt und abgestempelt. Ab jetzt war Jakob offiziell behindert. Wegen Entwicklungsverzögerung und Autismus stand im Attest. Sie hatte alle Definitionen, mit denen man Jakob beizukommen versuchte, demütig angenommen, und glaubte nun voreilig, sie habe den Schmerz bereits hinter sich, es käme nun eine neue, leichter erträgliche Zeit harter Arbeit, die nicht umsonst sein konnte, hatte doch bisher alles, bei dem sie ihre ganze Kraft eingesetzt hatte, schließlich Früchte getragen. Zehnmal härter würde sie arbeiten, als früher an ihrer eigenen Karriere. Und war sie nicht erfolgreich gewesen? Jetzt kommt eine neue Phase, sagte sie sich, aber sie rechnete nicht mit Jakobs hartnäckiger Weigerung sich den Normen zu unterwerfen, normal zu werden (pp. 110-11).

The repetition of 'schließlich' and the contritional way in which she half justifies herself are her attempts to blind herself to the way in which Jakob's enjoyment of his introverted world will lead Marta fatally away from all outside contacts and towards him as a form of self-justification on her part.

On holiday with him, Marta dedicates her entire future life to finding what will make Jakob happy—to become 'ganz und gar Selbstzweck und Glück' (p. 114)—while realizing that she can never hope for her own independent happiness. Her dependence on Jakob is demonstrated by her difficulties in struggling against another abstract concept drummed into her by experts:

> In diesem Sommer verlor sie die Normen, nach denen sie und alle andern, auch Felix und die Ärzte, Jakob gemessen hatten. Sie begann zu begreifen, daß keine Liebe sein konnte ohne die bedingungslose Annahme, und daß sie keine andere Aufgabe hatte, als dieses Kind glücklich zu machen, was immer Glück für Jakob bedeuten mochte. Und auch die Schuld sollte nicht mehr zwischen sie und das Kind kommen. Das Schuldgefühl abzulegen fiel ihr am schwersten (p. 113).

Whereas Jakob cannot express relationship to other children, Marta cannot break through the wall of silence and hostility of adults who have been restricted by expectations of proper behaviour or typecast by academic formulae. Jakob's inability to envisage an 'I'-figure, his particular echoism, develops into a transferable imagined self called Arni. Like Arni for Jakob, Jakob becomes for Marta the filter through which she experiences other people. His tantrum-like screaming in public when gripped with fear parallels the silent panic in Marta that this tug of war will never end; this later develops as hatred and anger with physical side-effects. Ironically she understands:

> Er brauchte Grenzen und stieß sich an ihnen, aber er besaß auch eine anspruchsvolle innere Welt, die oft so aufdringlich wurde und seine ausschließliche Anwesenheit verlangte. Kein Wunder, daß diese Grenzgänge zwischen zwei Wirklichkeiten anstrengend für ihn waren (p. 171).

By the time another man, Werner, enters Marta's life, Jakob's power of fantasy has laid bare to her the restrictive vision of a stable, socially acceptable world, and she suffers further guilt feelings towards her son, until Werner demands that she sends Jakob into a home. She opts for Jakob and becomes a sacrifice to a society which, as Felix puts it, will put up with a certain measure of eccentricity, but screaming is not included. By taking this option she turns her back on the potential second chance that an affair with Werner would represent. By giving in to her guilt towards Jakob, and her guilt that she is seen as a failed mother, she rebels against the more comfortable solution, that of entering into a relationship with Werner. Her rebellion thus emerges as an act of self-sacrifice that cannot win more than occasional moments of happiness when Jakob appears to come closer to normally acceptable, approachable behaviour. Ironically, such moments are ones when he is less true to his own special inner self. Her rebellion, because it is now linked so deliberately to his existence, cannot become complete, for both are now isolated. Furthermore, society defends itself with definitions, when such outcasts need immediate help. Thus when Marta's need for an operation and Felix's refusal to look after Jakob force him into a home, her litany of her son's qualities is answered with stern abstracts from the 'educators' of a home where Jakob is to spend a few weeks:

> Sie schaute besorgt in die Gesichter der Erzieher, zerstreut lächelnde Gesichter. Es gelang ihr nicht, in ihnen zu lesen, Güte zu finden, Geduld. Mein Kind ist nämlich, begann sie und stockte. Das waren keine Ärzte, und es ging hier nicht um

Symptome, sie mußte diese Menschen für Jakob gewinnen. Mein Kind ist nämlich sehr begabt, sagte sie, musikalisch, künstlerisch, sehr phantasievoll und sehr sensibel, er braucht viel Geduld, Lärm erträgt er nicht... Man schnitt ihr das Wort ab, die Diagnose? Autismus, Entwicklungsverzögerung. Mit spöttischen Augen hörte man zu, wie sie von Jakob schwärmte. Natürlich wird es ihm gut gehen bei uns! Man warnte sie, es wird ihm schwerfallen am Anfang, die Eingliederung, die Anpassung an die Gemeinschaft, ein derart verhätscheltes Kind, ein Muttersohn, sie konnte den Tadel nicht überhören, und manchmal sagte einer laut, kein Wunder, daß er zurück-geblieben ist, bei so viel Verweichlichung, so viel übertriebener Pflege, Überbemutterung. Härte sei nötig, belehrte man sie, ohne Härte kein Wachstum, ja, auch Abhärtung, Ernüchtigung!

Aber mein Kind ist so zart, wandte sie ein, so sensibel! Sie sah die Ungeduld in den Gesichtern, was erwartete denn diese Frau, was gab sie denn schon ab? Ein behindertes Kind. Und tat, als sei es ein Juwel. Erst am Schluß sagte sie leise, er wird sowieso nicht lange hier bleiben, sechs Wochen, zwei Monate höchstens. Häufiger Aufenthaltswechsel sei schädlich, erklärte man ihr, besonders für ein Kind wie Jakob (pp. 224-25).

Stylistically, this passage drifts between the formulaic absolutes of the teachers and Marta's own expression of consciousness, including some sentence structures that change perspective. The passage thus typifies this novel's imagined definition of third-party comments as a process of self-determination. In *Die Züchtigung* Vera, the daughter, mainly relies on memories of her mother—the self is examined and portrayed by internalization almost as an extension of the mother-figure. In *Das andere Gesicht* the double-narrator device, culminating in the use of the mistaken mirror episode at the end, produces self definition by absorption into the 'You'-figure. In *Ausgrenzung* Marta tries to overcome definition of herself by norms stated or suggested by experts indifferent to the chaos within her. There is, then, in broad terms, a development from the 'I'-centred, to 'You'-centred to 'They'-centred narrative. Yet in each case a central figure suffers and rebels because of the power of the mother, the partner and the experts; moreover, the central figure's inner world is constructed out of the struggle with these influences.

In the home Jakob is given drugs whose effects take him back seven years leaving Marta angry in her despair and helplessness, yet she insists: 'Lieber alle Schuld auf sich nehmen ...als sich mit ein paar Worten des Mitgefühls die Hoffnung zerschlagen lassen' (p. 238). Jakob begins to destroy all his things at home leading to a numbing anxiety that transfers on to her:

> Aber sie hatte dieses langsame Anwachsen des Chaos in ihm schon oft genug erlebt, um zu wissen, Verbote nützten nichts mehr; sie sah es in seinen Augen, er würde schreien müssen, um sich schlagen wie früher, die ganze Entwicklung noch einmal durchmachen und alle Stufen der letzten Jahre wieder von neuem überstehen, viele Male, um wieder aufzutauchen und selbstbewußt ich zu sagen. Sie spürte die Anspannung in ihm, die wachsende Unruhe, die Angst, eine sich immer noch steigernde Angst, sie spürte dieselbe Ausweglosigkeit in sich, ihre Angst und die seine, wie eine einzige Lawine, vor der sie sich duckte, unfähig sich zu erinnern, wie sie es früher überlebt hatten, wie es ihr manchmal gelungen war, den drohenden Ausbruch abzuwenden (p. 239).

She clings to the forlorn hope that his abstract drawings will allow him to achieve an independent place in the world.

Marta's pride in having brought up Jakob without violence is shattered when Jakob has to endure a mugging, and she finds her new home vandalized. They live on in terror unable any longer to summon up any rational defence, and are later driven out of the district. Anxiety now grows out of the emptiness surrounding the socially isolated mother and son and eventually undermines her reason. When, significantly, the telephone is cut off, Marta, despite encouraging questions by the police from whom she has sought protection, links together the various attacks on her relative peace of mind:

> Ob sie schon bei der Post angerufen habe, beim Entstörungsdienst? Aber die Anrufe, rief Marta, die Nägel, die Kratzer am Auto, die Exkremente, die Taschenlampen, die Angst, die wahnsinnige Angst schon seit Wochen! Sie schwitzte, sie fuhr sich mit der Hand über das Gesicht. Später sah sie dieses Gesicht im Spiegel, angespannt bis zum Wahnsinn und die schwarzen Spuren ihres Augenmakeups auf Wangen und Stirn, aber auch in den schnellen Blicken, die zwischen den Gendarmen hin und her gingen, hatte sie es gesehen: Die spinnt, die dreht durch (p. 269).

Jakob, she realizes is a 'Grenzfall' (p. 278), an outsider for specialists who drew the lines of normality to exclude him from society. Life on this frontier for twenty years has taken its toll, isolating her, giving her acute anxiety-ridden hearing abilities and almost destroying her faith in her fellow human beings. They are driven out, and in the final three pages Mitgutsch records Marta's unanswered accusatory questions: who drew the borderline that shut Jakob out? Is the image of a borderline fitting? Are norms a means of shutting out problems? Taking the lead from Jakob in his moments of trust, Marta rests her hopes not on a formula expressed in abstract terms, but 'daß der Planet bewohnbar und die Menschen vertrauenswürdig und liebenswert waren' (p. 280).

In all three novels an arrogant, selfish man is one of the root causes of suffering (in *Die Züchtigung*, however, only as a secondary factor in Marie's life, still less so for Vera). This is confirmed also in an excerpt from a longer story, 'Mit anderen Augen', with its portrayal of an acute form of suffering that refers us back to the 'particular female vulnerability' that Mitgutsch identified in Christine Lavant (1984: 100). In this story we find a young woman writer taking a translation manuscript to a male publisher's reader. She is painfully aware through her own previous experiences and through his body language that he is likely to treat her as a woman: 'Ich bin eine Frau. Also bin ich Jungfrau, Mutter, oder Hure' (1985: 117). She is in fact recovering from a recent abortion, and suffering from not knowing what she now wants in life. She rejects him or, as she puts it, springs off the roundabout of life, and in so doing loses something: 'Hoffnungen, Wunderglauben, Illusionen, oder die Ehrfurcht vor dem Gesetz, daß eine Frau eine Frau ist durch einen Mann. Gerd Brenner. Ein Mann. Ich werde nicht auf seinen Anruf warten' (p. 122). She returns to Barbara, her friend in Salzburg, who listens to her story, reassures her, and allows her to express her love as if transferred into another being: 'Und wenn ich in den Spiegel schaue, werde ich mit ihren Augen sehen' (p. 124).

In all four texts and in the three essays, the problems of withdrawal of another person, isolation of the self from the world and partial identification with a fallen idol are represented as retreats into inner worlds under threat. To break such bonds, to free oneself from the normal role-casting of relationships, whether between mother and child, woman and man, or woman and woman, the inner world needs to express itself independently. In the first two novels and in the story, there is an appearance of freedom, but in *Ausgrenzung* Marta's whole existence has been put beyond the pale. Despair and anger are typical reactions to the threatened inner world and represent, in their metaphoric expression, a revolt against the expectations of the world and of other people. Mitgutsch has shown one mode of revolt: the force of narrative distancing, where inner and outer worlds are not just merged to bring about a surrealist dream landscape, but allow the individual to try and set up her own laws. Mitgutsch's central figures start with attitudes and existences governed by traditionally hallowed modes of behaviour. These are enforced by the principles that structure society and human relationships and by male figures whose dominance and shortcomings are transferred on to female companions or authority figures (Marie, Jana, the *Ärztin*, even Barbara). These represent or reconstruct norms against which the central character can mirror herself. However, traditional devices such as mirroring, whether as narcissism or to reveal a 'Doppelgängerin' are not sufficient—only the continuous refusal to accept such identification can keep the self alive and open to development, and hence to suffering and an unfinished rebellion. The key to such refusal is found in Mitgutsch's essay on Sylvia Plath when she writes, 'Dein Leben, zersplittert in die Bilder Deiner Betrachter, nicht alle wohlwollend, aber je unsympathischer Dich Deine Betrachter fanden, desto mehr erkannte ich mich selber wieder'. Mitgutsch used Plath's poems as a mirror 'der mich erschreckte und anzog'. Plath's images helped her 'den Schritt über den Rand zu gehen und mir dabei zuzusehen, als Voyeurin meiner Vernichtung' (1990: 166). Plath's poetry is thus interpreted as a freeing of herself from everyday life, the result being something belonging to art rather than life: 'Sich auszulöschen als einzige Form des Überlebens: das Paradox der Kunst, der Triumph eines im Leben unmöglichen Ewigkeitsanspruchs' (1990a: 173-74). Such distancing is achieved (ambivalently) in a process

Mitgutsch calls 'Zersplitterung', and it is this above all that characterizes her narrative technique.

In *Die Züchtigung*, for instance, the tension between Vera's ties to her mother and her wish to break free becomes the key to her life and to her narrative, much of which is an attempt to understand her mother through her mother's eyes and values in order to overcome transference and dependence. Hence we find discussion in retrospect of individual events, querying of motives, uncertainty of interpretation, even recourse to traditional set phrases which, by their ambiguity of relevance, create uncertainty and distancing. In *Das andere Gesicht* the loosening of the perspective, especially after the awareness of a betrayal sparked off by jealousy, leads near the end of the novel to a false self-identification. In *Ausgrenzung* Marta's attempt to lead an authentic life through the demands of a dependent person produces a form of selflessness but not a total transference onto Jakob. In *Mit anderen Augen* the double focus of the woman watching herself as an object reacting negatively to the man's lust allows her to make the decision to return to Barbara. In all four texts the central figure needs to overcome the pleasures of narcissism, but this clearly is not always realized. Hence Marta in *Ausgrenzung* renounces personal happiness in order to win an ideal self differentiated from an evil world full of selfish people. In this she fails because, paradoxically, deliberate destruction of the self leads to heightened awareness. That destruction requires, as Mitgutsch found in the poetry of Christine Lavant, an understanding of the self as an outsider. For, in particular, the outsider figure is capable of constant renewal. Mitgutsch's search for constant renewal is also seen in the tone of some of the poetry she translated by Philip Larkin; it is perhaps most clearly represented in the resigned hope of 'Trees' or 'Bäume', where the lost ideal is shown as a natural process:

> Die Bäume setzen wieder Knospen an
> wie etwas fast Gesagtes;
> die jungen Triebe dehnen sich und sprießen,
> ihr Grün ist eine Art von Traurigkeit.
>
> Liegt's daran, daß sie immer wiederkehren
> und wir älter werden? Nein, sie sterben auch.

Ihr Kunststück jedes Jahr ganz neu zu sein
kerbt sich in Ringen in ihre Rinde ein.

Und doch, die ruhelosen Burgen schlagen
mit voller Dichte aus in jedem Mai,
das letzte Jahr ist tot, so scheinen sie zu sagen,
fang wieder neu an, neu.

WORKS CITED

Kecht, R.M.
　1989　' "In the Name of Obedience, Reason, and Fear": Mother–Daughter Relations in W.A. Mitgutsch and E. Jelinek'. *The German Quarterly* 62, pp. 357-72.

Larkin, P.
　1988　*Gedichte: Ausgewählt und übertragen von Waltraud Anna Mitgutsch.* Stuttgart: Klett-Cotta.

Lavant, C.
　1959　*Spindel im Mund.* Salzburg: Otto Müller.

Merwin, W.S.
　1971　*The Carrier of Ladders.* New York: Atheneum.

Mitgutsch, W.A.
　1977　'Weltverlust in der zeitgenössischen Lyrik, exemplarisch dargestellt an Paul Celan und Sylvia Plath'. *Sprachkunst* 8, pp. 251-72.
　1979　'Die Rezeption des Expressionismus in der zeitgenössischen amerikanischen Lyrik'. *Sprachkunst* 10 , pp. 87-108.
　1984　'Hermetic Languages as Subversion: The Poetry of Christine Lavant'. *Modern Austrian Literature* 17, 1, pp. 79-107.
　1985　'Mit anderen Augen', in H. Fink and M. Reich-Ranicki (eds.), *Klagenfurter Texte 1985*. Munich: List, pp. 115-24.
　1988a　*Die Züchtigung.* Repr. Munich: dtv (1985).
　1988b　*Das andere Gesicht.* Repr. Munich: dtv (1986).
　1989　*Ausgrenzung.* Frankfurt: Luchterhand.
　1990a　'An Sylvia Plath: "Wann weiß man, daß das Warten sich nicht mehr lohnt?" ', in G. Kreis and J. Siegmund-Schultze (eds.), *Es geht mir verflucht durch Kopf und Herz.* Hamburg: Hoffmann und Campe, pp. 166-81.
　1990b　Unpublished letter to Brian Keith-Smith, September.

'Die Bachmann hab' ich sehr gern mögen, die war halt
eine gescheite Frau. Eine seltsame Verbindung, nicht?':
Women in Thomas Bernhard's Prose Writings

Andrea Reiter

In 1980 a book entitled *Am Ende angekommen* caused considerable controversy among German literary critics. Applying
psychoanalytical techniques to textual criticism, its author Ria
Endres attacked Thomas Bernhard's intellectual hostility to
women. As the published form of a doctoral thesis, this slim
volume is strikingly unorthodox: its simple layout, descriptive
chapter titles, and lack of long theoretical sections belong more
to the world of journalism than to that of academia. Endres
failed to annotate her arguments adequately, and was accused
of treating the secondary literature haphazardly (e.g. Fueß
1981). A more serious objection was raised by Martin Lüdke
about her, as he put it, 'psychologistic and biologistic' view of
Bernhard's portrayal of women, one which was formulated in
crude, Freudian terms; yet the same reviewer was fascinated
not only by its unconventional format but also by the author's
courageous stance. This admiration was shared by other critics,
such as Rolf Michaelis, and even by Bernhard scholars, such as
Anneliese Botond (cf. Fueß 1981: 88-89).

In keeping with a then widespread trend, Endres makes
explicit the subjective and autobiographical aspects of her
approach. She starts her essay by linking it with the story of her
own life. Her recollections turn out to be strikingly reminiscent
of Thomas Bernhard's autobiography. Endres has never known
her father, an American soldier. Like Bernhard she grows up in
an environment which she recognizes retrospectively as
restricting her early development. Eventually she frees herself
by going to university, where she comes across Bernhard's

writings, in which she discovers her own anxieties expressed in words. Her book is the attempt to dissociate herself from the spell of this literature by deconstructing it. Yet she unwittingly achieves the opposite of what she intended: the more she attacks Bernhard the patriarch, the more closely she resembles him (cf. Fueß 1981: 89).

Because of her personal involvement in it, Endres approaches Bernhard's work from an extremely emotional standpoint. This may well explain why the book's long-term impact on Bernhard studies has been surprisingly insignificant. Although Bernhard's women figures have since been studied (e.g. by Mittermayer), there is still no comprehensive assessment of the theme. Endres deserves credit for being the first extensively to question Bernhard's attitude towards women. Unfortunately, her approach has led into a cul-de-sac, failing to show convincingly the connection between her condemnation of his portrayal of women and other features of Bernhard's work. Where she does refer to women in Bernhard's work she does so in a descriptive way, their relevance for her subject is only claimed without being properly argued (e.g. Endres 1980: 28).

'La femme n'existe pas' is Endres's pointed conclusion about Bernhard's books. Where the woman does appear, writes Endres, she snugly fits into the 'Tragödienzusammenhang männlicher Projektion' (Endres 1980: 98). Endres is correct in saying that women in Bernhard's prose do not, in the main, speak with their own voices. The narrator, behind whom the author largely hides, is always male. The same is true for their informers. However, there is a split half way through Bernhard's *œuvre*. In the early novels women are talked about, at best they are quoted. While the male narrators are philosophers or scientists or have some such academic background, the women figures are usually their social dependents. When it requires proof of Bernhard's hostility to women, the secondary literature frequently refers to the notorious landladies in his novels, although his prose is also populated by mothers, sisters and lovers. Specifically, they all seem to be designed as stereotypes; the majority remain nameless, a fact which reinforces this impression. And this is where Endres's criticism remains trapped. She is not prepared to do justice to the diversity of his portraits of them even in his early texts. Furthermore, Endres would have found it more difficult to launch her attack on the novels Bernhard published in the late 1970s and 1980s. Significantly, she fails to even mention *Ja* (1978), where this diversity starts to become more pronounced. In subsequent novels such as *Holzfällen* (1984) female characters like Joana and Jeannie Billroth are granted a certain individuality. The attempt to read the novel as a *roman à clef* identifying the characters as exponents of the Viennese cultural scene, testifies to this (Dittmar 1990: 270-78).

The landladies in Bernhard's texts belong to the so-called primitive folk, whom Bernhard and his narrators hold in especially high esteem (see Dittmar 1990: 9). A particularly clear example is Murau's view of the gardeners in *Auslöschung* (p. 334). Nevertheless, *Frost* (1963) creates a character pattern of such a woman which reduces simplicity to crude animality. The brutality with which the narrator of 'An der Baumgrenze' (1969) rejects the landlady's advances, however, also casts some light on the sexual phobias of these men. In two other texts, *Der Untergeher* (1983) and *Ja* (1978), it is not sexuality which threatens the narrators but a talkative landlady. These two later texts also indicate a change in the pattern in a different respect. Approvingly, one of the narrators refers to the intelligence and willpower of the landlady (1979b: 51). Moreover, it transpires that both landladies share with the narrators, as well as with their creator, an important biographical detail: in their youth they had suffered from a severe lung disease, which they had overcome through a strong will to survive. From *Ja* onwards, the narrators also display a new self-criticism. In *Der Untergeher* the introduction of the landlady is preceded by the following reflection:

> In der Theorie verstehen wir die Menschen, aber in der Praxis halten wir sie nicht aus, dachte ich, gehen mit ihnen meistens nur widerwillig um und behandeln sie immer von uns aus gesehen...weil wir tatsächlich immer jedem gegenüber voreingenommen sind' (pp. 189-90).

This self-critical tone becomes increasingly a hallmark of Bernhard's writings. The portrayal of the mothers, however, who feature only in his earlier novels, is not affected by that.

The mothers in Bernhard's texts share a common background with the landladies. Compared with fathers, who come from the landed gentry, mothers are descendants of butchers or green-grocers. Retrospectively, the narrator-sons take verbal revenge on their mothers. They accuse them of having been unpredict-able: Roithamer says about his mother, 'Überall war sie und immer unvorhergesehen, als ob sie sich angeschlichen hätte, auf einmal aufgetaucht' (1984c: 253). Murau, too, remembers that 'das Mißtrauen unserer Mutter ist das allergrößte gewesen' (1986a: 178). Both sons assert that their mothers displayed a special phobia for the written or printed word.

The son considers himself unwanted and unloved. As the 'substitute' heir he has felt rejected all his life. 'Sie hatte mich, wie ich immer gehört habe', writes Murau, 'nicht haben wollen, sich gegen mich gewehrt. Aber sie hatte mich gebären *müssen*' (Bernhard's italics) (1986a: 289). It is of some significance that Murau's mother expresses her dislike of her son with the same words that Bernhard claims to remember from his own mother. Murau's mother called him *'das überflüssigste Kind, das man sich vorstellen kann'* (Bernhard's italics) (p. 290). Bernhard remembers an abundance of invectives: *'Du hast mir noch gefehlt* oder *Du bist mein ganzes Unglück'* (Bernhard's italics) and observes, 'Tatsächlich hatte sie mir immer das Gefühl gegeben, daß ich ihr zeitlebens im Wege gestanden bin, daß ich ihr vollkommenes Glück verhindert habe' (1982: 38).[1] As is the case with other novels Bernhard has salvaged material for *Auslöschung* from his own life. Yet while his own disturbed relationship with his mother must be attributed to his illegitimate birth and the problems which it caused to a woman in a country village in the 1930s, in *Auslöschung* this plausible reason does not exist.

The representation of the mother in Bernhard's autobio-graphical writings undergoes a significant metamorphosis, which reveals the adult Bernhard in the process of coming to

1. The tension in the face of Bernhard's mother in a photograph showing them together in 1939 in Seekirchen supports these assertions (see Hofmann 1988). On the connection between the portrayal of women in Bernhard's fiction and the author's childhood, see Mittermayer 1988: 76.

terms with childhood experience. He wrote and published *Ein Kind* (1982), which depicts the first few years of his life, as the last autobiographical volume. Only in 1982, 32 years after his mother had died, could Bernhard bring himself to reflect on the experience on which the mother figures of his fiction appear to be modelled. In an autobiographical note from 1953 Bernhard calls his mother a wonderful woman (Dittmar 1990: 13), yet in the early volumes of his autobiography he admits that he did not have a relaxed relationship with her until he was eighteen. Tragically this was not to last. She died soon afterwards of cancer, while Bernhard himself was also critically ill with tuberculosis. 'Es war ja noch nicht lange her', he writes in *Die Kälte* (1981), 'daß ich den mir liebsten Menschen verloren hatte, meinen Großvater, ein halbes Jahr später hatte ich auch schon die Gewißheit, den zu verlieren, der mir nach ihm am nächsten war, meine Mutter ' (p. 39). His close relationship to his mother was not to come about before the death of his grandfather, the father figure and close ally of his youth whom Bernhard idealizes in his autobiography (1984a: 93-94).

Several of Bernhard's early novels centre on a problematic relationship between the narrator and his sister. This is true above all of *Korrektur* (1975), where Roithamer builds a cone-shaped house for his sister, the very sight of which kills her.

The latent constellation of incest in some of Bernhard's texts has been pointed out before. Konrad and his wife in *Das Kalkwerk* (1970) are half-brother and half-sister. 'An der Baumgrenze' focuses on a brother and sister who decide to die in the mountains in order to escape from society. These examples document the fact that relationships between brothers and sisters in Bernhard's prose texts have nothing in common with the treatment of the theme of incest in such literature as that of the pre-fascist *Freikorps*, where on the one hand the heroes' preference for their friends' sisters as brides implies fear of the potentially dangerous erotic encounter with the unknown female, on the other hand the woman's brother serves as guarantee for her 'purity' (see Theweleit 1977: 114-235). Indeed Roithamer's papers depict a relationship between the siblings which suggests that he does not speak of two independent individuals. Each takes a keen interest in the other's occupation, Roithamer in his sister's art and she in his science; thus enhancing and complementing one another. Furthermore Roithamer remembers talking about their shared reading experience, 'während wir in meinem oder in ihrem Zimmer aufundab gegangen sind' (1984c: 311). Normally pacing up and down in rooms points to the intense isolation of the solitary individual in Bernhard's prose. The symbiotic relationship of Roithamer and his sister thus makes them react like one single individual. The fact that they die almost at the same time is further proof that Roithamer's sister is none other than his alter ego.

In *Auslöschung* the narrator has two sisters. From early childhood, identification with either one of them is denied to him, as they both side with their mother against him: 'sie machten immer alles gegen mich, gleich was es war. Als ob sie von meinen Eltern *ganz bewußt gegen mich* [Bernhard's italics] erzeugt worden wären' (1986a: 98). Consequently, it is their mocking faces, in the only photograph he kept of them, in which Murau insists on recognizing their true characters (pp. 74-75).

Thus devoid of any ties with his sisters, Murau is able to form relationships beyond the family circle. A close friendship binds him to his pupil Gambetti and to Maria, who assumes the position of his artistic alter ego. Although we get some information about Maria's life, she remains curiously shadowy and intangible and is thus not dissimilar to Roithamer's sister.

In *Auslöschung*, the apotheosis of themes and personages of Bernhard's early prose texts, Bernhard presents a number of metamorphosed relationships between men and women. A close relationship with the sister is no longer possible; the relationship with the mother, albeit disturbed, has lost its destructive impact on the son. In *Auslöschung* she finds fulfilment herself in a relationship outside the family. Satisfying relationships in the case of the narrator are presented in artistic-intellectual friendships with the female poet who is the narrator's senior by a few years (pp. 214-27) and with the younger male pupil.

Ein Kind (1982) marks a turning point in Bernhard's portrayal of women; by now he had come to terms with his mother: all subsequent prose texts like *Wittgensteins Neffe* (1982) and *Der Untergeher* (1983) have male friendships at their centres. The last novels, *Holzfällen* (1984) and *Alte Meister* (1985), do not fit the pattern of the earlier texts either. Despite presenting the familiar personages, *Auslöschung* constitutes an exception in this group. Recent research has, however, shown conclusively that the novel was written in 1980, a fact which would put it at the transition between the early and the late novels and would also explain its striking resemblance to the earlier novels (see Weinzierl 1990: 455-61).

Friendship between men is an important motif in Bernhard's texts; *Holzfällen*, however, is the only novel in which the narrator actually alludes to a sexual relationship with another man. Although Bernhard categorically protests against speculation about the affair on which this part of the novel is allegedly based (Hofmann 1988: 15), one can hardly overlook the fact that in his fiction he generally presents friendship between men as a satisfying form of social relationship. He once admitted too to having had 'alle möglichen Beziehungen zu Frauen und zu Männern' (Hofmann 1988: 66). However, like the alliances of the narrators with women, those with men are generally desexualized. The friendships between men are instead characterized as intellectual relationships, which may have their roots in that of the maturing Bernhard to his grandfather.

Women, especially in Bernhard's early novels, are characterized as romantics, involuntarily linked with nature, and anti-intellectual:

> Dem Manne sei angeboren, was der Frau angelernt werden müsse in mühevoller, oft verzweifelter Lehrmethode, nämlich der Verstand als chirurgisches Instrument gegenüber der sich sonst unweigerlich auflösenden, ja sonst rettungslos zerbröckelnden Geschichts-und Naturmaterie (1973: 129).

With these words Konrad is said to have justified his oppression of his wife. By reading to her from Wittgenstein's *Tractatus* he forces her up to his own intellectual level. To complicate matters, however, there are women in Bernhard's prose who are the narrators' intellectual equals and whom they accept and admire, such as Roithamer's sister, or the Persian woman in *Ja* who impresses the narrator as 'Geh- Denk- und also Gesprächs- und Philosophierpartner', a role which is normally reserved for men in Bernhard's prose (as, for example, in *Gehen* [1971], *Wittgensteins Neffe*).

In Bernhard's prose writings, emotion is paired with intellect in those women who support the artistic socialization of the narrator: Joana and Jeannie Billroth in *Holzfällen*, Maria in *Auslöschung*. Murau accepts Maria as an authority, to whose judgment on his writings he listens (1986a: 541). 'Die Bachmann hab' ich sehr gern mögen', Thomas Bernhard admits to Kurt Hofmann, 'die war halt eine gescheite Frau. Eine seltsame Verbindung, nicht?' he adds archly (Hofmann 1988: 96).[2]

This admiration for the intelligent women, however, cannot be generalized. In his diary-like notes in 1959, Bernhard claims that 'Jedes intelligentere Mädchen stößt mich ab, hat mich immer abgestoßen' (1989a: 65-66). Even in later years he cannot stand intellectual ability in women. This is why he considers Ria Endres to be 'völlig unweiblich... Eine Frau, die wirklich natürlich ist, also das, was man unter einer Frau versteht, würde nie so einen Blödsinn schreiben und verzapfen' (Hofmann 1988: 95). The significant term here is 'natürlich', a key-word in Bernhard's works. While Bernhard uses it mainly in a negative context as contrasted with the artificial (see Schmidt-Dengler 1986: 70), it has a positive meaning for him here. However, in denoting the desired unintellectual quality of the woman, the term is derogatory. Endres, in Bernhard's view, is neither a real woman nor can she be like a man.

This analysis of female figures in Bernhard's prose will, it is hoped, call in question Endres's claim of the non-existent woman. Far from excluding women from his texts, Bernhard portrays them in rather complex ways. He could even be accused of inconsistency: on the one hand, characters like Roithamer are taken by the intellectuality of a woman; on the other, they seem to feel threatened by them. This contradiction becomes even more obvious in his later novels, notably in *Holzfällen*, where the narrator freely admits his exploitation of the intellectual woman. It is, however, also in these later texts that the narrators' self-critical remarks relativize their sentiments.

2. Bachmann admired the intellectuality of Bernhard's prose, as is shown in her brief essay 'Entwurf: Thomas Bernhard. Ein Versuch' (1969) (Bachmann 1978: 361).

> Ohne Erotik lebt nichts. Nicht einmal die Insekten, die
> brauchen es auch. Außer man hat eine ganz primitive
> Vorstellung von Erotik. Das ist nicht drin, weil ich halt immer
> schau', daß ich das Primitive auch überwinde. Ich brauche
> weder eine Schwester noch brauche ich eine Liebhaberin. Das
> hat man alles in sich selber, manchmal kann man's ja
> benutzen, wenn man Lust hat. Die Leute glauben immer,
> wovon nicht direkt die Rede ist, das ist nicht da, das ist ja ein
> Unsinn. Ein achtzigjähriger Greis, der irgendwo liegt und diese
> Liebe schon fünfzig Jahre lang nimmer g'habt hat, der ist ja
> auch in seinem sexuellen Leben drinnen. Im Gegenteil, das ist
> noch eine viel tollere Sache von sexuellem Dasein als das
> Primitive. Ich schau' mir das lieber bei einem Hund an und
> bleib selber stark (Bernhard, quoted in Hofmann 1988: 59-60).

In Bernhard's prose, sexuality and eroticism are portrayed, if
at all, in a negative way, as a threat against which the narrator
has to guard himself. (He once explained their omission in terms
of his fear of producing trash.) In the earliest prose the narrator
is still ashamed of his sexual desires (1989a: 80). Although
Bernhard's lung disease did retard his sexual development, he
later comments, 'zwischen zweiundzwanzig und dreißig war
das dann alles schon ganz richtig und normal da—auch mit
großem Genuß' (Fleischmann and Koch 1981: 4).

In his novels, beginning with *Frost* (1963), however, some
male characters transform self-discipline into the condemnation
of the erotic woman; sexuality assumes the negative character
which is familiar in Bernhard's work. Furthermore, it is associated with unpleasant odours (1972: 17). Bernhard's remarks
about the primitive sexuality of dogs fits into this context.

Although some relationships between siblings in Bernhard's
prose—like that between Roithamer and his sister—are
resonances of his belated affection for his mother (1984a: 94),
brutality is the keynote. This is connected with Bernhard's
idiosyncratic concept of love and eroticism. Already as a young
writer Bernhard interpreted love as a subtle form of oppression.
In his earliest prose he self-critically asserts,

> wenn wir einen Menschen gefunden haben, mit dem wir uns
> zusammentun, tun wir so, als besäßen wir ihn, als gehörte er
> uns, wir umgeben ihn mit Mauern, hohen Mauern, unendlich
> hohen Mauern, kerkern ihn ein, zementieren seinen Geist,
> seine Gefühle ein, am liebsten töteten wir ihn (1989a: 92-93).

There is no difficulty here in recognizing the original conception
of the cone-shaped house of *Korrektur*. In *Ja* a building becomes
the concrete image of a man's revenge on a woman. In this text
the immuring of the woman is quite openly presented as a
means of destroying her. While Roithamer insists that the cone
fully 'corresponds with' his sister, that it would meet her needs
perfectly, the Swiss power-station architect designs a house for
his common-law wife which meets his own requirements
(p. 108). Leaving her behind on her own in the half-finished
house, he destroys her: her suicide is the logical consequence. In
this short text which has, undeservedly, received little critical
attention, Bernhard makes one aspect explicit which is only
latent in the two earlier novels exploring the same theme: the
man's constructions are inevitably fatal to the woman without,
however, allowing the men to triumph.

These buildings can, of course, be read as metaphors. In
particular the cone invites a psychoanalytical interpretation,
such as that offered by Endres. The male houses denote male
intellectuality. Roithamer says that he designed the cone against
all reason, yet the very act of designing is an intellectual act. In
the lime works Konrad not only tyrannizes his wife with
experiments following the 'urbantschitsche Methode' but also
terrorizes her whenever the experiments do not work to his
satisfaction. Thus an erotic relationship is superseded by the
rigid order of the experiment in the course of which the
intellectual activity turns into an instrument of terror against
the woman.

The narrator of *Holzfällen* calls Joana's common-law
husband her 'Zufluchtsmensch', because he has stayed with her
even after she has taken to the bottle (p. 126). In *Wittgensteins
Neffe* the narrator claims that he owes everything to his

> Lebensfreundin... Ohne sie wäre ich überhaupt nicht mehr
> am Leben und wäre ich jedenfalls niemals der, der ich heute
> bin, so verrückt und so unglücklich, aber auch glücklich, wie
> immer. Die Eingeweihten wissen, was alles sich hinter diesem
> Wort *Lebensmensch* verbirgt, von und aus welchem ich über
> dreißig Jahre meine Kraft und immer wieder mein Überleben
> bezogen habe, aus nichts sonst, das ist die Wahrheit (pp. 30-31).

'Zufluchtsmensch' as well as 'Lebensmensch' are to be understood in an existential sense: as terms for a person who sustains the survival of another by offering spiritual support. Thus the woman in *Wittgensteins Neffe* is said not to have spared any effort to visit the narrator in hospital while he was critically ill (p. 31). The narrator in *Holzfällen* also remembers with some gratitude the intellectual stimulation by a 'Lebensmensch'. The later despised, indeed hated Jeannie Billroth, he says, had introduced him to almost all the great writers of the twentieth century (p. 217). The so-called 'Philosophennichte' (p. 216) was the first '*Kunstmensch*' (Bernhard's italics) who gave the young writer any guidance when he first arrived in Vienna (p. 215).

A 'Lebensmensch' halts not only physical deterioration but also psychological derangement. The common-law wife of the Swiss architect was just such an 'entsprechender Mensch' for the narrator of *Ja*. He met her at the moment of his total desperation, took her on his walks and was for once able to talk to somebody. Yet when she turned out to suffer from the same personal problem as the narrator himself he reacted in terror and disillusion (1979b: 135). The excited narrator in *Holzfällen* also ends relationships as soon as he no longer benefits from them. He justifies his disloyalty in terms of self-defence (p. 220). 'Hätte ich mich der Jeannie nicht entzogen', he grumbles, 'sozusagen auf dem Höhepunkt meiner Beziehung zu ihr, ich wäre unweigerlich von ihr verschlungen und also vernichtet worden' (p. 218). Similarly, he terminates his relationship with Joana and with the Auersbergers.

Bernhard's narrators thus give the impression that they treat relationships, even the most intimate ones, as purely utilitarian, formed only for selfish reasons and terminated as soon as they have served their purpose. In *Holzfällen* the narrator proudly insists: 'ich selbst habe mir diese ideale Entwicklung genommen, diese für mich ideale künstlerische Entwicklung' (p. 223). Totally controlled and calculated, the relationships are removed from the influence of pure chance. This approach seems to be supported by a statement Bernhard made in an interview, in which he referred to relationships between the sexes as a series of experiments which are far removed from anything natural (Hofmann 1988: 66). Yet Bernhard's interviews have to be seen in the context of his other public statements, in which he indiscriminately attacks politicians, diplomats and representatives of the establishment in general. These invectives take much the same form as his fictional attacks. To a large extent, however, the author's 'views' resemble the narrators' not because they are identical in substance but because their verbal formulation is similar. A random example can be found in Bernhard's invectives against the Austrians in *Auslöschung*:

> Die Österreicher haben nicht den geringsten Geschmack, jedenfalls schon lange Zeit nicht mehr, wo man hinschaut, herrscht die allergrößte Geschmacklosigkeit. Und was für eine allgemeine Interesselosigkeit. Als ob der Mittelpunkt nur der Magen sei, sagte ich, und der Kopf völlig ausgeschaltet. Ein so dummes Volk (p. 112).

Like Bernhard in his interviews, Murau extends his criticism of his family estate Wolfsegg by analogy 'zu einer Beschimpfung alles Österreichischen und schließlich dazu auch noch alles Deutschen, ja letzten Endes alles Mitteleuropäischen' (p. 111). The similarity between Bernhard's public tirades and those in his novels is due to the fact that neither can be verified, nor are they meant to be. Indeed they are part of his narrative style. In an early interview Bernhard asserts, 'In meinen Büchern ist alles *künstlich*, das heißt, alle Figuren, Ereignisse, Vorkommnisse spielen sich auf einer Bühne ab' (1989b: 82, Bernhard's italics; see also Reiter 1990). This is reiterated by the term 'Übertreibungskunst' which Bernhard, through Murau, applies to his work. Exaggeration, a 'Kunst der Überbrückung...der Existenzüberbrückung' (1986a: 611), he maintains, help him overcome his depressions. Bernhard is thus not asking the reader either to accept or to reject the particular views of his narrators. His aim is to provoke.

It is hardly surprising that Bernhard's conception of a 'Lebensmensch' and of marital partnership have nothing in common. The mere thought of the latter seemed insane to the young Bernhard (1989a: 23). From an early stage he rejected any social ties for himself. From 1965 he retreated to his farmhouse in Upper Austria, sought greater anonymity in Vienna or escape to Madrid or Mallorca. Only towards the end of his life did he become more sociable and, from the late 1970s, give the occasional interview. His last novels display self-critical, more companionable narrators who have a certain amount of sympathy for their surroundings (see Reich-Ranicki 1990: 88).

Marriage for himself had been out of the question: 'Mit einer Frau zusammen können's ja nicht Bücher schreiben, oder halt blöde' (Hofmann 1988: 14). Corresponding passages can be found in Bernhard's prose:

> Wie weit müsse ein Mensch gekommen sein, wegen der geringsten Unsinnigkeit seine Studie im Stich zu lassen, nur weil seine Frau oben einen Polster gerade gerichtet haben will, weil sie etwas zu trinken will, weil sie ein Stück aus dem Ofterdingen vorgelesen haben will, weil sie die Vorhänge auf—oder zugemacht haben will, weil ich ihr eine Brotscheibe abschneiden, die Haarschleife zuziehen, das Strumpfband zubinden, weil ich ihr die Zuckerdose anfüllen, die Brille aufsetzen, den Rücken mit Melissengeist einreiben soll (1973: 59).

Like the statement in the interview, this passage has to be approached with caution. A glimpse of Bernhard's plays, where the stubborn grumblers are in the main men, suggests that he is not to be taken at face value. Bernhard does not stop short of attacking anyone and anything, exaggeration being his main weapon. Whether in a public statement such as his letters to the editors of various newspapers (see Schmidt-Dengler 1986: 93-106), or in his literary work, his aim is to provoke a complacent public. It is in this context that his portrayal of women, and of men's relationships with them, has to be understood. His attitude is rooted in the experience of his illness. 'Es ist nichts zu loben, nichts anzuklagen, aber es ist vieles lächerlich; es ist alles lächerlich, wenn man an den *Tod* denkt' (Bernhard's italics) (quoted in Botond 1970: 7). All of Bernhard's literary and public statements have to be seen in the light of this introductory sentence from his speech on the occasion of his receiving the Österrreichische Staatspreis für Literatur in 1968. Faithful to this conviction Bernhard has alienated people on the left and the right of the ideological spectrum, not least the Austrian Minister of Education Dr Theodor Piffl-Perčević, who left the room during Bernhard's acceptance speech. Ironically, feminists thus find themselves aligned with conservatives: Bernhard represents an assault on the values of both. Yet he never excludes himself from his own attacks, just as in his prose he does not portray his narrators as superior to the other characters, indeed, in his later novels the narrators are increasingly self-critical.

It is particularly in the portraits of marriages that Bernhard's self-criticism becomes evident through his criticism of the male partners. The married men in novels such as *Auslöschung* and *Korrektur* are shown to have become attached to their partners for egotistical reasons and soon suffer for it. Endres correctly observes that a man may abuse his wife as 'Gebärwerkzeug für seine Nachkommen' (Endres 1980: 64), however the wives do, in most cases, come out on top or at least prevent their husbands from doing so.

Bernhard's view of marriage is a pessimistic one. Marriage always means oppression in the end. Any close relationship in Bernhard's prose is eventually doomed to fail. This pessimism seems to result from his high expectations of a relationship, his idealistic notion of the 'entsprechender Mensch'. Human relationships are so fragile that every attempt to make them permanent is bound to end up in suppression, as is demonstrated in a number of novels. The total equivalence between two persons can, in the end, only result in destruction because it dissolves the boundary between individuals. Bernhard experienced this himself with his much-loved grandfather. Although he talks about him with great admiration, he realized that he could not develop his own artistic personality until his grandfather had died. Only when the older man had left his desk could the younger take his place. It is significant that Bernhard hardly ever criticizes the character of his grandfather although he must have suffered from his overpowering personality. His disappointment with the relationship is embodied, however, in the portraits of the old men in his plays.

It was Bernhard's intimate relationship with his grandfather too which convinced him of the necessity of social contacts (Hofmann 1988: 15-16). After his grandfather's death he literally discovered his mother, and after she died he started making friendships outside his family circle. The first of these was with a lawyer who, like Bernhard himself, suffered from tuberculosis; the best known of his friends was Paul Wittgenstein. Every now and then he would prescribe himself a kind of social therapy.

Retrospectively, he interprets his enrolment at the Mozarteum as a 'Flucht zum Menschen' (Hofmann 1988: 47). Later the theatre offered him the opportunity to make contacts (Hofmann 1988: 86),

'The woman makes the man': what might be dismissed as a cliché is taken literally in a number of Bernhard's later novels; in particular, where the relationship between man and woman is not conventionalized by marriage and the upbringing of children. Although the woman gains the upper hand, she does not use her power to realize herself but her partner. Female domination of the male manifests itself in a subtle way. The woman sacrifices herself, she dispenses with a career of her own like the Persian woman in *Ja* or Joana in *Holzfällen*. The influence which the woman exercises over the man, even if it eventually leads to the man's success, is described as suppression. The Persian woman is said to have forced the Swiss man into a career as an architect (1979b: 99). Her sacrifice, which eventually was to become her own purpose in life (p. 115), thus takes on a different meaning. The narrators of both texts are concerned to explain that the sacrifices of the women are voluntary, if rooted in their upbringing and mentality.

As seen from the woman's point of view, men cause women's misery by withdrawing from their influence. In *Holzfällen* Bernhard contrasts this with the man's interpretation: the narrator claims that he had to leave Jeannie Billroth as he felt overpowered by her. This act of male desperation is a more subtle form of Konrad's way of disposing of his wife. Narrators and characters seem to share this fear of the woman with their creator, who, in his interview with Kurt Hofmann, expressed his fright in the image of the balloonist, who was unaware of a woman cutting the rope (Hofmann 1988: 29). Can this particular version of the stab-in-the-back legend be traced perhaps to Bernhard's work as a court reporter? A passage in his early prose, where a waitress defends herself quite suddenly and unexpectedly against an importunate lover (1989a: 92), suggests this may be the case. While the revenge of the woman remains in the man's fantasy or dream (apart from this last example), his revenge has harsh consequences for the woman: he defends himself by murder (*Das Kalkwerk*), walling up (*Ja*) or disappearance (*Holzfällen*). The man's love proceeds from his taking possession of the woman to the point of her physical destruction (*Korrektur*). One must not, however, overlook the fact that the men who act in such ways do so in utter desperation, a point Endres disregards. The male philosophers and scientists are shown to be imprisoned by their intellectual aims which they never achieve. Unable to cope with this insight either, they abuse their wives like Konrad in *Korrektur*. Yet despite the absence of critical comments by the narrator Konrad comes over as the weaker part of the relationship, making a total fool of himself by nearly drowning in the cesspool after killing his wife. Narrators of later novels frequently question the validity of their perception as shown in *Der Untergeher*:

> Wie immer, übertrieb ich auch jetzt[,] und es war mir vor mir selbst peinlich, Wertheimer aufeinmal als den Quälgeist und den Zerstörer seiner Schwester bezeichnet zu haben, so, dachte ich, gehe ich immer gegen andere vor, ungerecht, ja verbrecherisch (1986b: 215).

Bernhard's men thus *are* shown or even admit to be weak; they do not have to be unmasked.

In conclusion, then, women play a more diverse role in Bernhard's prose works than Ria Endres suggests. Far from being absent they are—especially in the later ones—given distinct personalities. Where the relationship between a man and a woman is described as one of patriarchal oppression, it hardly ever has the unequivocal approval of the narrator. In the earlier novels the oppressors' deaths are shown as the immediate result of that of their victims (*Das Kalkwerk, Korrektur*). In the later ones like *Ja*, which Endres characteristically overlooks, (though she does cite other texts published in 1978), and *Holzfällen*, which she admittedly could not have known, the narrators have become increasingly self-critical.

A purely psychoanalytical approach, like Klaus Theweleit applied in his *Buch der Könige* to interpret the work of certain male writers as the exploitation of their girlfriends and wives, does not do justice to the problem. Bernhard does not use women as Theweleit has, for example, shown to be the case with Franz Kafka (Theweleit 1988: 974-1046). When the narrator in *Holzfällen* boasts of having left Jeannie Billroth at the right moment, he finishes his reflections and the account of the 'künstlerische Abendessen' (around which the book revolves) on a note which relativizes all his earlier attacks. The narrator reflects,

> daß ich Wien hasse und daß es doch rührend ist, daß ich diese Menschen verfluche und doch lieben muß und daß ich dieses Wien hasse und doch lieben muß[,] und ich dachte, während ich schon durch die Innere Stadt lief, daß diese Stadt doch meine Stadt ist und immer meine Stadt sein wird und daß diese Menschen meine Menschen sind und immer meine Menschen sein werden (pp. 329-30).

Bernhard repeatedly stresses the 'Künstlichkeit' of all his literary works. This artificiality manifests itself in a highly manneristic style. Especially his earlier novels are sophisticated perspectivized constructions. In *Das Kalkwerk* the first-person narrator, a life-insurance agent, reports what the two witnesses Fro and Wieser told him about Konrad. In their turn they report the conversations they had over the years with Konrad and with each other. Rather like a court hearing (the influence of Bernhard's experience as a court reporter is evident) the novel thus offers the opinion and evidence given by several witnesses. Konrad's treatment of his wife is neither confirmed by the narrator nor commented on. The whole text is written in reported speech, leaving the final judgment to the reader. It is characteristic of Endres's approach that she does not seem to attach great importance to this telling feature of Bernhard's style. She dismisses it in a mere seven lines, ending with the following remark: 'Viele Maschinenbeine als Zitatenstränge. Ein monströser männlicher Körper' (Endres 1980: 28).

In the novels starting with *Ja*, Bernhard relinquishes this perspectivistic narrative technique for a first-person narrator who reports and reflects in a quasi-autobiographical manner about his own experience. It is in these texts that the narrators become increasingly self-critical with respect to the point of view from which they report. Like the perspectivistic narrative technique of the earlier texts, this self-criticism is rooted in the author's/narrators' awareness of the problem of perception and of relating it to a third person. It is generally accepted that Bernhard's linguistic scepticism has been influenced by the philosophy of Ludwig Wittgenstein. All Bernhard's works must be considered in relation to this fundamental distrust of the narrator's ability to express experience reliably. Endres fails to recognize this phenomenon of 'Sprachskepsis' which has affected Austrian writers at least since Hofmannsthal's 'Brief des Lord Chandos'. Instead, what she detects in Bernhard's language is, quite unhistorically but predictably, a cover-up of male impotence. It has become clear that Endres's preoccupation with Bernhard's male chauvinism has left her blind to all other features of his work, features which could have helped put this chauvinism into perspective. Paradoxical statements echoing Derrida, such as 'Die Sprache schweigt sich mächtig aus' (Endres 1980: 29), or 'Masturbation und Inzest sind in ihrer Anwesenheit immer abwesend' (p. 82), make her damning conclusions even more questionable.

WORKS CITED

Bachmann, I.
   1978   *Werke. IV. Reden, vermischte Schriften*. Ed. C. Koschel, I. Weidenbaum and C. Münster. Munich: Piper.
Bernhard, T.
   1972   *Frost*. Frankfurt: Suhrkamp (1963).
   1973   *Das Kalkwerk: Roman*. Frankfurt: Suhrkamp (1970).
   1977   *Gehen*. Frankfurt: Suhrkamp (1971).
   1979a   'An der Baumgrenze' (1969), in *Erzählungen*. Franfurt: Suhrkamp. pp. 102-11.
   1979b   *Ja*. Frankfurt: Suhrkamp (1978).
   1982   *Ein Kind*. Salzburg: Residenz.
   1984a   *Der Atem: Eine Entscheidung*. Munich: dtv (1978).
   1984b   *Holzfällen: Eine Erregung*. Frankfurt: Suhrkamp.
   1984c   *Korrektur: Roman*. Frankfurt: Suhrkamp. (1975).
   1985a   *Alte Meister: Komödie*. Frankfurt: Suhrkamp.
   1985b   *Die Kälte: Eine Isolation*. München: dtv (1981).
   1985c   *Wittgensteins Neffe: Eine Freundschaft*. Frankfurt: Suhrkamp (1982).
   1986a   *Auslöschung: Ein Zerfall*. Frankfurt: Suhrkamp.
   1986b   *Der Untergeher: Roman*. Frankfurt: Suhrkamp (1983).
   1989a   *In der Höhe: Rettungsversuch, Unsinn*. Salzburg: Residenz.
   1989b   *Der Italiener*. Frankfurt: Suhrkamp (1971).
Botond, A., (ed.)
   1970   *Über Thomas Bernhard*. Frankfurt: Suhrkamp.
Dittmar, J., (ed.)
   1990   *Thomas Bernhard Werkgeschichte*. Rev. edn. Frankfurt: Suhrkamp.

Endres, R.
1980   *Am Ende angekommen: Dargestellt am wahnhaften Dunkel der Männerportraits des Thomas Bernhard.* Frankfurt: Fischer.

Fleischmann, K., and W. Koch
1981   'Monologe auf Mallorca, Thomas Bernhard—eine Herausforderung'. *ORF-Nachlese* 4, pp. 2-8

Fueß, R.
1981   ' "Wo hab ich jemals einen Kontakt wollen?" (Thomas Bernhard) Vom Mythos des "Einsamen in der Bergwelt" und seinem Ausverkauf', in *Literaturmagazin*. XIV. *Die Literatur blüht im Tal. Gespräche—Essays—Neue Prosa und Lyrik.* Reinbek: Rowohlt, pp. 78-92.

Hofmann, K.
1988   *Aus Gesprächen mit Thomas Bernhard.* Vienna: Löcker.

Lüdke, M.
1980   'Thomas Bernhard und die Metropolenfrau. Ria Endres "Am Ende angekommen" und Bernhards "Erzählungen" '. *Frankfurter Rundschau*, 23 August.

Mittermayer, M.
1988   *Ich werden: Versuch einer Thomas-Bernard-Lektüre.* Stuttgart: Heinz.

Reich-Ranicki, M.
1990   *Thomas Bernhard: Aufsätze und Reden.* Zürich: Ammann.

Reiter, A.
1990   'Thomas Bernhard's "Musical Prose" ', in A. Williams, S. Parkes and R. Smith (eds.), *Literature on the Threshold: The German Novel in the 1980s.* New York: Berg, pp. 187-207.

Schmidt-Dengler, W.
1986   *Der Übertreibungskünstler: Zu Thomas Bernhard.* Vienna: Sonderzahl.

Theweleit, K.
1977   *Männerphantasien. I. Frauen, Fluten, Körper, Geschichte.* Frankfurt: Roter Stern.

1988   *Buch der Könige. I. Orpheus und Euridike.* Basel: Stroemfeld/Roter Stern.

Weinzierl, U.
1990   'Bernhard als Erzieher. Thomas Bernhards *Auslöschung*'. *The German Quarterly* 63, 3/4, pp. 455-61.

'Dieses verfluchte Land':
Felix Mitterer's Austria, Past and Present

Thomas E. Bourke

It might be ill-considered to proffer an extrapolation of a sharp and clear picture of Austria from Felix Mitterer's works, because he addresses himself to specific problems rather than attempting a literary stock-taking of the 'state of the nation', and focuses his attention more on rural rather than urban life and more on his native Tyrol than on Austria as a whole. Nevertheless, when one traces the author's concerns and preoccupations in his work, the configuration that begins to emerge is a distinctly bleak one.

Mitterer's subject matter stretches back in history to the year 1678. The play *Die Kinder des Teufels* dramatizes the 'Zauberer-Jackl' trials held in the archdiocese of Salzburg between 1675 and 1690, as a result of which some 200 people from the Alpine regions, one-third of whom were under 15 years of age, were tortured and executed. But although the trials constituted one of the last great outbreaks of systematic witch-hunting in Central Europe, the play is less about the end of the Middle Ages than the beginning of modern times, and thus bears relevance to the patterns of the persecution of minorities and marginalization of outsider figures that crop up continuously in Mitterer's works about the more recent past as well as the present.

The inquisition of the so-called malefactors, though proceeding from the basis of mediaeval demonology, had become secularized at the stage of history in which the play is set. Although the witchcraft commissioner Dr Sebastian Zillner uses the language of the Church, it is no longer primarily ecclesiastical interests that he serves but rather those of the new bureaucratic state in the early Absolutist epoch in its efforts to register all its subjects and keep them under surveillance (cf. Schindler 1987). The commissioner makes constant use of the infinitive imperative so beloved of German and Austrian officialdom to this day: 'Fremde Bettler fortschaffen, die inländischen mit Abzeichen versehen!' (Mitterer 1987b: 30). He manifests that ecstatic relationship to systematization shared by so many latter-day functionaries: 'Wir haben die absolute Politik, die absolute Wissenschaft, die absolute Theologie! Die Verwaltungsgeschichte ist das oberste Prinzip der Ordnung!' (p. 109). We see through his attempt to rationalize the motive of wiping out the growing population of vagrants as a holy campaign against the works and pomps of the Devil (p. 94). He even betrays himself verbally by referring to the beggar children as 'der ganze christliche Auswurf unseres Landes' (p. 80) or mentioning in passing the option of extermination: 'Entweder wir rotten sie aus, oder wir schaffen Arbeitshäuser!' (p. 32).

From this to the Austria of the Final Solution is a long but straight road. Dr Zillner and his scribe Gregori Finsterwalder, who in the course of the play almost disappears behind growing stacks of files, are the prototypes of the modern 'Schreibtischtäter'. As the accused Dionysus Feldner says, 'Sie schreiben und schreiben—und schreiben uns zu Tod!' (p. 28). The historian Wolfgang Behringer has written on this continuum between the witch-hunts of old and those of our century:

> Bei den Verfolgungsbefürwortern finden wir regelmäßig die Denkfigur der 'Vernichtung des Ungeziefers', der 'Ausrottung des Unkrauts mit Stumpf und Stiel'... Viele dieser Denkfiguren finden wir bei den extremen Konservativen des 18. und 20. Jahrhunderts unverändert wieder, nur daß die Feindbilder von Zeit zu Zeit modernisiert werden: Freimaurer, Illuminaten, Jakobiner, Kommunisten, Sozialdemokraten, Juden, Zigeuner, Ausländer, Gammler, Terroristen etc. (Behringer 1988: 326).

It is precisely this legacy that Mitterer exposes in his writings. The brandmark for vagrants ordered by the witchcraft commissioner would in time become the Star of David for Stefan Adler in *Kein schöner Land*. In his historical plots Mitterer touches upon the deep-rootedness of anti-Semitism in former centuries. The beggar children of *Die Kinder des Teufels*, in their attempt to blaspheme, abuse the one social group that stands in lower social esteem than themselves when they call the crucified Christ 'du schiacher Jud' (p. 62). In *Stigma*, which is set in the early nineteenth century, even the demon Saggera Taggera, which first possesses the stigmatized Moid and then the would-be exorcist Monsignore, is itself anti-Semitic, reacting to the sight of the crucifix with the words 'Den Juden weg!' and 'der narrete Jud' (pp. 70, 75). Walter Methlagl has referred to this as an elemental hate projection 'nahe am Ursprung von Feindbild-Projektionen, deren fast mechanisches Zustandekommen den Sprachgebrauch zwischen Menschen und Völkern heute gefährlich vereinseitigt' (Methlagl 1983: 112).

In the play *Kein schöner Land*, set in a Tyrolean village, these forces erupt in the conducive climate of Austrofascism and Nazism. The plot is based loosely on an actual case, that of Rudolf Gomperz, who had been such a prominent and tireless promoter of skiing in and around St Anton that he was named affectionately in an annual report of the Skiing Club of Arlberg in 1930–31 as 'Vater Gomperz' (cf. Thöni 1987: 104). After the Anschluss, however, the web of persecution closed in on him relentlessly, mainly due to the remorseless snooping of one National Socialist neighbour, Frau Grete Feldmeier. He was removed in 1938 from his job as manager of the local tourism office, in 1941 ordered to wear the Star of David, in January 1942 forced to travel to Vienna and transported in May to the concentration camp at Minsk where he was eventually shot. Mitterer made his theme the absurd fact that 'ein bisher beliebter, geachteter und verdienter Bürger plötzlich zum Schurken und Volksschädling gestempelt und zuletzt ermordet wird, weil sich herausstellt, daß er Jude ist' (1987a: 91).

Tyrol, with its 0.1% Jewish population, had had much practice in an 'anti-Semitism without Jews' (Köfler 1987: 121). The Antisemitenbund, which had a strong backing there, anticipated as early as its programme of 1919 many of the Nuremberg Racial Laws of 1935–38 (Köfler 1987: 124). The Alpenverein had had an 'Aryan Clause' forbidding Jewish membership from the turn of the century (Köfler 1987: 125-26). The scale of anti-Semitic activity in Tyrol led in 1938 to an approving mention in *Der Stürmer*:

Sämtliche Judengeschäfte—ohne Ausnahme—sind als jüdisch gekennzeichnet. In jedem Schaufenster prankt groß ein gelbes Schild.

Jüdisches Geschäft

Der Besucher staunt. Das haben die Tiroler schon in den wenigen Wochen durchgeführt! Und wir im Altreich, wir sind heute noch nicht so weit! (Mitterer 1987a: 144)

In the play the cattle trader Stefan Adler, whose two sons are in the Hitler Youth, is a respected and popular member of the Catholic parish until his revelation that he is a Jew. His main adversary is the Nazi schoolmaster Hopfgartner, the classic example of what Theodor Adorno and colleagues delineated in *The Authoritarian Personality* (1950). But with regard to Mitterer's portrayal of Austria and the Austrians, the character of the village mayor and pub-owner Rudolf Holzknecht is far more damning. Living according to the motto 'Schlau muß ma sein, Bua, wenn ma in schweren Zeiten überleben will!' (1987a: 20), he represents the staying power of parish pump pragmatism, contriving by wheeling and dealing to remain mayor from the clerical triumphalism of Dollfuß's *Ständestaat* and Austrofascism through the clinical savagery of the Nazi period to the postwar reconstruction of the Second Republic.

Kein schöner Land ends with harrowing scenes in which Hopfgartner's mentally handicapped son Toni, strapped to an operating table, is injected with poison (accompanying documentation demonstrates that the euthanasia programme was carried out with chilling efficiency by the Gauamt für Volksgesundheit in Tyrol-Vorarlberg in the years 1942–45), and Stefan Adler, now an inmate of a concentration camp, encounters his own son Hans, an SS officer. To spare his father what is awaiting him, Hans shoots him and then himself. The curtain falls; the audience is to be given the impression that the play is over. The mayor appears through the curtains in Tyrolean costume and with the colours of the Second Republic on his armband, waves down the applause, and makes a speech which, in evincing the art of expedient forgetfulness, has implications far beyond the boundaries of Tyrol, as proven by an amnesiac President some time after Mitterer published the text:

Mitbürger, Freunde, Österreicher! Dank des Vertrauens, das unsere amerikanischen Freunde mir entgegenbringen, bin ich nun wieder euer Bürgermeister! Dieses Vertrauen besteht nicht ohne Grund, wie ich meine! Ihr wißt es selbst, daß ich vielen geholfen habe, in dieser schweren Zeit! Vielen! Ohne Unterschied von Stand und Anschauung, stets um Einigung und Ausgleich bemüht!—Freunde, wir haben alle Furchtbares hinter uns! Viele unserer Söhne—auch mein Sohn!—, viele unserer Väter sind gefallen für eine Idee, an die sie geglaubt haben, mit jeder Faser ihres Herzens! Darum laßt uns ehren diejenigen, die ihre soldatische Pflicht erfüllt haben—in den Tundren des Nordens, in den Schneefeldern Rußlands, im heißen Wüstensand Afrikas! Mag da auch manches passiert sein, was jetzt von manchen breitgetreten und maßlos übertrieben wird—der Krieg, liebe Mitbürger, ist nun einmal kein Honigschlecken! Keinen soll ein Vorwurf treffen! Keinen unserer tapferen Landser, keinen von denen, die in der Heimat in Not und Hunger die Wirtschaftsschlacht schlugen oder in der Verwaltung Ordnung und Gesetz zu vertreten hatten! Denn keiner, keiner von uns wußte, daß wir von einem Wahnsinnigen angeführt wurden! Alle, alle wurden wir mißbraucht: ausgenützt hat man unseren Idealismus, unseren Glauben, unsere Treue!—Liebe Mitbürger, ich weiß, es gab in dieser schweren Zeit Haß und Streit und Mißgunst in unserem Dorf! Vergessen wir das jetzt, ich appelliere an euch! Streichen wir durch diese Zeit, löschen wir sie aus in unserem Herzen und in unserem Gedächtnis! Vergessen wir Hader und Zwist und kleinliche Rache! Denn nun, Freunde, geht es an den Wiederaufbau; und nur mit vereinten Kräften werden wir diesen Wiederaufbau schaffen!—Darum bitte ich euch: Halten wir alle zusammen, laßt uns gemeinsam, mit neuem Mut, mit neuer Kraft, mit neuem Schaffensdrang das neue, zukünftige Österreich aufbauen! (pp. 85-86)

Mitterer chose as prescript for his play George Santayana's famous dictum that those who forget the past are condemned to relive it. The past *is* relived in the New Austria as depicted in Mitterer's writings. *Kein Platz für Idioten* is based on an actual incident in 1974 in which a mother and her handicapped child were barred from a Tyrolean inn in case the sight of the child drove away tourists. In the play, the fascistically inclined mentality described by Adorno features once more—and not for the last time—in the shape of a guest who is instrumental in having the old man Plattl-Hons and the mentally retarded boy Wastl barred from the local pub.

But notwithstanding historical continuities in behaviour patterns, the ideology of the Master Race has been replaced by that of Economic Growth. The figure of the mayor is correspondingly altered: he is now what is known in rural Ireland as a gombeen man—the village go-getter who would 'sell his grandmother' to enrich himself and extend his power. He represents the spirit of entrepreneurship, economic expansionism and monopolization in the microstructure: he is building a ski-lift, a skiing instruction centre, a bowling alley and a discotheque 'mit bunte Liachta und Negermusik und so' (1979: 35). He personifies a problematic to which Mitterer will return again and again in his writings: tourism, an industry that currently comprises over half of the world's gross national product, and is probably one of the most alienating of all means of profit-spinning in that it turns not only people but entire cultures into consumer goods. It dictates that ruralism should be reduced to rusticity, cultural diversity to pastiche. Experiences have to be cosmetically packaged to be marketable: the German tourist's wife is disappointed because the village has no Tyrolean evening to offer. People are reified to ethnic motifs. The German guest says of Plattl-Hons, 'Schaut ja auch ziemlich pittoresk aus. Gefällt mir gut. Ein Gesicht hat der wie aus einem Wurzelstock geschnitzt!' (1979: 27), whereupon his wife expresses the wish to buy such a carving to hang in their living room. While the human is barred from the pub, the piece of kitsch replacing him is sought after. For the German guest even the mentally backward Wastl belongs among the props of the Alpine world: 'Vor dem brauchst du keine Angst zu haben! Scheint der Dorftrottel zu sein' (p. 27). The use of the definite article '*der* Dorftrottel' connotes the clichéed expectation of one idiot per village.

The village mayor promotes this commodification of all and sundry to his own ends. He will soon see to it that the tourists' voyeuristic desires are sated in his expanded leisure centre: 'Und herobn wer i donn Heimatobende veronstoltn. Mit Schuach-plattla und so, wißt's eh!' (p. 35). In his headlong commercial-ization drive he is destroying exactly that which tourism is supposed to make purchasable: the country life. In the name of progress two mountain farmholders have been pushed off their land by compulsory expropriation to make way for the ski lift. 'Dia lebn do obn am Berg, hobn koa Ohnung vom Tutn und Blosn und sein um fünfazwanzg Johr hintn! Die hobn total die neue Zeit verschlofn!' (p. 34).

The short prose piece *An den Rand des Dorfes* describes how the eccentric road-sweeper Matthias is gradually marginalized due to the deterioration of the informal social network typical of some small communities and its replacement by the same hard-nosed business instinct that causes all interactions to become transactions:

> Die Bewohner des Dorfes hatten keine Zeit mehr. Sie mußten Pensionen bauen und Betten machen und Souvenirs verkaufen und die Gäste vom Bahnhof abholen... Die jungen Burschen sind Schilehrer geworden und müssen sich am Abend den Gästen widmen. Sie schlüpfen in Lederhosen und lernen Tänze, die man den fremden Gästen gegenüber als Volkstänze ausgibt (1981: 65).

Matthias, like Plattl-Hons, is barred from his local because he could soil the newly laid floor or freshly cushioned chairs. Ultimately, he is removed, both literally and metaphorically, to the edge of the village community.

The monologue *Der Umbau* develops a similar theme: the conversion of a farmhouse into a road house with streamlined *Lüftlmalerei* ('Bleamln... und Schnörkl und lauta so Glump', 1981: 85), car park, neon signs with the words GRILL, DANCING, COCA-COLA and DORTMUNDER AKTIEN BIER. The old farmer, who is edged out of both the *Stube* and the kitchen because of step-by-step renovation, appears after his death on a tourist brochure in a four-colour photo, caught unawares in front of the new establishment. In the short play *Weizen auf der Autobahn*, in which the farmhouse is now 'Hotel Alpenblick' and, to compound matters, a motorway is built through its fields, the farmer ends up in the psychiatric clinic due to his spreading manure and sowing wheat on the tarmac. An adapted version of the play was staged in September 1989 in the village of Schönberg up against the sound protection wall of the

Brenner motorway. Mitterer commented in his diary on the difficulties arising from the production:

> Es spielt nun dort, wo es spielt. Der alte Bauer bricht aus der Anstalt aus, setzt sich auf die Bank vor der Autobahn, auf die Bank, die er selbst gezimmert hat, zwischen zwei Birken, die er selbst vor Jahren pflanzte. Seine Tochter findet ihn, will ihn überreden, freiwillig in die Anstalt zurückzukehren. Das Stück hat Aufsehen erregt. Dafür und dawider. Viele Schönberger haben von der Autobahn profitiert, viele leiden darunter. Am Schluß rollt ein Bagger auf den Bauern zu, hebt drohend die Schaufel. Bei der nächsten Vorstellung wird der Bagger nicht mehr dabeisein. Der Fahrer und zugleich Besitzer bangt um seine Aufträge (1990: 55).

Mitterer has been criticized for what has been seen as the questionable ideology of his plays, his revolt against technology and propagation of a cosy humanitarianism (Kruntorad 1980: 38). It is true that Mitterer reappraises rural traditions that are passing out of existence, such as that of the extended family, and sets them against modern trends, like that of the nuclear family, to find the latter wanting. One of his most recurrent themes is the problem of old people's homes, which he treats on the basis of documentary evidence provided by Magdalene Stöcker of *Pro Senectute Austria* (Mitterer 1989: 6). But it is an integral part of his overall critique of an increasingly achievement-oriented society that shelves the economically redundant. In its more acute manifestations he even implies connections with the eugenics of the Hitler period, a parallel none too far-fetched since the Lainz scandal of 1989. The old man in *Sibirien* talks of his old people's home in metaphors of planned if gradual extermination: 'Gnadenschuß', 'Deportation', 'Spritzen', 'Euthanasie', 'Altenvernichtung', 'Insassen', 'Lager', 'Wachpersonal', 'Gefangenschaft'. The day-to-day happenings conjure up images of the Holocaust:

> Heute zwei innerhalb von einer Stunde!
> Die Burschen von der Bestattung
> gut gelaunt mit dem Blechsarg herein,
> beide nackt aufeinander hineingeschmissen,
> schwer sind sie ja nicht,
> diese ausgemergelten Männchen,

und noch einmal gehen zu einem zweiten Sarg,
das ist zu lästig,
und wieder ab durch die Mitte!
Das ist eine Totenfabrik,
Frau Schwiegertochter,
Eine Totenfabrik! (p. 63)

In *Sibirien* the figure of the political 'Wendehals' reappears, if on a much higher plane than in *Kein schöner Land*. At the première of *Sibirien* in August 1989 in Telfs, the irony of the old man addressing (whether in his imagination or not) the President of Austria with the following words will not have escaped the audience:

Sie müssen wissen,
man überlebt hier nur durch Bestechung.
Sie mußten nicht
die Lagerwache bestechen, oder?
Hatten Sie Schwierigkeiten
mit der Lagerwache?
Hat man versucht,
auf Sie zu schießen?
Das will ich nicht annehmen.
Man schießt nicht auf einen Bundespräsidenten.
Schon gar nicht auf seine reizende Gattin.
Ich nehme an,
Sie haben Ihre diplomatischen Beziehungen
spielen lassen.
Diplomatie ist alles.
Man überlebt nur durch Diplomatie.
Durch Diplomatie und Bestechung.
Ihnen brauche ich das ja nicht zu sagen,
Sie wissen das besser als ich (p. 66).

Mitterer could be perceived at times to take sides in his writings with the old and fusty against the young and dynamic and to lament the erosion of traditionalist values and regional peculiarities by a pan-European cultural homogenization. Typically, the elderly Willi in the play *Munde* is the only one who drinks 'Obstler' while his younger workmates Gerhard, Tommi and Petra drink Johnny Walker, Bacardi Rum and Cinzano. Clothing styles too serve to signal the socially 'in' or 'out'. On their outing to the top of the 'Hohe Munde' Gerhard wears blue jeans and a new, garishly coloured rucksack, Petra wears trainers, thin, narrow trousers, handbag with make-up mirror and lipstick, and only Willi the traditional green knee-socks, knee breeches and an old-fashioned green rucksack. Willi thinks of the TV mast on the summit, the playing of pop music on a cassette recorder or the burning of rubber tyres in the midst of the Alpine peaks as a desecration, while Petra, the fan of cable TV and chairlifts, can hardly do without her aural and optical stimulants and is utterly blind to the natural splendour about her: 'Nit amal a Musig habts mit! Hat koaner a Gitarre mit!' (1990: 22).

However, it would surely be a misreading of Mitterer's text to infer from this a rejection of contemporary modes of behaviour per se in favour of more traditional modes. Although Mitterer does not subscribe to the notion that technological and economic 'progress' of the purely quantitative kind is necessarily beneficial, his *œuvre* as a whole manifests as much dissatisfaction with inherited patterns as it does with modern trends. *Kein Platz für Idioten*, for instance, can be interpreted, among other things, as an arraignment of traditionalist, authoritarian child-rearing and of the utilitarian thinking typical of small-farmer milieus. Mitterer's criticism is directed at *all* inhumane forms of social relations, past or present.

In *Munde* the case is made that labour relations have not necessarily improved in recent years but might even have become more alienated. Willi represents an outmoded work ethic as the master roofer who takes an aesthetic pleasure in good craftsmanship, while the up-and-coming Gerhard exemplifies the new socialization type of the eighties in his aggressive drive for self-assertion. Willi's comparison of the new owner of the company with his father before him amounts to an authorial comment on the times: while the older man had worked shoulder to shoulder with his apprentices, the yuppie son obeys only the commandment of profit maximization, drives around in his Mercedes complete with car telephone, secures contracts by bribes, lives in a copper-roofed villa and uses the growing unemployment figures as a bogey to depress wages. He plans to discard his former master roofer Willi: 'Der Chef moant nämlich, daß es vorbei is mit dir. Du bist schon zu langsam. Und manchmal packt di der Schwindel. Und der Schweiß bricht dir aus. Nit?' (1990: 34).

Whether deservedly or not, Mitterer's works convey an image of a New Austria in which Social Darwinism is alive and kicking. The protagonists of *Besuchszeit* have all been thrown on the rubbish heap of human obsolescence: in the old people's home, the women's prison, the psychiatric clinic and the cancer ward. The woman in *Man versteht nichts* is never told by the senior consultant that she is terminally ill or what she is dying from. Her aging husband is threatened with redundancy after 23 years with his firm, although the company has a favourable order situation, because his labour is to be replaced by new machines. (The fact that the owner is a German who flies in by helicopter and practices massive tax evasion is Mitterer's comment on economic imperialism.) And yet the elderly couple agree at the end of Scene 3 that former times were much harder. But immediately afterwards we encounter the husband reading the following letter with its managerial euphemisms for sacking:

> Die Konjunkturschwankungen der letzten Zeit zwingen uns leider zu einer längst fälligen Rationalisierung und zum stufen-weisen Abbau der Arbeitskräfteüberkapazität. Wir danken Ihnen für Ihre langjährige, treue Mitarbeit (1985: 66).

Seen in this context, the metaphor of coldness that recurs frequently in other works assumes the nature of an indictment of the culture at large. The pyromaniac in the radio sketch *Der Feuerteufel*, who has had a desolate family history and is now a social outcast, gives as his reason to the police for burning down hay sheds that he felt the cold too much (1981: 69). The warmth that Christine craves in the short narrative *Christines Schoß* is that which is lacking in the world around her (pp. 115-22). And coldness becomes the central leitmotif of *Sibirien*. The old man says of the regime in the old people's home:

> Gleichgültigkeit.
> Das schlimmste aller Gefühle.
> Nein, kein Gefühl.
> Der absolute Mangel an Gefühl.
> Gefühlskälte.
> Tausendmal kälter
> als die klirrende Kälte Sibiriens. (p. 39)

The pervading cold of Siberia and that of the old people's home begin to merge in his mind into one ubiquitous iciness that even freezes the words on their way from person to person (p. 67). It seems to take on the significance of a generic metaphor for Austria, old and new.

The Jewish cattle dealer Stefan Adler says of Tyrol, 'Des is a schönes Land! I kenn koa schöner's!' (1987a: 72), unwittingly echoing the popular folksong 'Kein schöner Land in dieser Zeit/Als hier das unsere weit und breit'. But despite his heartfelt love of his country he ends his life in the concentration camp. As in all of Mitterer's works, the potentials of beauty and warmth yet again fall tragically short of realization. And the fear that George Santayana's dictum has come true is once more reinforced by the 'Gastarbeiter' Memet in *Munde* when he exclaims in Turkish after realizing that Willi has been driven to suicide: 'Warum bin ich nicht zu Hause geblieben? Warum mußte ich in dieses verfluchte Land kommen? Keine Liebe! Keine Liebe!' (p. 40).

WORKS CITED

Adorno, T., *et al.*
    1950   *The Authoritarian Personality*. New York: Harper.
Behringer, W., (ed.)
    1988   *Hexen und Hexenprozesse in Deutschland*. Munich: dtv.
Köfler, G.
    1987   'Die Juden in Tirol', in Mitterer 1987a: 119-35.
Kruntorad, P.
    1980   'Österreichische Beerenauslese, Most und Heuriger beim "Steirischen Herbst 1980"'. *Theater heute* 21, 12, p. 38.
Methlagl, W.
    1983   'Fragment über *Stigma*', in Mitterer 1983: 104-13.
Mitterer, F.
    1979   *Kein Platz für Idioten: Volksstück in drei Akten*. Munich: Friedl Brehm.
    1981   *An den Rand des Dorfes: Erzählungen—Hörspiele*. Vienna: Jugend und Volk.
    1983   *Stigma: Eine Passion*. Feldafing: Friedl Brehm.
    1985   *Besuchszeit: Vier Einakter*. Munich: Friedl Brehm.
    1987a   *Kein schöner Land: Ein Theaterstück und sein historischer Hintergrund*. Innsbruck: Haymon.
    1987b   *Die Kinder des Teufels: Ein Theaterstück und sein historischer Hintergrund*. Innsbruck: Haymon.

1989   *Sibirien: Ein Monolog*. Innsbruck: Haymon.
1990   *Munde: Das Stück auf dem Gipfel*. Innsbruck: Haymon.
Schindler, N.
1987   'Die Entstehung der Unbarmherzigkeit. Zur Kultur und Lebensweise der Salzburger Bettler am Ende des 17. Jahrhunderts', in Mitterer 1987b: 93-117.
Thöni, H.
1987   'Der Anlaß zum Stück. Das Schicksal des Rudolf Gomperz', in Mitterer 1987a: 93-118.

Ghosts, Fairies and Magicians:
Elements of the Old-Viennese Popular Comedy in Contemporary *Volksstücke*

Herbert Herzmann

Critics tend to distinguish between two types of *Volksstücke*. According to Hugo Aust, Peter Haida and Jürgen Hein, there is, on the one hand, the 'phantastische Volksstückstrang' (Aust *et al.* 1989: 290), to which belong the Old Viennese Popular Comedies with their magical apparatus. On the other hand there is a type of *Volksstück* which is more concerned with social issues and which uses realistic devices (Aust *et al.* 1989: 340-41). The realistic type has supposedly become the dominant one since the middle of the nineteenth century (Aust *et al.* 1989: 290). However, the dividing line between these two subgroups of the genre is blurred. Some of the contemporary playwrights whom Aust, Haida and Hein regard as representatives of the socially critical and realistic type—for example, Franz Xaver Kroetz, Gustav Ernst, Heinz R. Unger and Felix Mitterer—make frequent use of fantastic elements traditionally associated with the Old Viennese *Zaubermärchen* of the eighteenth and early nineteenth centuries.

In those old Viennese plays the world appeared as divided into two spheres. The higher sphere was inhabited by supernatural beings while in the lower sphere dwelt ordinary people with their everyday problems. Contact between the two spheres usually resulted from the fact that an inhabitant of the higher sphere needed the help of a human being. In order to secure this help a spirit might interfere in the life of a human thus giving him or her the opportunity to improve him- or herself. In Mozart's and Schikaneder's *Die Zauberflöte* for example the Queen of the Night enlists the help of a human prince to free her daughter, Pamina, from a magician who has taken her away. The prince is promised Pamina's hand as reward. What may strike today's reader or theatre-goer as strange is the familiarity with which spirits and humans deal with each other in these plays. The dualism between high and low seems to be softened by common interests as well as by similarities in language and behaviour—the spirits behave and speak like humans, very often in Viennese dialect.

Johann Nestroy started a new trend in the history of the Viennese Popular Comedy which—as I intend to show—still has its effects on the contemporary scene. In Nestroy's plays, like in those of his predecessors, something 'miraculous' happens in people's lives. However, whereas in Ferdinand Raimund's *Der Bauer als Millionär*—to name but one example—inhabitants of the higher sphere actually enter the humble hut of the peasant Fortunatus Wurzel, the 'miraculous' in Nestroy's plays has no supernatural causes and thus on closer scrutiny loses the aura of the miraculous. A wig, for example, is a man-made object. In Nestroy's *Der Talisman*, however, it literally works miracles which can easily compete with those worked by a genuine magical object such as the magic flute in Mozart's opera. A talisman originally was a magical object which had the power to keep evil at bay and to bring luck to the bearer. With the help of such an object man could get into contact with the higher sphere to which it belonged. Modern man no longer seriously believes in miracles and magical objects, yet he is prepared to treat a talisman as if it had such magical powers. Superstition fills a gap which opens when, on the one hand, religious convictions have lost their power and, on the other hand, the new rational explanations which only allow for natural causes do not satisfy the psychological needs of supposedly 'enlightened' man.

In spite of the disenchantment and/or parody of magical objects there are events in Nestroy's plays the causes of which cannot be determined. Certainly, the wig is the clearly determined cause of many of the 'miraculous' events in *Der Talisman*, but the fact that Titus happens to be present at the right moment to save the life of the hairdresser who then gives him the wig as a token of gratitude, is pure chance (*Zufall*). Chance, however, is, like fate (*Schicksal*), beyond the scope of human planning. Yet, while chance has no identifiable cause, fate is seen as being sent by some higher power. The German word *Schicksal* which derives from *schicken* ('to send') retains this notion. The original title of Nestroy's play, *Die Schicksalsperücken* (see Basil 1967: 100) seems to point towards the involvement of higher powers in Titus's life, although the irony cannot be overlooked. One might sum up the relationship between fate and chance as follows: to people who do not believe in higher powers, inexplicable events appear as chance and thus as natural. The inclination, on the other hand, of many people to presume the involvement of higher powers where it is easy enough to prove human or other natural causes might well be the result of a desire for a supernatural world for which modern thinking has left no place. In secularized times (supernatural) fate becomes chance, and, in a kind of counter movement, chance is turned into fate sent by higher powers in whom nobody seriously believes. Nestroy skilfully plays with modern man's oscillation between secularism and religiosity, and he makes good use of the magical apparatus of the Old Viennese Popular Comedy. When, for instance, Titus, having put on the black wig, enters the garden of the castle, he exclaims: 'Meine Karriere geht an, die Glückspforte öffnet sich' (Nestroy 1968: 258). This clearly recalls the scene in *Die Zauberflöte* when Tamino enters the Temple of Wisdom. The portal of the temple has shrivelled down to a garden gate and has become a turn of phrase. The higher sphere continues to live on petrified in a phrase. The banishment of daemonic forces into language, however, does not render them completely harmless. If one takes the idioms literally, the banished forces may well come to life again. The warning of the hairdresser to Titus—'vergessen Sie ja nicht, daß Ihr Schicksal am Haare hängt' (Nestroy 1968: 283)—is highly appropriate.

The fantastic devices of the old Viennese plays are alive and well in the work of Ödon von Horváth, the acknowledged father of the modern *kritisches Volksstück*. His best known play, *Geschichten aus dem Wienerwald*, is, certainly, a socially critical piece close to the realist/naturalist tradition. Yet, Marianne's father bears the nickname 'Zauberkönig' because he deals in 'Scherzartikeln' and magical toys. His business is going badly because he lives in a disillusioned age where people no longer have any time for what he has to offer. Nevertheless, almost everybody in the play hopes for miracles. Alfred lives in permanent expectation of a big win at the horse races, the Rittmeister is a regular lottery gambler. Are these hopes not a shrivelled remainder of transcendental desires, containing even in their reduced and, perhaps, perverted form something of the attractions of genuine religiosity? At the same time such perverted belief, such trust in false hopes seriously impedes the judgment of the real situation. Marianne really thinks that 'Gott' has sent her Alfred as a saviour (Horváth 1972: 191)!

Horváth's characters see themselves as determined by outside forces. Like the figures of the Old Viennese Comedies they have a dualistic world view: here are we, the ordinary people, and above us higher powers are at work. Yet, these supposedly higher powers turn out on closer inspection to be economic and social circumstances (that is, of human origin). However, these circumstances have become so complex that to Horváth's lower-middle-class characters they appear much less transparent than the spirits and fairies were to Raimund's Biedermeier figures.

In the so-called *kritische Volksstücke* of our time we constantly come across people who treat human events as if they were fate sent by a transcendental power. In the one act play *Man versteht nichts* by the Tyrol playwright Felix Mitterer the man loses his job because the owner of the factory is no longer willing to invest. He tells his wife about it as she lies in hospital:

ER Und der Besitzer will anscheinend nix mehr einistecken...
SIE Aso? Wia hoaßt jetzt der?
ER Gottlieb. Des is a Deutscher, glaub i. Im Betrieb hoaßns ihn den 'Lieben Gott'. Hab i dir doch eh erzählt.
SIE Ahja. Der 'Liebe Gott'. Weil er immer mitn Flieger kommt.
ER Ja, weil er immer mitn Hubschrauber auf'm Betriebs-gelände landet, wenn er nachschaun kommt. So viermal im Jahr taucht er auf. Wie der liebe Gott kommt er vom Himmel. Dann rauscht er durch die Fabrik, hinter ihm zwei Mandln mit Aktentaschen, und nach zwei Stunden verschwindet er wieder in den Wolken.
SIE Wieso will er denn nix mehr einistecken?
ER Des woaß i nit. Ma verstehts nit. (Mitterer 1985: 64)

If that which has been created by humans becomes strange or alien to them, if society, politics, work situation and so on are no longer understood by the individual, then the realm of the familiar becomes seriously diminished. The Bavarian Franz Xaver Kroetz shows in many of his plays how even the intimate sphere is affected by this process of alienation. The third scene of *Mensch Meier* is entitled 'Koitus interruptus'. While having sex with his wife, Martha, Otto remembers his expensive ballpoint pen which he has lent to his boss, who then forgot to give it back to him. Otto did not have the courage to ask his boss for it. The worry about this ballpoint pen which has cost him, he recalls exactly, DM28.70 spoils the intimate encounter with Martha. A longish discussion follows, the result of which is that the loss of the pen has to be accepted as 'Schicksal' (Kroetz 1979: 18).

The extent to which one's own actions can be experienced as something completely dissociated from one's will is shockingly exposed in Felix Mitterer's one act play *Verbrecherin*. A woman is in prison because she has rammed a kitchen knife into her husband's stomach after he had criticized her cooking. When the husband visits her in prison she can only say, 'I woaß es nit, Kurt, warum i des tan hab! I woaß es nit!' (Mitterer 1985: 23). The reader or theatre-goer can clearly see that her action was the result of stress due to the burden of being a housewife, mother and lover. To her, however, the causes remain obscure. The complete separation of will and action are also reflected in the newspaper article which describes in somewhat sensational language what had happened, and which the husband reads out to her: 'Während der Mann sich schwer verletzt in seinem Blut am Boden wälzte, erledigte die Frau seelenruhig ihren Abwasch' (p. 23).

Another example as to how that which comes from within man can affect him like some daemonic force coming from outside is given in Mitterer's short play *Die wilde Frau*. Here Mitterer takes up Alpine legends of *die Saligen* or *die wilden Frauen*, daemonic female beings who interfere in the lives of human beings, usually men (see Mitterer 1986: 68-76). In Mitterer's play five woodcutters take a strange dark-haired and dark-eyed woman, who silently asks for shelter from the snow storm, into their hut. She stays several days without ever speaking one word. It never becomes clear whether she cannot speak or does not want to. In any case, she understands what is being said to her. She carried out the 'feminine' activities (washing, cooking, sewing) and is sexually (ab)used by all the men except by the youngest, Wendl, who worships her with almost religious fervour. The silent presence of the strange woman has disastrous effects. It brings out latent aggressions, power wishes and frustrations. Finally the men kill each other in dramatic fighting scenes. Only Wendl survives. At the end the woman goes away, nobody knows where.

The pattern is reminiscent of that of the Old Viennese *Zaubermärchen*. A spirit (a daemon) makes him/herself available to human beings as a 'dienstbarer Geist' so to speak. However, the pattern has become 'secularized', that is to say it has been transferred into a real material and social context. The 'wilde Frau' is probably a gypsy or, perhaps, an Italian, 'a Walsche' (Mitterer 1986: 12), as one of the woodcutters surmises. Because she never speaks and lets everything happen to her, the men can project anything onto her they wish. From her these projections return to the men as a quasi daemonic force and destroy them.

In his play *Sennentuntschi*, the Swiss writer Hansjörg Schneider makes use of similar Alpine legends, but takes them more literally than Mitterer. Three 'Sennen' in their isolated mountain hut make a female dummy (the 'Tuntschi') which comes to life. It offers sexual gratification to the men but in the end kills one of them and pulls off his skin. In Schneider's play it also becomes clear that the 'Tuntschi' is a projection which assumes a life of its own. Thus the final catastrophe is, in the last analysis, of human origin, even if it appears to be the work of an outside power.

The alienation of modern human beings from their creation and from themselves is dramatized by these southern German (Austrian, Swiss, Bavarian) authors with the help of devices which have their origin in the Old Viennese Popular Comedy and in Alpine folklore. The phantasmagoric projections of repressed anxieties and desires take on a life of their own which makes them resemble the spirits and inhabitants of a magical sphere in the old plays. Of course, the difference must not be overlooked. The spirits in, for example, the plays by Ferdinand Raimund, have a genuine life of their own. By contrast, the phantasmagoric projections only *function* like spirits.

In a somewhat more transparent fashion the old magical apparatus reappears in some of the plays of the Viennese Heinz R. Unger. *Hoch hinaus* is a play about the homecoming of a soldier to Vienna shortly after the end of the Second World War. One of the characters he encounters is a professional magician, Charivari, who can no longer support himself and his wife with his art: 'Als Zauberer hat man's eh schon schwer genug heutzutag'. Nämlich, wenn das Unmögliche erst einmal möglich 'word'n is', war's dann gar nix Besonderes mehr' (Unger 1987: 174).

Charivari is, like the *Zauberkönig* in Horváth's *Geschichten aus dem Wienerwald*, a 'secularized' magician. While in Horváth's play people have too many economic and financial worries to be bothered with what the *Zauberkönig* can offer, the new reality after the Second World War seems to be more fantastic than anything an old-fashioned magician can provide. The new reality seems to better satisfy people's dreams and desires for the miraculous. Charivari says to another character in the play who thinks that people nowadays do not as readily fall for illusions as they used to, 'Aber konträr, lieber Herr, ganz im Gegenteil! Es macht si' heutzutag' ein jeder solchene Illusionen, daß man als Illusionist direkt daneben verblaßt!' (Unger 1987: 174).

Another character tells us more about the nature of the contemporary illusions:

> Heut' muß man handfest denk'n! Was's wiegt, das hat's! Net träumen, kalkulier'n muß man! Schaut's euch die Amis an, Eiskast'n hab'n's', so groß als wie a Kredenz und voller Fress'n! Die kennen ka' Träumerei, cool bis ans Herz hinan, dafür hab'n's' a Traumfabrik! (Unger 1987: 185).

As in the plays by Mitterer and Schneider something real is experienced as something miraculous. However, while in the above-mentioned plays a reality normally hidden in the human psyche is projected outside and takes on mysterious qualities, in Unger's play it is the external reality which has been transferred to the level of the wonderful. Yet, ironically, none of the characters in this play succeeds in benefiting from this supposedly readily accessible new miraculous reality.

Mass-produced dreams enter a symbiosis with individual desires, become independent of their creators and re-enter the lives of human beings as if they came from a higher sphere. A striking example is the scene 'Mit Gästen' in Franz Xaver Kroetz's play *Mensch Meier* (Kroetz 1979: 10-15). Otto, the father, Martha, the mother, and Ludwig, the son, are sitting in the living-room watching the live TV broadcast of the wedding of the son of the Swedish king to a woman from the German bourgeoisie. To the persons in the living-room this show, made by mortals for consumption by other mortals, appears like something out of a fairy tale. Martha in particular experiences the spectacle on television as if it actually were taking place in the living-room and as if she and her family were partaking in it. As in a play by Raimund, higher beings enter the dwelling of humble people. However, whereas in Raimund's plays spirits actually make contact with humans, the Swedish royal couple are first not spirits but human beings and secondly they do not enter the lower-middle-class home in person but only as 'Phantome' in the sense in which Günther Anders uses the term, namely as something which exists in appearance only but is taken for real (Anders 1956: 1-2, 97-211). Once again it is clear that human beings in the old plays were much closer to the spirits and magicians of another world than to the phantas-magoric projections and phantoms which they themselves have created.

A further variation of this new kind of dualism can be seen in the plays of the Viennese Gustav Ernst. At first sight his plays appear to be very different from those of Mitterer, Kroetz or Unger. Ernst categorically rejects the usage of well-tried genres and schemes:

> Wer etwas Neues sagen und sicher sein möchte, daß es als Neues auch verstanden wird, der muß es auf eine neue Art sagen. Ein brisanter Inhalt kann brisant sein nur in einer brisanten Form (Ernst 1989).

Ernst's comic effects result from the discrepancy between hopes and what becomes of them. His world is radically split into 'above' and 'below', into ideal and trivial reality. In his play

Mallorca the trade union official Willi, a hospital patient, looks at the wounds of his room-mate, a socialist intellectual by the name of Brettschneider, and says, 'Grauslich, wie sowas ausein-anderbricht. Zuerst denkt es, dann stinkt es.' In spite of his rejection of tradition, Ernst appears, perhaps without being aware of it, to use the traditional motif of vanity. Hilde Spiel has pointed out that some contemporary Austrian authors—she refers specifically to Peter Turrini—can be placed within a baroque, Catholic tradition (see Spiel 1967). This seems to apply to Gustav Ernst also.

While Willi is waiting for the operation on his stomach ulcers he is also preparing for the twentieth jubilee celebration of his section of the union. The hospital possibly stands for Austria or for the Austrian Socialist movement, in any case for an organization in which hardly any of the ideals which were upheld at its beginning have survived. The title awakens associations with the 'Insel der Seligen' which Austria supposedly was under the chancellorship of Bruno Kreisky, Mallorca incidentally being the place to which Kreisky retired. The slides which Willi sorts out for his jubilee speech, and which he projects against the wall, show persons and events of a long gone era. They bring back dead comrades and dead (because betrayed) ideals. Willi holds long conversations with his deceased friend Hansl. Hansl is a projection in a triple sense. First, his image is created by a technical projection similar to that of the wedding of the royal Swedish couple. Secondly, it is, like the latter, a phantom in the above mentioned sense of something unreal which is experienced as if it were real. Thirdly, it is not so different from the phantasmagorical projections of secret desires, anxieties, guilt feelings and so on such as we have encountered before. The projected image of Hans is a source of irritation for Willi who is trying to make himself all too comfortable in a corrupt reality. One may also consider Willi to be analogous to the ghosts and spirits in the old plays who, in so far as they were kind spirits, offered help to humans in order to encourage the realization of laudable ideals. It may be argued that a ghost of a human being returning from the hereafter is not the same thing as a spirit who has always been part of the other world. Yet it cannot be denied that a person who has become a ghost is in some way partaking in the other world and thus instils the same awe in a human being (when returning to earth) as a genuine spirit would.

The *kritische Volksstücke* of the sixties, seventies and eighties are eminently suited to dramatize the paradoxical relationship between secularization and continuing belief in (and hope for) miracles, between the ever increasing degree of acceptance of individuals' responsibility for their own affairs (in other words the ongoing process of emancipation) and the equally increasing messianic hopes of people of today. The reason appears to be that the authors who all come from either Austria, Bavaria or Switzerland, can make use of the literary devices of the Old Viennese Popular Comedy and of Alpine folklore with which they are familiar. Especially the Old Viennese Popular Comedy drew its effects from the symbiosis of fantastic and realistic elements. It requires comparatively small modifications of the well-tried structures and elements of this old and still popular tradition to represent the modern dualism of freedom and determinism, familiarity and alienation, transparency and opacity, high-flown ideals and banal everyday reality in a fashion which is convincing to a contemporary audience.

WORKS CITED

Anders, G.
  1956 *Die Antiquiertheit des Menschen: Über die Seele im Zeitalter der zweiten industriellen Revolution*. Munich: C.H. Beck.

Aust, H, P. Haida and J. Hein
  1989 *Volksstück: Vom Hanswurstspiel zum sozialen Drama der Gegenwart*. Munich: C.H. Beck.

Basil, O.
  1967 *Johann Nestroy in Bildzeugnissen und Dokumenten*. Reinbek: Rowohlt.

Ernst, G.
  1985 *Mallorca*. Unpublished manuscript. First performed 1985/86.
  1989 'Wir warten auf das Volk!'. *AZ*, 9 December.

Horváth, Ö. von
  1972 *Gesammelte Werke*, I. Ed. T. Krischke and D. Hildebrandt. Frankfurt: Suhrkamp.

Kroetz, F.X.
  1979 *Mensch Meier/Der stramme Max/Wer durchs Laub geht...Drei Stücke*. Frankfurt: Suhrkamp.

Mitterer, F.
    1985   *Besuchszeit: Vier Einakter*. Munich: Friedl Brehm.
    1986   *Die wilde Frau: Ein Stück*. Munich: Friedl Brehm.
Nestroy, J.
    1968   *Werke*. Ed. O.M. Fontana. Darmstadt: Wissenschaftliche Buchgesellschaft.
Raimund, F.
    n.d.   *Sämtliche Werke*. Ed. F. Schreyvogl. Munich: Winkler.
Schneider, H.
    1980   *Stücke I: Sennentuntschi. Der Erfinder. Der Schütze Tell*. Basel: Matthyas Jenny, Nachtmaschine.
Spiel, H.
    1967   'Zweimal Rattenjagd—Uraufführung von Turrinis Rozznjogd in Wien'. *Frankfurter Allgemeine Zeitung*, 1 February. Reprinted in P. Turrini, *Lesebuch*. Ed. U. Birbaumer. Vienna: Europa, 1978, p. 73.
Unger, H.R.
    1987   *Die Republik des Vergessens: Drei Stücke*. Vienna: Europa.

Christine Nöstlinger: Kids' Stuff?

Mike   Rogers

On the spectrum that runs from high priest to desecrator, Christine Nöstlinger is much closer to the destructive end, as one might expect from somebody who was awarded the 1986 Nestroy-Ring of the City of Vienna for 'satirical services' to the city.

In the world of children's literature in German, she is a very important figure. First, her books sell very well. Secondly, she has been awarded the Hans Christian Andersen Medal, the Deutscher Jugendbuchpreis and the Österreichischer Staatspreis für Kinder- und Jugendliteratur.

Though she is popular in Germany too, many of her works have a specifically Viennese setting, and draw on its atmosphere and recent history, especially from the 1920s through the Anschluss up to the first few years of the postwar period. However, she does not write books that are actually set in the past; instead, there are detailed references to historical events which have a deep significance for the adult characters. The way in which she assumes familiarity with Vienna and its social and political history, as well as her uncompromising use of Austrian vocabulary and turns of phrase, has sometimes caused trouble for her German publishers (she has at least three regular publishers, only one of whom is based in Vienna), who often provide a glossary. Only a small selection of her large output (over fifty works to date, since her debut in 1970) has appeared in English, perhaps for similar reasons. Nöstlinger has published three volumes of poetry in Viennese dialect, has written series for Austrian television and scripted films of her own works; she contributes daily and weekly columns to popular newspapers and magazines, collections of which are published in book form, and in 1991 her teenage musical, *Franz und Frey*, was performed at open air venues throughout Vienna and elsewhere in Austria.

Children's literature is often regarded in academic circles as something second-rate; as a useful field for sociological or cultural analysis but not on a par with 'Real' literature written for adults (see Mattenklott 1989). In *Nußknacker*, the 1986 almanac of Beltz and Gelberg, a publisher dedicated to children's literature, which celebrated Nöstlinger's fiftieth birthday, the academic judgment of children's literature as 'zielgruppenorientierte Trivialliteratur' is quoted with disapproval (Gelberg 1986: 25). The publishers, who display a certain amount of idealism, do not wish to see their products compared to thrillers, westerns and romances. They certainly do not wish it to be thought that they are purveying a similar kind of narcotic escapism with dubious overtones. On the other hand, an examination of Nöstlinger's texts alone would make it clear that the publishers are not trying the other kind of brain-washing, either: they are not dispensing adult propaganda in sugared pills. Instead, they are taking the child's point of view seriously, and offering books which engage with the world and its problems from that point of view.

The possibility of doing that in children's literature is explored by Alison Lurie in her collection of essays *Not in Front of the Grown-ups*, in which she presents many of the 'classics' of children's literature in English as subversive works whose authors champion the child against the adult and especially against 'schwarze Pädagogik' (to use the term coined by Alice Miller, but now employed generally in discussions of children's literature or education). For Lurie, the fact that these works throw fixed values into question and stimulate us to further thought means that they fulfil very important criteria by which the value of literature generally should be judged.

Indeed, the richness and quality of children's literature in English is universally acknowledged by writers on the subject, and even by writers for children in other languages, who look to the English model. German 'classics' for children—aside from Erich Kästner, who clearly supports the clarity of the child's mind against the obfuscation of compromising adults—tend much more to reinforce the adult point of view, as in *Die Biene Maja*, the tale of a bee who deserts the hive in order to be independent, but is forced to return and integrate herself into (bee) society again. Even such a work as Michael Ende's *Die unendliche Geschichte*, despite its international success as an apparent championing of the child's point of view and the validity of the child's imagination, shirks a confrontation between the hero and the real world from which he fled.

Nöstlinger too has written and still writes fantasy stories, but they are not escapist. They use imaginative transposition to explore the nature of problems from the real world, and sometimes even to suggest solutions.

She also writes stories that are set in the everyday contemporary world and deal with divorces, compulsive eating, the sexual activities and sexual problems of teenagers *and* parents, and the disappointments of growing up, though a mere enumeration of 'up-to-date' themes will not suffice to demonstrate her quality as a writer, nor guarantee that the themes are not just used as window-dressing to attract the progressive parent. Her approach to contemporary reality is fairly scathing and cynical, and is certainly not toned down 'for the kiddies'. In *Andreas* (1978) the mother is obsessed with furniture, her 'Wohnlandschaft' and her all-white bedroom, named by her husband 'die unteren sieben achtel des Eisbergs' (which, with grim irony, is the subtitle of the book). If the working class on its way up is satirized, so is the working class that has stayed where it is, for example the overweight, stupid mother in *Pfui, Spinne!* (1980). Mothers, this text also points out, are responsible for throwing things away: a clear criticism of parental authoritarianism, from the point of view of the oppressed child.

It would be possible to produce a long list of such satirical *aperçus*, some of them derived from the narrative perspective, others from the natural rebelliousness of teenagers, whose point of view is often relativized in the long run, but usually not before the more perceptive adults have been forced to recognize the justice of their criticisms.

Alison Lurie sees the taking of the child's part against the adult world as being subversive, and certainly Nöstlinger does this without exception. However, the process is more convincing in fantasies than it is in realistic works: the eponymous heroine of *Ilse Janda, 14* (1974) may be right in believing there is no love for her at home, but she is not going to find it with the man in the red BMW who takes her off to Italy and then abandons her when he finds out she is under age.

What Nöstlinger basically attacks is authoritarianism, especially as it is manifested in the parent–child relationship. Her adaptation of Carlo Collodi's *Pinocchio* as *Der neue Pinocchio* (1988) removes the sadistic 'educational' elements of the original, and defends the child's right to play, which the original dismisses in favour of 'useful' activity. Indeed, as will be seen in later examples, she uses the concept of the freedom of childhood to undermine the conformism, authoritarianism and worship of order which she presents as typical of German-speaking (adult) society.

In her fantasy stories Nöstlinger uses the 'freewheeling' alternative subversively to question normal assumptions. This questioning relates directly to children's innate desire to question everything, which is all too often dismissed and suppressed by parental authority, instead of being welcomed as imaginative and inventive.

Nöstlinger's first work, *Die feuerrote Friederike* (1970), concerns a girl teased at school about her red hair (a traditional source of prejudice in Austria; see Nestroy's *Der Talisman* of 1840). She discovers it is magic, can burn those who tease her, and also gives her the ability to fly. Naturally, her powers do not make her any more popular, and finally she flies away with her aunt (who also has magic hair), her cat (who had lost the ability to fly through overeating, but goes on a diet), and their friends the redundant postman and his wife, to the land of happiness at the world's end. This is a kind of socialist paradise, where no one has to work if they do not want to, but most do, because they enjoy it. Supply and demand even out miraculously. (Nöstlinger's own political views, made explicit in postscripts, articles and interviews, are not as naive as this might suggest: she is essentially a socialist disillusioned with Social Democratic Party politics.)

This wish fulfilment escape from persecution is linked with

satirical elements: for example, an attack on bureaucracy, and the actions of the mayor, who is so disturbed by the departure of Friederike and her companions on the crowded town square at 10 am on a Sunday morning straight after mass, that he orders in a circus and a choir to make people forget what they have just seen. Authority figures do not come off well: their response to Friederike's being teased is to do nothing and hope it will go away, which the narrator describes as no response at all. Even the aunt needs the stimulus of Friederike's (and the cat's) example to recover her magic powers. The process involves her hair being coloured its original red; rejuvenation, which is presented in a more problematic way in *Mr Bats Meisterstück oder die total verjüngte Oma* (1974), obviously represents the need for adults, even sympathetic ones, to get back in touch with their childhood.

As in fairy-tales, it is often, though not always, the generation of the grandparents that has the time and the insight to relate properly to children; parents are incapable of it. On the other hand, in *Andreas* the socialist grandfather is not happy about the way he brought up his daughter, the mother of the eponymous hero.

Das Leben der Tomanis (1974) goes even further than *Friederike* in its rejection of conventional adult society; but this time no paradisiacal world is found. The totally adapted Meier daughters do everything a parent could wish of a child. But then they read a book called *The Life of the Tomanis*, which describes blue-skinned humanoid creatures with tails who do nothing useful, but instead sing, laugh and run around naked. The daughters abandon their dutiful lives and turn into Tomanis. The father defends them against the conformism of their housing estate: 'Alle Kinder können nicht gleich aussehen!' (p. 27). The mother is ashamed; but the persecution she too experiences makes her side with her daughters. The parents sell everything to buy a boat, read the book until they too turn into Tomanis, and the whole family sails away to look for the land where the Tomanis live. Whether they ever find it is left open; they are mentioned as appearing periodically like the Flying Dutchman, still asking the way.

Here again the child's point of view is taken seriously. The child's reaction against the conventional world unleashes that world's violence and prejudice, and the adults who are already emotionally close to the children learn from them and respond accordingly. This clearly reverses the normal expectation that the child will learn from the adult who has all the answers.

On the other hand, it could be argued that this is all childish self-indulgence, flight in the face of reality, a refusal to grow up. Unresolved psychological conflicts in the author, which should have been sorted out in the course of the transition from childhood to adulthood, are being allowed to assert themselves, and are being taken too seriously. A little bit of bullying is insufficient reason to make one despair of the world.

If we consider one aspect that could be regarded as an unresolved childhood trauma, namely the question of obesity, then we should be able to see how Nöstlinger adopts the child's point of view, not as some glorification of the 'natural' child, but as a common-sense position, free from prejudice and authoritarian thinking.

In *Friederike*, the heroine, her aunt and her cat are all overweight, and have to lose that weight in order to be able to fly properly and carry other people with them. It is implied that being overweight is the result of oral gratification to make up for lack of true fulfilment; sluggishness, mental and emotional, also plays its part, the result of losing sight of the true objective in life, the paradisiacal land. In *Das Leben der Tomanis*, on the other hand, weight gain symbolizes the rejection of bourgeois norms. The father (usually the more perceptive parent in Nöstlinger's work, reflecting her relationship to her own parents, as she freely admits) observes that the children, once they begin to change into Tomanis, look happier than they used to and are no longer so skinny either. The contrast between the two stories is essentially more apparent than real, though, as emerges from the title of Nöstlinger's non-fiction work on eating disorders: *Einen Löffel für den Papa, einen Löffel für die Mama, einen Löffel für die Oma, einen Löffel für den Opa. Jeder Löffel für die Katz* (1989). In other words, whatever may be Nöstlinger's own experiences as a child with fatness or thinness, she relates these conditions, together with eating disorders in general, to the attitudes of adults. These themes are emotionally charged—for everybody—which is why she explores them; but it is a conscious exploration, and not a compulsion, which is why she dedicates the book on eating disorders to all those good people who, throughout her childhood, neither refused her food and drink nor forced it on her, but gave her the freedom to eat every day. The book itself is a comic account, in the manner of her semi-didactic articles for the popular press, of children's responses to food, and is clearly intended to educate parents away from authoritarian and prescriptive attitudes.

In the same way, her championing of the child is an identification of the child as a member of a persecuted and misunderstood minority. This emerges most clearly in *Hugo, das Kind in den besten Jahren* (1983). Hugo is a child who has not been allowed to grow up, in the positive sense, and is still treated as if he were about eight by his two male parents, Miesmeier 1 and Miesmeier 2. The names make clear the nature of the 'parental role': the grumbler, the scold, the spoilsport. In intellectual terms an adult, Hugo absents himself from home during the night on a giant paper aeroplane, pursuing his long-term aim of forming a union of all the children who have never grown up in the negative sense. Some of the nightmare elements in the story derive from the illustrations by Jörg Wollmann which in fact inspired it,[1] but the explanations of the pictures are Nöstlinger's own, and the deeper problems which she touches on in the course of the work are certainly of her invention: these include the multi-layered racial prejudice in the country where Hugo lives (it seems like a kind of Switzerland), which is inhabited by all kinds of animals who go around as if they were human beings, but are debarred from various jobs and squabble amongst themselves. This culminates in the question of rabbit ancestry, which the Miesmeiers hotly deny, and in the revelation that there are two kinds of rabbits: 'Kampfhasen' and 'Angsthasen'. The 'Angsthasen' are kept safe from the outside world in a special camp. The fact that one of the 'Kampfhasen' is called Rabbitsky makes the parallels to anti-Semitism even clearer.

1. This is not the only work by Nöstlinger to have been written around existing illustrations. *Der gefrorene Prinz* is based on drawings by F.K. Waechter originally published in the children's magazine *Der bunte Hund* as a stimulus for children to write their own stories.

Thus, time and again, Nöstlinger defends the position of the child, and also everything for which the child stands. She opposes the authoritarianism which finds its ultimate expression in the absolute power that parents have over the child, and its theoretical legitimation in the notion of 'upbringing' or 'education'.

This issue is examined in the greatest detail in *Konrad, oder das Kind aus der Konservenbüchse* (1975). The premiss is the delivery of a ready-made, seven-year-old, fully conditioned child in a can (just add water). It might be every would-be parent's dream: no nappies, no sleepless nights, no discipline problems.

The delivery, however, is made to the wrong address: to Frau Berti Bartolotti, a weaver of artistic rugs and wall-hangings who lives a life of total disorder. Her shower is full of houseplants that need their tropical rainstorm, the washbasin is full of goldfish who have been let out for exercise, the only cleanliness possible is a kind of dry-cleaning: she wipes off the previous day's make-up and puts on a new layer.

The well-schooled Konrad's entry into this disorder raises some questions for Frau Bartolotti; but not many, because most of the time she dismisses the notion of what a seven-year-old should or should not do, and simply asks him what he would *like* to do. But Konrad does not in fact *know*; and even more problems arise when she sees that her behaviour is causing Konrad pain or difficulty, as when he asks her to teach him the sort of songs children sing, and all she can recall are rather vulgar playground rhymes. This places him in a painful dilemma, because he has been conditioned at the factory to pay attention to whatever father or mother say, but also not to listen to anything vulgar.

Nöstlinger is clearly on the side of Frau Bartolotti, who does not try to force her non-conformism on Konrad, even if it always represents her first reaction (though she does try to tone down her language). Sharper satire is reserved for the friend and neighbour, Egon, the pharmacist, whose naturally 'adult' personality has internalized his childhood lessons all too well, and who therefore entirely approves of Konrad.

Konrad's gradual education in the ways of the normal world, so as not to be so unbearably good that people wonder what dreadful thing he's done, proceeds until his manufacturers try to reclaim him. At this point, he has to be submitted to a ruthless Pavlovian retraining in naughtiness, so that the agents from the factory will be appalled by Konrad's disgraceful behaviour and not wish to reclaim him. The result is so impressive that the factory director disclaims all responsibility, in a phrase that gives an ironic twist to the famous line of Moritz's father at his son's funeral in Wedekind's *Frühlings Erwachen*: 'Der Junge war nicht von mir!' (p. 115) becomes 'Dieser Junge kann nicht aus meiner Produktion hervorgegangen sein, das ist unmöglich!' (Nöstlinger 1975: 147)

This story, in particular, touches on many of the problems of childhood and parent–child relations, especially in a society such as that in German-speaking countries, where, according to Alice Miller, physical violence towards children is still generally approved of, and the notions of the need for discipline and absolute parental authority are widely believed in. However, it also demonstrates the shortcomings of the completely anti-authoritarian view unless it is modified (as here) by respect for those who think and feel otherwise. It also makes clear that 'naughtiness' of the extreme kind is indeed a form of rebellion against what is perceived as repression, lack of understanding or lack of attention; and Konrad's 're-education' is also presented as a mechanical process which could be applied to inculcate anything. The point of the story is to establish Konrad's freedom to choose between the two kinds of behaviour which are now available to him: only if he genuinely *can* choose will his choice be meaningful in any moral or personal sense.

Konrad was dramatized, and early productions were attacked quite vehemently by the Katholischer Familienverband. More recent ones (it has been performed widely in Germany as well as in Vienna) have not attracted such attacks, which may be a sign of increasing liberalism, or simply indicate that the Katholischer Familienverband realized it was giving the play free publicity.

In *Konrad*, finally, the behaviour of the adults is shown to relate to the way they were themselves treated as children. Frau Bartolotti is clearly in some sense childlike (she is an artist, after all) in her rejection of order and cleanliness; and whenever she wants to get herself to do anything, she has to address herself as 'liebes Kind', the words with which her parents and her husband had addressed her.

Nöstlinger's more recent works (and all the older ones discussed are still in print, a tribute to her staying power in a volatile market) continue these critical themes. The canine hero of *Der Hund kommt!* (1987) assumes, in the course of various disruptive adventures, the role of a primary school teacher; his unconventional, child-centred methods are enormously success-ful with the children, who help him escape when the authorities, who of course never appointed him, try to have him arrested.

Der gefrorene Prinz (1990) addresses the problem I mentioned at the beginning of this paper, and which led me to focus on Nöstlinger's fantasy narratives: that the child's point of view may cut through the thicket of adult conventions in a satirical way, and may be more authentic and emotionally fulfilling, but that it may not be complex enough to do justice to the problems concerned. The eponymous hero has to face up to the breakdown of his parents' marriage: 'Prinz Franz war wirklich das ganze Glück seiner Eltern. Wäre er nicht gewesen, hätten sie gar kein Glück gehabt, denn miteinander hatten sie großes Unglück' (p. 7). The subsequent battle for his affections leads the Prince to place his bed across the stream that divides his father's half of the kingdom from his mother's. The bed falls in, the stream carries him away, and only after terrifying adventures does he return. With the aid of a wise old man and a speaking tree he establishes a *modus vivendi*; the tree criticizes the parents for causing their child such emotional pain (the Prince not wishing to hurt them by saying that), and gives them leaves to chew when they are angry with each other. Not exactly a conventional fairy tale solution, but then nor are the open endings of *Tomanis* or *Hugo*; and *Konrad*, after all, ends by rejecting all extremism, whether of order or disorder.

The qualities that this analysis has shown to be present in these works, that is, an imaginative treatment of the child's point of view and an ability to relate this to other instances of author-itarianism and blind obedience, are present in all Nöstlinger's works, whether they are fantasies or set firmly in reality.

In accordance with Alison Lurie's criteria, Nöstlinger's works unsettle fixed categories and stimulate further questioning.

Together with the quality of the writing and the verbal ingenuity, this should qualify them to be judged as 'literature'. However, they also offer us the special gift of children's literature: they remind adults that they were children once: not in the cosy way in which that phrase is often used, but in terms of reminding adults that their present characters were moulded by their own childhoods, just as they may be moulding their own children. Nöstlinger suggests that adults should learn from their own children, before they transmit to them that long line of error that stretches back to Cain and Abel.

WORKS CITED

Gelberg, H.-J.
    1986   *Nußknacker.* Weinheim: Beltz and Gelberg.

Lurie, A.
    1990   *Not in Front of the Grown-Ups.* London: Sphere Books.

Mattenklott, G.
    1989   *Zauberkreide: Kinderliteratur seit 1945.* Stuttgart: Metzler.

Nöstlinger, C.
    1970   *Die feuerrote Friederike.* Vienna: Jugend und Volk.

    1974a   *Mr Bats Meisterstück oder die total verjüngte Oma.* Hamburg: Friedrich Oetinger.

    1974b   *Ilse Janda 14.* Hamburg: Friedrich Oetinger.

    1975   *Konrad, oder das Kind aus der Konservenbüchse.* Hamburg: Friedrich Oetinger.

    1978   *Andreas, oder die unteren sieben Achtel des Eisbergs.* Weinheim: Beltz and Gelberg.

    1980   *Das Leben der Tomanis.* Ravensburg: Otto Maier (First published 1974).

    1983   *Hugo, das Kind in den besten Jahren.* Weinheim: Beltz and Gelberg.

    1987   *Der Hund kommt!* Weinheim: Beltz and Gelberg.

    1988   *Der neue Pinocchio.* Weinheim: Beltz and Gelberg.

    1989   *Einen Löffel für den Papa, einen Löffel für die Mama, einen Löffel für die Oma, einen Löffel für den Opa. Jeder Löffel für die Katz.* Vienna: Jugend und Volk.

    1990   *Der gefrorene Prinz.* Weinheim: Beltz and Gelberg.

Wedekind, F.
    1919   *Gesammelte Werke. II. Frühlings Erwachen.* Munich: Georg Langen.

Index of Names